WEBER'S
BIG BOOK OF
BARBECUE

WEBER'S
BIG BOOK OF
BARBECUE

OVER 200 BRAND-NEW RECIPES

BY **JAMIE PURVIANCE**   PHOTOGRAPHS BY **TIM TURNER**

hamlyn

An Hachette UK Company
www.hachette.co.uk

First published in Great Britain in 2014 by
Hamlyn, a division of Octopus Publishing Group Ltd,
Endeavour House, 189 Shaftesbury Avenue,
London, WC2H 8JY

www.octopusbooks.co.uk

ISBN 978-0-600-62883-5

A CIP catalogue record for this book is available from the
British Library

Printed and bound in China

10 9 8 7 6 5 4 3 2 1

www.weber.com®
www.sunset.com

CONTENTS

FOREWORD

BY MIKE KEMPSTER

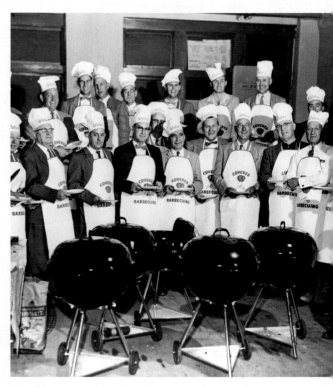

I was born in the early wave of baby boomers. It was the early 1950s, not long after our troops returned home from World War II. It was a time when the American dream really took root and people began settling into new homes and optimistic new lives. Back then, you knew you were doing well if you had a car with gigantic fins parked in front of a new home, a lush lawn, and a backyard patio decked out with a barbecue grill and picnic table. Life was good. Dads everywhere were stepping up to the grill, and a passion for grilling was beginning to burn across the land.

I grew up watching my dad use some of the first grills that were mass-produced for home-owners. Little did I know back then that grilling would become such an integral part of my adult life.

The year was 1952. George Stephen, a metalworker and father of twelve, loved to barbecue, but grills on the market at the time were far from ideal. Most were open braziers, making it impossible to control flare-ups. George thought that a lid with vents might help control airflow, prevent flare-ups and keep the ashes and the elements at bay.

It's been said that necessity is the mother of invention, and that was certainly true when George invented the Weber® kettle. He was working at his father's company, Weber Brothers Metal Works, at the time, welding metal spheres into buoys. He was just about to weld two sphere halves together when it hit him: he could make a grill out of the two halves. So he did just that, and the classic Weber kettle was born. Over the next two decades, George grew his invention from a curiosity into a backyard staple.

I started selling Weber® grills when I was a teenager working in a Kansas City hardware store. I never imagined that I would be hired by George Stephen and go on to become a lifelong Weber salesman and barbecue fanatic. In the early 1970s, growing the business meant hauling grills around from store to store conducting grilling demonstrations. We even published little paper pamphlets that we sold for fifty cents.

MIKE KEMPSTER AND GEORGE STEPHEN CIRCA 1974

Each had a dozen or so recipes and grilling tips, and boy, were they popular. So we decided to go a little bigger. We published our first hardcover cookbook, *Barbecuing the Weber® Covered Way*, in 1972. This was also the first cookbook with instructions on how to use something very new – a Weber® gas grill. Our grills are now sold around the globe, and our cookbooks have become international best sellers. No matter the country, grilling enthusiasts have shown their excitement for great recipes and for becoming better outdoor grillers.

As the years have passed, traditional barbecued meals have evolved. Grilling enthusiasts are more adventuresome, and their palates expect to be treated to the wide range of food and flavours that were not popular or didn't even exist ten or twenty years ago. It's my pleasure to introduce you to this latest collection. Decades of hands-on grilling, answering grilling questions and feeding the fire are behind every word and photo. I think you will enjoy this book as much as we have enjoyed bringing it to life.

Mike Kempster

INTRODUCTION

BY JAMIE PURVIANCE

In the beginning there was fire. Then we threw some burgers and hot dogs on it, and there was dinner.

When I was a boy in suburban New Jersey in the 1960s, this is how my family grilled. Those were the days when meat came off the grill, and pretty much everything else came out of the kitchen. Americans were still revelling in post-war, modern conveniences like Jell-O® salads, instant rice, orange juice powders and boxed cake mixes that were 'ready in a jiffy'.

As the decades came and went, so did many food trends, including our passing interests in things like nouvelle cuisine and east–west fusion foods. If nothing else, these trends brought some great ingredients to ordinary supermarkets. Remember that back in the 1980s, items such as real balsamic vinegar, chipotle chillies, and panko breadcrumbs were 'ethnic' foods that you could only find in specialised shops, if at all. Now they are supermarket staples and, as a result, grilling staples.

This book is a collection of delicious but doable recipes built on today's supermarket staples. Trust us, we get it. We know you have better things to do than going on a crazed hunt for rare groceries. We all want to be at home, enjoying our downtime with good food, family and friends. In this era of financial uncertainty, market upheavals and debt crises, the home is a safe haven. The backyard is our oasis. The grill is our hearth.

This is where memories are made. This is what is real. In these pages you'll find many classic dishes that have been popular for years, but we gave each one a twist. Nothing crazy, just riffs on popular themes – think Cheeseburgers with Mango-Chilli Salsa, Coffee-Rubbed Rib-Eye Steaks with Stout Glaze and Prawn Kebabs with Pistachio-Tarragon Pesto.

Grilling tools and cookware have come a long way, too. It used to be that all the food went right on the cooking grate and we moved it with one of two items: tongs or a spatula. Now we have more accessories and much more fun. Have you ever used your grill to make cioppino in a wok or made bread on a pizza stone? This ingenuity, the old-meets-new ethic – is the new experience of grilling.

So welcome to the party! Grilling is more a part of the outdoor living dream than it's ever been. We've been cooking this way since the beginning of time, but how we see it now – as a gateway to the good life, as a tasty means to our contented end – has evolved. Grilling is how we entertain, how we relax, and how we reconnect with what means most. This book captures all those contemporary elements of grilling while staying focused on what really never changes. It's fun, and it's delicious. That's why we grilled back then, and that's why we grill today.

Jamie Purviance

GRILLING EVOLVED

THE EVOLUTION OF FIRE

What began with a spark turned into flames . . .
and then the flames sparked some clever designs.

CHARCOAL GRILLS

Our classic kettle is a purist griller's dream, but for those who dream even bigger along came a few bells and whistles. To some charcoal grills we added the convenience of gas-assisted ignition and plenty of grill-side charcoal storage. A large work surface on some recent models answers the ever-present 'where do I put my tongs?' call, and a lid holder provides a safe place for the lid while you tend to your fire.

GAS GRILLS

Back before we introduced the Genesis® grill in the mid-80s, predecessor gas grills used lava rocks to distribute heat. While, um, groovy in theory, they were a little too hotheaded in practice, causing volcanic flare-ups and torching food beyond recognition. The gas grill market was booming and just starting to outpace charcoal grill sales, as busy folks everywhere sought convenient options. Riding that wave – but steering clear of the lava thing – we engineered the Genesis grill with a set of precisely angled bars set over the flames. These Flavourizer® bars channel juices falling from the cooking grates down on to the heating element where they sizzle and smoke, creating that coveted grill flavour but all the while deterring flare-ups.

That first Genesis model was a runaway hit, but it keeps on getting better. For instance, a Sear Station® allows you to cook food at extremely high temperatures – a must for that perfect steak. A tank scale provides an accurate reading of how much gas is available, which is nice to avoid panicked propane runs. Sideburner technology rivals the kitchen stove with the ability to cook at super low or super high temperatures.

SOME OF WEBER'S MORE MEMORABLE HITS AND MISSES OVER THE LAST 60+ YEARS

1952
Original Kettle

1965
The Ranger™

1966
The Wishing Well™

1972
Barrel-Barb-B-Q™

SMOKERS

Where the kettle leaves off, the smoker picks up, and that is at the next level of low-and-slow grilling intensity. The first smokers were fashioned out of old oil drums cut in half and rigged with a cooking grate. Like any good idea, it was taken in all sorts of directions – vertical smokers, water smokers, electric smokers – that all did pretty much the same thing: cook food at a low temperature for a very long time. The Smokey Mountain Cooker™ smoker is designed simply but smartly, enabling consistent temperatures to be obtained using a spot-on thermometer and vents to control airflow.

ELECTRIC GRILLS

Apartment dwellers, campers and the otherwise space-challenged need love, too. Enter the portable and compact Q® electric grill. Having a tiny footprint is great, but not when you can't get the thing hot enough using a standard household current. Innovations to grill design, however, have yielded searing hot results. The popular Q® grill produces food that tastes just as if it was grilled on a standard-sized grill.

CHARCOAL VERSUS GAS

The debate has left many a house divided, but it's finally been settled. Which is better? Both.

Before you slam this book shut, hear us out: charcoal and gas allegiances have less to do with one fuel's superiority than your personal taste and lifestyle. If it's mostly weeknight burgers and chicken breasts you want, then you may be partial to the flick-of-a-switch ease of a gas grill. Perhaps you're more of a low-and-slow type, relishing the smoke and strategy behind coals in a kettle – then charcoal it is. Gas gets a bad rap for being too mild in smoke flavour, but juicy meat plus fire equals smoke every time, regardless of the grill type. And if all else fails, there's always the smoker box.

Charcoal's many varieties, from no-frills briquettes to the knock-your-socks-off smokiness of lump coals, give us good options. Each type uniquely flavours food and impacts how much hands-on time and money go into grilling it (pricier charcoals tend to burn hotter – and faster). For these reasons, cost isn't always a good argument for charcoal versus gas because of all the variables attached to your style and frequency of grilling. When in doubt, embrace both. There's no need for rivalry talk when everybody wins.

1985
Genesis®

1990
Performer®

2000
One-Touch®

TODAY
Summit®

USING A WOK

Wok cooking on your grill may sound like new-fangled fusion cuisine, but in fact it's steeped in tradition. For thousands of years, the focal point in a typical Chinese kitchen was a round hole over a firebox of burning wood and embers with a wok fitted snugly inside the hole, making efficient use of a small amount of expensive fuel. And you can replicate the ancient art of stir-frying over live fire by using a grill-proof wok on your backyard barbecue.

WHAT YOU'LL NEED

- ▶ Gas or charcoal grill
- ▶ Cooking grate with removable centre
- ▶ Grill-proof wok *Use enamel-coated cast iron. It retains heat without reacting with acidic ingredients as uncoated cast iron can.*
- ▶ Utensils *Spatulas with a shovel-like shape that fit the sloped sides of a wok work best.*

1 Prep everything first. Then cook. Stir-frying happens in a short burst of time. Once it starts, you won't have time to slice or dice anything, so arrange all your chopped ingredients, sauces and even serving plates near the grill first. Chop all the ingredients into cubes or strips of about the same size (no bigger than bite-size) so they cook evenly.

2 Get the wok hot. Smoking hot. It's pretty simple, really. Light 50 to 75 briquettes and let them burn until they are lightly coated with ash. Arrange the charcoal one or two layers deep in the centre of the charcoal grate. Put in place the cooking grate with a hole in the centre. Set the wok in the hole and close the lid. Let the wok get smoking hot for about 10 minutes. When you flick a few drops of water into the wok, they should dance vigorously and disappear within just a second.

3 To stir or not to stir? That is the question. Stir-fry masters have a keen sense for when to stir with zeal and when to exercise patience. In most cases, when you add meat or other protein to a wok, you should quickly spread out the pieces to get as many of them as possible in direct contact with the hot wok surface. Then wait for 20–30 seconds so the food has a chance to sear.

4 Scoop and toss. Next, scoop to the bottom of the wok with two wok spatulas to lift the ingredients into the air and let them tumble back down repeatedly until the outside is evenly browned. Move the meat up the cooler sides of the wok to finish cooking it, and then add the vegetables to the blazing hot bottom of the wok. Again, let the new ingredients sear for a matter of seconds and then toss them with your spatulas.

TRY THESE WOK RECIPES:

Five-Minute Pepper Steak Stir-Fry, *page 99*

Chicken and Broccoli Stir-Fry with Peanuts and Spring Onions, *page 184*

USING A PIZZA STONE

It's a long fall from the culinary heights of the Italian masterpiece known as pizza to the lows of modern convenience food made of frozen, lifeless dough covered in icy toppings. Why take that fall when nowadays many supermarkets carry the components that used to take us so long to make? When you can buy fresh dough, good tomato sauce and grated cheese, a pizza worthy of its authentic roots is really only about 30 minutes away. The key is using the impressive heat retained by a solid stone slab to fill each pizza with light, doughy air pockets and to toast the bottom with a golden brown crust.

WHAT YOU'LL NEED

▸ Gas or charcoal grill

▸ Pizza stone

▸ Wooden or metal pizza paddle

TRY THESE PIZZA STONE RECIPES:

Grilled Pizzas with Sausage, Peppers and Herbs, *page 144*

Spinach and Ricotta Calzones, *page 282*

Beer and Cheddar Bread, *page 286*

1 Preheat the pizza stone first. Prepare your gas or charcoal grill for grilling/direct cooking over high heat, and preheat the stone for at least 15 minutes. The grill temperature should rise to at least 260°C/500°F. Meanwhile, roll out the dough and prepare your other ingredients.

2 Roll out the dough on a lightly floured surface. Turn the ball of dough in the flour a few times so it is not so sticky. Flatten into a disc and use a rolling pin to roll to a thickness of about 8 mm/⅓ inch, flipping the dough over once or twice to make sure it's not sticking.

3 Lightly coat a pizza paddle with flour, too. Then slide the paddle completely under the dough. Spread a thin layer of sauce almost all the way to the outer edge of the crust. Don't use too much sauce; otherwise, the dough will soak it up and turn soggy.

4 Scatter the toppings over the sauce. Don't use any toppings (like raw meat) that would not be safe to eat after only 10 minutes of cooking. Make sure the pizza can slide a little on the paddle. If any areas of the dough are sticking, lift them up and flick a large pinch of flour underneath.

5 Slide the pizza on to the hot stone. Tilt the paddle so that the pizza slides easily away from you and the edge of the crust lands near the part of the stone farthest from you. Then slowly pull the paddle towards you and lay the rest of the pizza on the stone. Close the lid and let the pizza cook for 4–5 minutes.

6 Rotate the pizza once or twice. Slide the paddle or a large spatula underneath and rotate the pizza a half turn for even cooking. You will know it is ready when the underside of the crust is golden brown in spots and the cheese is completely melted.

USING A GRIDDLE

Is there anything that appears as ordinary as a
black slab of metal? You might be surprised to learn
that there is also probably no other accessory that
opens up as many cooking possibilities on the grill.
For example, what if your vegetables are cut so small that
they might fall through the cooking grates? What if a fish
is too thin or delicate to put right on an open grate? What
if you need a hot flat surface to toast panini crust evenly?
What if you feel like making breakfast with eggs, bacon
and pancakes on the grill? A griddle handles all these
jobs and more easily.

WHAT YOU'LL NEED

▸ Gas or charcoal grill

▸ Grill-proof griddle *Make sure it fits your grill's dimensions.*

▸ Long-handled spatula or tongs

▸ Grill press *Use one you can hold in your hand for good control
when toasting grilled cheese sandwiches, flattening bacon and
crisping chicken skin.*

1 Preheat a grill-proof griddle for at least 10 minutes. It takes that long for the thick metal to get hot. Cut any vegetables small enough so that they cook in less than 10 minutes, and coat them with oil before sliding them on to the griddle.

2 Don't flip the vegetables too often. Spread them out and leave them in place for at least 1 minute to let them brown. Then turn them over with a wide spatula. If each vegetable cooks differently, separate them into piles.

3 Remember to toast the bread. Brush the cut sides with oil or butter and lay them flat on the griddle. Meanwhile, you can grill the meat right on the cooking grate.

4 Bring it all together. As a final touch, warm the sandwiches on the griddle until the outsides are crusty. If you like, flatten the sandwiches with a grill press.

TRY THESE GRIDDLE RECIPES:

Cheesesteaks with the Works, *page 87*

Black Forest Ham, Brie and Pear Panini, *page 154*

Griddled Cod with Sweet Pickle Tartare Sauce, *page 253*

French Toast with Grilled Peaches and Blueberry Syrup, *page 301*

BRASING

Grilling can dazzle us with its flickering, sparkling flames. Its dry, searing heat creates charred crusts and smoky aromas to admire – but don't overlook what a grill can also do with moist, gentle heat. Those same flames can simmer a flavourful liquid for braising and tenderising meats and vegetables of many kinds, even the toughest of all, like beef brisket. By combining both dry and moist heat, you can develop layers of flavours and textures that one kind of heat alone could not achieve. In the kielbasa recipe shown here, the sausages benefit first from the char of a sizzling hot cooking grate. Then they are submerged in a tasty stew of red onions, sauerkraut and beer. What happens next is close to magic, as all those ingredients blend into something much greater than the sum of their individual flavours.

WHAT YOU'LL NEED

▸ Gas or charcoal grill

▸ Large cast-iron frying pan

▸ Disposable foil tray

▸ Heavy-duty aluminium foil *When you want to simmer the liquid without much of it evaporating, it's good to cover the pan tightly with aluminium foil.*

1 Use a heavy, grill-proof pan. In a large cast-iron frying pan braise the onions in simmering sauerkraut and beer. This softens the onions and builds a rich base of flavours for braising the sausages later.

2 Sear the meat on the side. While the onions are braising, brown the sausages over grilling/direct heat. Cutting each sausage in half lengthways exposes more surface area for browning and charring right on the hot cooking grate.

3 Combine the meat and vegetables. Chop the browned sausages into bite-sized pieces and push them into the braising pool. Nestle the sausages into the liquid and let them simmer in the juices.

4 Move the pan for the right heat level. To slow down the cooking, slide the frying pan over roasting/indirect heat and close the grill lid. Your food will stay warm and moist for at least 30 minutes. When you are ready to eat, toast some buns over grilling/direct heat and pile them high with sausages and onions.

TRY THESE BRAISING RECIPES:

Braised and Glazed Short Ribs, *page 117*

Polish Sausage Sandwiches with Beer-Braised Onions, *page 148*

USING A ROTISSERIE 🔥

Rotisseries may conjure up images of medieval knights cranking a spit by hand to slow cook a wild beast over a bed of embers, but so much has changed since the days of King Arthur. For one thing, we cook in a covered grill now, which means that the meats are surrounded by circulating heat to cook them more quickly and evenly. Rotisserie cooking today is much more like oven-roasting large cuts of meat and whole birds in mid-air, with the significant advantage that as the food turns (with a motor, by the way), its juices are slowly redistributed to baste the food inside and outside.

WHAT YOU'LL NEED

▸ Gas or charcoal grill that accommodates a rotisserie

▸ Electrical socket and an extension cord

▸ Insulated barbecue mitts or oven gloves

▸ Kitchen string

ADAPTING RECIPES FOR THE ROTISSERIE

Almost any recipe that calls for roasting/indirect heat does really well on the rotisserie. As long as the meat can be evenly balanced on the spit, it's a prime candidate for the rotisserie.

1 Truss any unwieldy meats. If you are cooking something that holds together naturally, such as a beef rib roast, there is no need to truss it. But if it could fall apart or flop around and cook unevenly on the revolving spit, such as this pork loin, you must truss.

2 Secure the food with forks. Run the spit right down the centre and insert the forked tongs into each end. If necessary, first turn the spit so that the tongs are inserted into a dense section of the meat that will hold the tongs in place.

3 Press the tongs all the way into the meat. The meat will shrink as it cooks and could potentially slide off the tongs, so begin with the tongs pressed in as deep as possible.

4 Centre the roast. There should be an equal distance of metal on each side. Tighten the screws on the tongs.

5 Put the roast on the grill. Place the tip of the spit into the mount of the rotisserie motor and lower the other end of the spit into place.

6 Catch the drippings with a disposable foil tray. To make room for the tray, you may need to remove the cooking grates first.

TRY THESE ROTISSERIE RECIPES: **Leg of Lamb with Apricot and Chickpea Couscous,** *page 118* **Summer Herb-Roasted Chicken,** *page 202*

GETTING STARTED

STARTING YOUR GRILL

STARTING A CHARCOAL FIRE

The time required to fire up a charcoal grill can be as little as 15–20 minutes, if you use the right equipment.

1 The easiest method is to use a chimney starter, an upright metal cylinder with two handles on the outside and a wire rack inside. Simply fill the space under the wire rack with wadded-up newspaper or a few paraffin cubes, then fill the space above with charcoal briquettes.

2 Light the newspaper or the paraffin cubes, using a taper or match. This is when some impressive thermodynamics channel the heat evenly throughout the briquettes.

3 When the briquettes are lightly covered with white ash, use insulated barbecue mitts or oven gloves to grab hold of the two handles on the chimney starter. The swinging handle helps you lift the chimney starter and safely aim the coals just where you want them.

HEAT CONFIGURATIONS

The most flexible charcoal configuration is a two-zone fire. That means the coals are spread out on one side of the charcoal grate. This allows you to cook with both direct and indirect heat.

There are times when you might prefer a three-zone split fire, where the coals are separated into two equal piles on opposite sides of the charcoal grate. This gives you two zones for direct heat and one zone between them for indirect heat. This works well for cooking a roast over indirect heat, because you have the same level of heat on both sides of the roast.

After the coals are fully lit, put the cooking grate in place, put the lid on the grill, and wait for about 10 minutes until the temperature rises to at least 260°C/500°F on the lid's thermometer. Your charcoal grill's temperature depends on how much charcoal you use and how long it has been burning. The coals are at their hottest when they are newly lit. Over time they will gradually lose heat.

FUEL CHOICES

Briquettes are inexpensive and available practically everywhere. Most commonly, they are compressed black bundles of sawdust and coal, along with binders and fillers like clay and sodium nitrate. They produce a predictable, even heat over a long period of time. A batch of 80–100 briquettes will last for about an hour.

Pure hardwood briquettes are considered the gold standard of charcoal. They have the same pillow shape of standard briquettes, but they burn at higher temperatures and with none of the questionable fillers. They are usually made of crushed hardwoods bound together with nothing other than natural starches.

Lump charcoal is made by burning hardwood logs in an oxygen-deprived environment, such as an underground pit or a kiln. This type of charcoal lights faster than briquettes, burns hotter and burns out faster. It also tends to spark and crackle like real wood. Fortunately, it creates smoky aromas like real wood, too.

STARTING A GAS GRILL

Lighting a gas grill, in most cases, is as simple as lifting the lid, turning on the gas and igniting the burners. After you have opened the valve on your propane tank all the way, wait a minute for the gas to travel through the gas line, and then turn each burner to high, making sure one burner has ignited before turning on the next. Close the lid and preheat the grill for 10–15 minutes. For both gas and charcoal grills, this makes the cooking grate much easier to clean, and it improves the grill's ability to sear.

If you smell gas, that might indicate a leak around the connection or in the hose. Turn off all the burners. Close the valve on your propane tank and disconnect the hose. Wait 5–10 minutes, and then reconnect the hose. Try lighting the grill again. If you still smell gas, shut the grill down and contact the manufacturer.

HEAT CONFIGURATIONS

For direct cooking, simply leave all the burners on and adjust them for the heat level you want. For example, if you want to cook with direct medium heat, turn all the burners down to medium and wait until the thermometer indicates that the temperature is in the range of 180–230°C /350–450°F. For indirect cooking, you can leave some of the burners on and turn one or two of them off.

GRILL SAFETY

Please read your Owner's Guide and familiarise yourself with and follow all 'dangers', 'warnings' and 'cautions'. Also follow the grilling procedures and maintenance requirements listed in your Owner's Guide.

If you cannot locate the Owner's Guide for your grill model, please contact the manufacturer prior to use. If you have any questions concerning the 'dangers', 'warnings' and 'cautions' contained in your Weber® gas, charcoal or electric grill Owner's Guide, or if you do not have an Owner's Guide for your specific grill model, please contact Weber-Stephen Products LLC Customer Service at (0)1756 692611 before using your grill. You can also access your Owner's Guide online at www.weber.com.

GAS AND CHARCOAL GRILLS

After preheating the grill, put on an insulated barbecue mitt, and use a long-handled grill brush to scrape off any bits and pieces stuck to the cooking grates. There's no need to oil the grates before grilling; it would just drip into the grill, causing flare-ups. Improve the chances of your food releasing easily by oiling the food, not the grates.

Once your grill is preheated and brushed clean, bring out all the food and other supplies you will need and organise them nearby. If you have everything chopped and measured beforehand, the cooking will go faster, and you won't have to run back into the kitchen. Don't forget clean plates and platters for serving the grilled food.

DIRECT AND INDIRECT COOKING

When it comes to cooking with direct and indirect heat, there's good news and there's bad news.
Bad news first: the difference between direct and indirect heat is the most complicated part.

Good news: it's not complicated at all.

When a recipe calls for 'grilling/direct heat', this means that the grill's heat source – be it the hot coals of a charcoal grill or the fired-up burners on your gas grill – is directly underneath your food.

This hot blast of energy is what gives it a great caramelised crust and grill marks, all the while cooking your food all the way through. Cooking over direct heat works best with thinner, more tender items that cook quickly: thin steak, hamburgers, boneless chicken pieces, fish fillets, shellfish, cut vegetables and fruit.

Now, we dabble in some more technical talk. Direct heat cooking is the product of both conductive and radiant heat. The fire from the coals or burners zaps the cooking grates, which conduct the heat directly on to the surface of your food, giving it those distinct, tasty grill marks. The radiant heat is the oven effect that is created when hot air is swirling around food under the grill's closed lid. This brings us to our next point – keeping the lid on. With few exceptions, the lid should be closed as much as possible. The lid keeps air from getting to the fire, which controls flare-ups and allows the food to cook from both the bottom and the top.

While food will always cook faster from the bottom (this is why we flip!), a closed lid keeps that radiant heat in play and speeds up cooking times. Quicker cooking means fewer chances of burning or drying out our food. And of course, eating sooner, too.

CHARCOAL: GRILLING/DIRECT COOKING

With direct heat, the fire is right below the food. The heat radiates off the charcoal and conducts through the metal of the cooking grate to create those dark handsome grill marks.

CHARCOAL: ROASTING/INDIRECT COOKING

With indirect heat, the charcoal is arranged to one side of the food, or it is on both sides of the food. A large disposable foil tray catches the drippings underneath.

If you're a charcoal griller, consider setting up a two-zone fire, in which all the coals are pushed to one side. This way, even if you're not planning on needing roasting/indirect heat, you have that option if your food begins to cook too fast. For gas grillers, the principle is the same. Turn on all the burners to your desired heat level for direct heat. On-the-fly heat adjustments are a little easier on a gas grill so, if you feel that the fire is too hot, you've got the option of either lowering the heat on the burners or turning some off altogether.

This set-up also benefits all us steak lovers out there. We like having a two-zone fire for the 'sear and slide' grilling method. For thick-cut steaks and chops, a few minutes on each side over direct heat will take care of the sear; then, slide it over to the side without the fire to finish the cooking. This is the secret to a perfectly cooked steak.

In the case of indirect heat, you've probably already figured out what this means. Whereas direct heat puts your food directly above the heat source, indirect heat has it off to the side. This is a good option for larger, tougher cuts of meat that take a while to cook, such as roasts, whole chickens and racks of ribs. There tend to be fewer overcooking surprises when using indirect heat, as this method uses the grill's slightly gentler, oven-like radiant heat to do the bulk of the work. We still like to start these bigger, tougher items over direct heat, but then send them over to the indirect side to hang out for a while. It's the best of both worlds approach – getting those flavourful grill marks while your meat is still thoroughly cooked, but not overcooked.

GRILL MAINTENANCE

'Grill, you had us with the food'.... But you kept us with the easy upkeep.

In order to get those great grill marks, to keep food from sticking to the grill, and to prevent remnants of yesterday's brisket attaching to today's burgers, the cooking grates should be cleaned before every use. With the lid closed, preheat the grill to about 260°C/500°F for 10 minutes. Wearing an insulated barbecue mitt or oven gloves, open the lid and scrape the grates with a long-handled grill brush to loosen charred bits and pieces. That's it. You're done.

Your grill may need a more thorough cleaning every month or so, which is still really easy to do. Always check the instructions in your Owner's Guide first, but start by wiping the outside of the grill down with warm, soapy water. Scrape any accumulated debris from the inside of the lid. Remove the cooking grates, brush the burners and clean out the bottom of the cooking box and drip pan. For the full upkeep and maintenance treatment, consult your Owner's Guide.

Charcoal grillers, take note: ash contains a small amount of water. All ash sitting at the bottom of the kettle should be removed regularly to prevent rust.

GAS: GRILLING/DIRECT COOKING

To use direct heat on a gas grill, simply light the burners right below the food and adjust the knobs for the temperature level you want.

GAS: ROASTING/INDIRECT COOKING

To use indirect heat on a gas grill, light the burners on the far left and far right of the grill, and cook the food between them. If your grill has just two burners, turn one on and keep one off. Place the food over the unlit burner.

SMOKING ON THE GRILL

Barbecue masters and 'sultans of smoke' (almost always self-proclaimed) tend to talk a big game and lead you to believe that their smoking techniques are far beyond the understanding of backyard grillers. Don't be intimidated by the bravado and secrecy. Smoking is much simpler than it looks – and it doesn't require a gigantic barbecue rig either. Smoking is really just a form of seasoning, like rubbing meat with spices or soaking it in a marinade. Think of smoking as cooking your food in an aromatic cloud of seasonings. The keys, then, are knowing which seasonings (woods) to use and how much of them to use.

FOR A CHARCOAL GRILL

All you need to get started on a charcoal grill is to soak your wood chips in water for at least 30 minutes. Then shake off the excess water, and use tongs to scatter the chips on top of the burning charcoal. Many smoking recipes are true barbecue, taking a few hours or more over roasting/indirect low heat to cook, and so they will require some new additions of soaked and drained wood chips (and charcoal) to keep the smoke flowing.

FOR A GAS GRILL

You will need some sort of box for smoking soaked, drained wood chips on a gas grill, whether it's a built-in smoker box inside your grill, a stainless steel smoker box that you place on top of the cooking grate, or a disposable foil tray covered with aluminium foil and poked with holes to allow the smoke to escape. If you need to add more chips to a smoker box, do it while some of the old chips are still burning. The old chips will help to light the new ones.

SMOKING WITH WOOD

WHICH WOOD TO USE

Like herbs and spices, each type of wood has its own
strengths or intensities, from mild to moderate to strong.
It's a good idea to match the intensity of the smoke to
the intensity of your food. The chart opposite provides
some of our favourite combinations. We're talking about
personal preferences here, so there really is no wrong
choice of wood. Well, actually . . . some woods, such as
pine and aspen, are so soft and resinous that their smoke
is bitter and potentially toxic. Stick with the hardwoods
listed opposite instead.

HOW MUCH WOOD TO USE

The most common rookie mistake is oversmoking
food, which is particularly easy to do with seafood and
light meats, because they soak up smoke in a matter of
minutes. At some point, the smoke creeps over a line and
changes from being pleasantly fragrant and woodsy to
being aggressively bitter and sooty. To stay clear of that
line, add a few handfuls of water-soaked and drained
wood chips every hour, but stop smoking your food after
the first half of its cooking time so it doesn't get too
smoky. That's a good guideline.

FOR A WATER SMOKER

Wood chunks are a good choice when using a water
smoker. They last much longer than chips, so you
won't have to replenish them as often. Another little
convenience with chunks is that you don't need to soak
them. As dry as they are, they don't flame up the way
wood chips do.

WOOD TYPE		CHARACTERISTICS	PAIRS WITH
	Alder	**Mild:** Delicate flavour	Pork, poultry, salmon, swordfish, other fish
	Apple	**Mild:** Slightly sweet but also dense, fruity smoke flavour	Beef, pork (particularly ham), poultry, game birds
	Hickory	**Moderate:** Pungent, smoky, bacon-like flavour	Beef, pork, poultry, wild game, cheeses
	Oak	**Moderate:** An assertive but pleasing flavour; sometimes a little acidic; blends well with sweeter woods	Beef (particularly brisket), pork, poultry
	Mesquite	**Strong:** In a class by itself – a big, bold smoke bordering on bitter	Beef and lamb

Choose your wood wisely as it can affect the taste, smell and smoking times of your food. The above are some of our favourites.

KNIFE SKILLS

Knife skills are to grilling what wielding a bat is to baseball: fundamental. Without getting a handle on those basics, there's no chance of a win. Understanding how to use and to care for your knives, and knowing which knives are right for your cooking task, will make you a better, happier and more efficient cook ... with all your fingers intact. A huge knife collection isn't necessary, nor is spending too much on them. But having a few quality tools you enjoy using? That's like scoring a home run.

SHARPENING STEEL
A few glides down the sharpening steel before using your knife will grind and realign its edges back to sharpened life.

CHEF'S KNIFE
Above all others, this is the one to have. Slicing, dicing, carving and cutting, it's the kitchen workhorse.

SERRATED KNIFE
Its saw-like teeth cut through bread without crushing, through tomatoes without squishing, and through meat without toughening.

SANTOKU KNIFE
A little smaller than a chef's knife, this is a good one for smaller (or less sure) hands.

BONING KNIFE
This thin, almost flexible blade allows for more precise work along the edges of bones and in tight spaces.

PARING KNIFE
Use this short, handy little tool for peeling, trimming and chopping vegetables and fruits.

USING A SHARPENING STEEL

All knives lose their sharp edges when you run them across chopping boards again and again. They dull just from cutting food. If your knives are dull, you will need to work harder and longer to cut your food, raising the chances that you will slip while exerting too much force. A steel doesn't sharpen a knife as much as it straightens crooked edges. The safest way to do this is with the 'butcher's method', shown below. It's an easy, inexpensive way to ensure that your knives remain more of an asset than a liability.

1 Point the narrow end of the steel facing down on a chopping board. Position the heel of your knife at an angle of 15–20 degrees near the handle of the steel.

2 Swipe the blade down one side of the steel, pulling the knife towards you at the same time so that every part of the blade runs along the steel.

3 Repeat the swiping action on the opposite side of the steel.

4 Continue to swipe on both sides of the steel a few times or until the knife can easily cut through a piece of paper.

CHOPPING AN ONION

They're round, they're slippery and they make us cry: onions aren't doing anyone any chopping favours. But this vegetable, above all others, benefits from a good trip under the knife. Finely chopped, sliced, diced or rough-chopped, onions do so much of the flavourful heavy lifting in our recipes. Knowing how to properly prep them is integral and will make chopping all other vegetables a walk in the tear-free park.

1 Trim about 1 cm/ ½ inch from the stem end, but keep the root end intact; otherwise, the onion will fall apart.

2 Cut the onion in half through the stem and root ends.

3 Peel off the skin and possibly one layer of each half with your fingers or a paring knife.

4 Lay each half, flat side down, on a chopping board. Hold the onion steady with the fingertips of one hand.

5 Using the knife in your other hand, make a series of horizontal cuts, working from the bottom up and from the stem towards the root end, to but not through it.

6 Then make a series of vertical cuts, with the tip of the knife cutting almost but not quite through the root end.

7 Then cut each half crossways to create evenly sized dice.

8 The size of the dice depends on how far apart you make each horizontal, vertical and crossways cut.

ESSENTIAL TOOLS

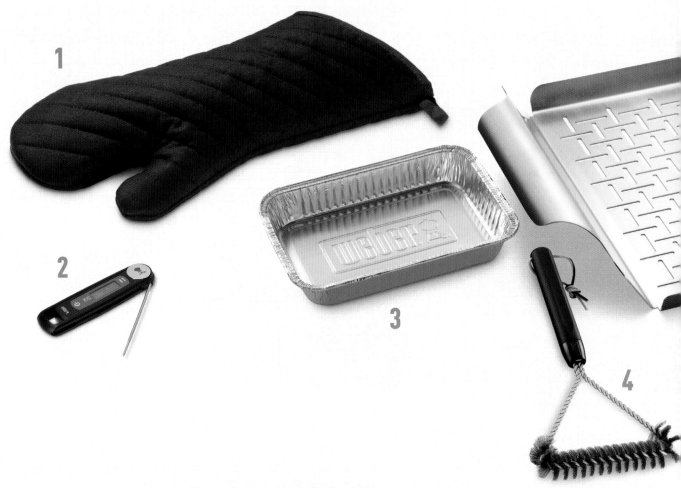

1

2

3

4

True, once you've got a grill, you don't need much else, but in order to prevent burnt food, scorched fingers, flare-ups and flameouts, you're going to really want the following items.

1 Barbecue Mitts
When in doubt, wear 'em. The good ones are insulated and protect both hand and forearm.

2 Thermometer
Small and relatively inexpensive, this gadget is essential for quickly gauging the internal temperature of the meat when grilling it.

3 Disposable Trays
Available in a variety of sizes, disposable foil trays offer many conveniences. Use them to move food to and from the grill and to keep food warm on the cooking grates.

4 Grill Brush
A must-use before you even dream of grilling. A quick once-over on hot grates prevents the charred remains of meals past from sticking to any of your meals present.

5 Grill Pan
Designed for food that is either too small or too delicate for the cooking grates, a perforated grill pan keeps food right where it ought to be – on the grill, not in it.

6 Brush
Look for a basting brush that has heat-resistant silicone bristles and a long handle.

7 Tongs
Consider these to be an extension of your hand. The best tongs should have an effortless tension mechanism, comfortable hand grips and a lock to keep them compact.

8 Spatula
Look for a long-handled spatula designed with a bent (offset) neck so that the blade is set lower than the handle. This makes it easier to lift food off the cooking grates.

9 Chimney Starter
Take some briquettes, lighter cubes or crumpled newspapers, and a match, and you've got a safely and quickly lit fire without lighter fluid.

THE GRILLER'S STORE-CUPBOARD

Extra-Virgin Olive Oil
You won't be getting far without this invaluable ingredient and handy tool (no more food sticking to the cooking grates). It's always good to have basic extra-virgin olive oil on hand because of its mild, fruity flavour, its health benefits and its availability just about everywhere.

Sea Salt
Alongside extra-virgin olive oil, this is on the 'desert island' list. Coarser and purer tasting than standard table salt, and with a larger grain, sea salt covers more surface area on your food and with fewer additives than the stuff that comes out of a shaker. It also dissolves beautifully.

Black Peppercorns
Salt's superhero sidekick, peppercorns give our palate the 'pow' we need to properly taste food. Have a stash of whole peppercorns to hand that can be tossed into a pepper mill and coarsely ground. Easier still, throw a handful into a spice grinder and you've got fresh pepper for the week.

Herbs and Spices
These are the quickest and easiest routes to serious flavour and are the basis for a good rub. You don't need every kind the supermarket store has to offer, but the essentials – thyme, oregano, chilli powder, cumin and paprika (try smoked paprika) – ought always to be on your shelves.

Mayonnaise
Mayonnaise elevates other ingredients' games while still being great on its own. It makes a delicious spread mixed with garlic or horseradish for grilled steak sandwiches, but it can also be slathered on lean cuts before grilling to lock in moisture. Some styles of barbecue even use it abundantly in sauces.

Dijon Mustard
Sophisticated Dijon mustard boasts a creamy, spicy tang and makes a great 'glue' to keep rubs and other seasonings on meats. Great for a glaze, in mopping sauces and in marinades, it's also often that note of creamy complexity found in salad dressings.

Soy Sauce

Brewed from fermented soya beans, soy sauce is a favourite in marinades for its ability to really sink into food and blast it with flavour. It's a staple in Chinese recipes, but it's also great for the pungent 'umami' it lends to so much more. Just a teaspoon in a vinaigrette can wake up the other ingredients' flavours.

Worcestershire Sauce

This ranks alongside soy sauce in the 'umami' major league. One tiny bottle contains vinegar, spices, herbs, anchovies and more – the combo of which perks up otherwise bland recipes and even makes meat taste meatier (it's great in burgers). A little goes a long way.

Tomato Ketchup

No self-respecting griller would be caught without this one. This classic topping for burgers and hot dogs is also the main ingredient in homemade barbecue sauces. Store-bought brands are about as good as you can make at home.

Sugar (Granulated and Brown)

Thank sugar for that sweet little note you get in the perfect barbecue sauce or in the caramelised crust on your slow-cooked pork shoulder. Brown sugar is used more often than granulated sugar because it has a deep, molasses flavour that complements spicy ingredients.

Balsamic Vinegar

Vinegar is everything oil is not – thin, acidic, pungent – but it so beautifully highlights everything oil is, which is why they're not often apart. Vinegar is a must in marinades, dressings and mopping sauces. Balsamic and cider vinegars are good choices for both their flavour and their availability.

Barbecue Sauce

This can be the griller's be-all and end-all. A good sauce can steal the spotlight, but a better one makes your meat the star. Tangy, spicy, or sweet and spicy, barbecue sauce should have both subtle and intense layers of flavour. Brush it on your meat towards the end of its cooking time, or serve it as a side.

SALT, PEPPER AND OIL

Good ole salt, pepper and olive oil. Rare is the recipe that doesn't involve this terrific trio. Why? Well, they're a griller's dream – tasty and practical. Salt is both a natural preservative and a mineral that our bodies require in proper doses (those crisp cravings are no coincidence). Salt draws moisture out of whatever it is sprinkled on to, concentrating the natural flavours of our food and allowing items, such as meat and fish, to develop a well-seasoned crust on the grill. Pepper, while not exactly life-sustaining, provides a kicky little palate pick-me-up. The slight tickle it leaves on the tongue enables it to be more receptive to flavours – like jump leads for our taste buds. Olive oil acts as a barrier protecting your food from the intense heat of the grill – no sticking, no burning and little-to-no effort. Its mild, fruity flavour, availability and health benefits (olive oil is the ultimate 'good' fat) are what make it so indispensable in recipes, from marinades to salad dressings and everything in between.

Sea salt and freshly ground black pepper have a purer taste and a larger grain than table salt and pre-ground pepper, which covers more surface area and cuts down on the chance of over-seasoning. Sea salt dissolves easily enough when you whisk it rigorously in water, but it dissolves slowly on meats, making it great for both brining and seasoning. If you prefer to use table salt in a recipe, be sure to cut the amount called for in half – it weighs twice as much as sea salt and is easy to overdo. Use the easy-to-find, inexpensive extra-virgin olive oils for grilling. The scorching hot temperature of the grill would ruin the nuances of really expensive, cold-pressed olive oils that are made for dressings; however, the less expensive olive oils hold up well on the grill and taste better than flavourless vegetable oils.

TOP TEN GRILLING DOS AND DON'TS

1 **Do preheat the grill.** If your cooking grates aren't hot enough, some food will stick and will never have a decent chance of searing properly or developing handsome grill marks. Even if a recipe calls for medium or low heat, you should preheat the grill on high first. Open the grill's lid, fire up the charcoal or the gas burners, close the lid, and then let the cooking grates get screaming hot for about 10 minutes. The grill temperature should reach at least 260°C/500°F.

2 **Don't start with dirty grates.** Tossing food on to the cooking grates before they have been cleaned is a great way to experience dinner déjà vu – if you're into that sort of thing. Leftover 'stuff' on the grates acts like glue, binding both your new food to the old and all of it to the grates. After you have preheated the grill for about 10 minutes, brush that stuff off entirely so that whatever you are grilling now has a clean, smooth surface to brown evenly. The best tool for the job is a sturdy long-handled brush with stiff stainless steel bristles.

3 **Do get your act together.** Bring everything you need near the grill before you actually grill. If you have to run back into the kitchen while your food is cooking, you might miss (that is, overcook or burn) something important. So bring your tools, bring your food that is already oiled and seasoned, bring your glaze or sauce or whatever. Don't forget clean platters for the cooked food. French chefs call this *mise en place* (meaning 'put in place'). We call it getting your act together.

4 **Do give yourself at least two heat zones.** If you set up your grill for one type of heat only, your options are limited. What if something is cooking too fast? What if your food is flaring up? What if you are grilling two very different foods at the same time? You should have at least two heat zones: one for direct heat (where the fire is right under the food) and one for indirect heat (where the fire is off to the side of the food). That way, you can move your food from one zone to another whenever you like.

5 **Don't overcrowd the grill.** Packing too much food into a tight space on the grill restricts your flexibility. You should leave at least one-quarter of the cooking grates clear, with plenty of space between each food item so that you can get your tongs in there and easily move them around. Sometimes grilling involves split-second decisions and the ability to jockey food from one area to another. So give yourself enough room to work.

6   **Do use the lid.** Believe it or not, a grill's lid is for much more than just keeping the rain out. Its more important job is preventing too much air from getting in and too much heat and smoke from getting out. When the lid is closed, the cooking grates are hotter, the grilling times are faster, the smoky tastes are stronger, and the flare-ups are fewer. So put a lid on it. Having said that, don't forget to open the charcoal grill's lid vent at least halfway. Every fire needs a little air to keep on burning.

7   **Don't touch the food too much.** We all like food when it is seared to a deep brown colour with plenty of beautifully charred bits. The trouble is, many people move their food so often that it doesn't get enough time in one place to reach that desirable level of colour and flavour. In nearly all cases, you should turn food just once or twice. If you're fiddling with it more than that, you are probably also opening the lid too much, which causes its own set of problems. Step back and trust the process.

8   **Do take charge of the fire.** On its own, a charcoal fire climbs to its hottest temperatures first and then loses heat either quickly or slowly, depending on your type of charcoal and, more importantly, on you. So make some proactive moves like refuelling the fire before you lose too much heat, rearranging coals to suit your needs, sweeping away the ashes that could clog the bottom vents, and adjusting the vents on the lid for ideal airflow. A grill master is always in charge.

9   **Don't serve rubbery chicken.** When grilling, sometimes the most important thing is knowing when to stop. If you specialise in chicken breasts so overcooked that they bounce, it's time to learn some doneness clues, as in the gently yielding firmness of perfectly grilled chicken when you press the surface with a fingertip. If you want an even more reliable test of doneness, get an instant-read meat thermometer. This slim little gem will help you pinpoint that critical moment when your food is at its best.

10   **Do use the grill for more than grilling.** Back in the 1950s, grilling meant one thing: meat (and only meat) charred over open flames. A true measure of a griller today is the depth and breadth of the menu. That means appetizers through to desserts cooked on the grill and, in some cases, that means learning how to braise, roast, smoke, simmer and even sauté or stir-fry. When you have learnt how to harness the heat of the grill to do all this and more, you're officially a master of Weber®-style grilling.

STARTERS

GRILL SKILLS
PERFECT SHELLFISH

PRAWNS

Terms like 'small', 'medium', and 'large', as well as 'king' and 'jumbo' are used inconsistently where prawns are sold. Occasionally prawns are given a size, as in the US, where a label that reads '16/20' means that it takes 16–20 of those prawns to make a pound. The larger the prawn the better it is for grilling, as they will not dry out as quickly as small ones.

WHEN IS IT DONE?

Shellfish don't flake, but they turn an opaque, pearly white colour at the centre when they are cooked. The only way to know for sure how the centre looks is to cut into it, so plan on sacrificing one or two shellfish. In this photo, the prawn on the left is underdone, the prawn on the right is overdone and the prawn in the middle is just right.

As with prawns, bigger is usually better because bigger scallops allow for more time on the grill to develop flavours. However, avoid 'wet-packed' scallops that have been treated with a phosphate-and-water solution that causes them to swell with liquid. Wet scallops tend to steam (and stick) rather than sear on the grill, so look for 'dry-packed' scallops instead.

The easiest way to cook any of these bivalves (meaning they have two shells) is to lay them directly over the fire. When they get hot, their briny juices boil and the steam released puts pressure on their shells, causing them to open. When the shells burn just a little, the smoke carries magical aromas.

1 Check your scallops for a small tough muscle along the side. This is the adductor muscle that helps the scallop hold on to its shell. It is quite chewy, so pull it off with your fingers and discard it before grilling.

2 Marinate your scallops for extra flavour and moisture, but don't overdo it. If your marinade has a fair amount of acidity, your scallops could turn mushy. One to two hours of marinating is usually a good time frame.

A tightly closed mussel shell is a good sign of freshness. If any mussel is gaping open a bit, tap it with a finger. If the shell closes immediately, the mussel is alive and fresh.

3 Going onto the grill, scallops should be well oiled or buttered, but not dripping wet. Too much liquid causes sticking. If you have used a wet marinade, lightly pat the scallops dry on kitchen paper.

Some mussels come with the added issue of a 'beard'. To remove the beard, use your thumb and index finger to grasp the beard, and pull sharply, perpendicular to the mussel. Do this shortly before grilling, because once its beard has been removed, a mussel begins to spoil.

4 Grill scallops over grilling/direct high heat with the flattest side down first. Wait at least 2 minutes for that side to brown. Turn them over only when you can lift each scallop along its edge with tongs. Don't scrape under a scallop with a spatula and tear it.

Clams and mussels often have some sand and grit inside and outside. The easiest way to clean them is to soak them in salt water (200 g/7 oz sea salt to 1 litre/2 pints of water) for 30 minutes to 1 hour. Then rinse and scrub the outside of the shells with a stiff brush.

5 The sweet succulence of a perfectly grilled scallop is spectacular. When it reaches its ideal doneness, the pearly colour is opaque, and the texture is both creamy and wet.

Big, juicy oysters do best on the grill. After you have shucked each one (see page 225) and have released the flesh from the shell, grill it with the deeper shell balanced over grilling/direct high heat, with or without

CLAMS CASINO
WITH TOASTED BREADCRUMBS

SERVES: 4–6 | PREP TIME: 20 minutes, plus about 30 minutes to open the clams | GRILLING TIME: 6–8 minutes
SPECIAL EQUIPMENT: clam knife (optional)

36 American hard shell clams, scrubbed

TOPPING
4 rashers bacon, finely diced
1 red pepper, finely diced
2 garlic cloves, finely chopped or crushed
2 tablespoons white wine
50 g/2 oz fresh breadcrumbs
2 tablespoons finely chopped fresh flat-leaf parsley
1 tablespoon finely chopped fresh oregano
Sea salt
Freshly ground black pepper

1 Open the clams: cover your left hand (if you are right-handed) with a double or triple thickness of kitchen paper. Using the paper, grip one clam so that the thickest edges, or lips, are pointing outwards, away from your palm. Holding a clam knife in your right hand, place the sharp edge of the blade (not the tip) between the lips. Slide the blade between the two halves of the shell. (The paper should be positioned so that it will protect your hand in case the knife slips down the side of the shell.) Work the knife blade around the edges of the shell to cut through the adductor muscles, and then give the knife a twist to prise open the shell. Use your fingers to finish opening the shell and gently scrape the clam from both halves of the shell using the tip of the knife. Break off one half of the shell, leaving the clam and its juices in the remaining half. If you are having difficulty opening the clams, you can put three or four clams at a time on a microwave-safe plate and microwave on high for 15–25 seconds. This will cause the clams to open slightly, creating an opening so you can insert the knife and proceed as directed above.

2 Prepare the grill for roasting/indirect cooking over high heat (230–290°C/450–550°F).

3 In a large frying pan over a high heat, cook the bacon for 7–8 minutes until crisp, stirring occasionally. Using a slotted spoon, transfer the bacon to kitchen paper to drain. Carefully remove about half of the bacon fat from the pan and discard. Add the diced pepper and cook over a high heat until it begins to soften, about 3 minutes. Add the garlic and cook until fragrant, about 1 minute, stirring occasionally. Add the wine and cook for about 10 seconds. Add the breadcrumbs, parsley and oregano and cook for about 4 minutes until the breadcrumbs are lightly toasted, stirring often. Remove the pan from the heat, add the cooked bacon and mix well. Season with salt and pepper and set aside.

4 Lightly crumple one or two large pieces of aluminium foil and use them to line a large roasting tray or rimmed baking sheet. Nestle the clams in the foil and spoon a generous teaspoon of the topping over each. Grill the clams on the roasting tray over *roasting/indirect high heat* for 6–8 minutes, with the lid closed, until the breadcrumbs have browned and the juices are bubbling, taking care not to overcook the clams. Serve warm, with lemon wedges, if desired.

A crumpled sheet or two of aluminium foil inside a roasting tray will hold the clams in place, replacing the rock salt used for this purpose in many shellfish recipes. Nestle the opened clams in the foil and spoon some of the bacon-and-crumb mixture over each.

BACON-WRAPPED JALAPEÑO PRAWN POPPERS

SERVES: 4 | PREP TIME: 15 minutes | GRILLING TIME: 6–8 minutes | SPECIAL EQUIPMENT: 16 cocktail sticks

16 large prawns, peeled and deveined, tails left on
8 rashers bacon, each cut crossways in half
50 g/2 oz Monterey Jack or Cheddar cheese, cut
   into 16 sticks
16 pickled jalapeño pepper rings (from a jar)

1 Soak the cocktail sticks in water for at least 30 minutes.

2 Butterfly each prawn by cutting along its curved back from the head end to the tail end, cutting almost all the way through the prawn. Leave the tail section intact.

3 Prepare the grill for grilling/direct cooking over medium heat (180–230°C/350–450°F).

4 In a microwave oven on high, cook the bacon for 2–3 minutes until the fat is slightly rendered.

5 Place one piece of the cheese and one jalapeño ring inside each butterflied prawn. Close the prawn, and then wrap one piece of bacon around each prawn so that the cheese and the jalapeño are enclosed. Insert a cocktail stick into the prawn, pushing it through the exposed end of the bacon strip so that the bacon is held in place and the prawn is held closed. Grill over *grilling/direct medium heat* for 6–8 minutes, with the lid closed, until the prawns are firm to the touch and just turning opaque at the centre and the bacon is crisp, turning once. Serve immediately.

Wrapping prawns in bacon seems like a great idea until you realize that the prawns are fully cooked before the bacon gets crispy. Solution: precook the bacon for a few minutes before wrapping the prawns. Also, secure both ends of each piece with a cocktail stick so the bacon does not fall off.

FIESTA PRAWN SALSA
WITH TORTILLA CHIPS

SERVES: 4 | PREP TIME: 20 minutes | GRILLING TIME: 12–16 minutes | MARINATING TIME: 1–4 hours

1 poblano chilli, about 175 g/6 oz
24 large prawns, peeled and deveined, tails removed
Extra-virgin olive oil
2 tomatoes, deseeded and finely diced
1 small Fresno chilli, deseeded and finely chopped
1 jalapeño chilli, deseeded and finely chopped
½ red onion, finely diced
1 large garlic clove, finely chopped or crushed
3 tablespoons fresh lime juice
½ teaspoon sea salt
½ teaspoon freshly ground black pepper
4 tablespoons finely chopped fresh coriander
Tortilla chips

1 Prepare the grill for grilling/direct cooking over medium heat (180–230°C/350–450°F).

2 Grill the poblano over *grilling/direct medium heat* for 10–12 minutes, with the lid closed, until blackened and blistered all over, turning occasionally. Put the poblano in a bowl and cover with clingfilm to trap the steam. Let stand for about 10 minutes. Peel away and discard the charred skin, cut off and discard the stem and seeds, and then cut the poblano into 5-mm/¼-inch dice. Put the diced poblano back in the bowl.

3 Increase the temperature of the grill to high heat (230–290°C/450–550°F). Lightly brush the prawns on both sides with oil. Grill over *grilling/direct high heat* for 2–4 minutes, with the lid closed, until they are firm to the touch and just turning opaque in the centre. Cut the prawns into 5-mm/¼-inch pieces.

4 To the bowl with the diced poblano, add the prawns, 1 tablespoon oil, the tomatoes, Fresno and jalapeño chillies, the onion, garlic, lime juice, salt and pepper; toss to combine. Cover and refrigerate for at least 1 hour or up to 4 hours. Just before serving, stir in the coriander. Serve the salsa immediately with tortilla chips.

TIP If preferred, substitute the Fresno chilli with another jalapeño chilli. Be sure to take a small taste of the chillies to determine how hot they are, and then adjust the amount you use accordingly.

SEARED CALAMARI
WITH CHILLI SAUCE AND MINT

SERVES: 4 | PREP TIME: **30 minutes** | GRILLING TIME: **2–4 minutes** | SPECIAL EQUIPMENT: **perforated grill pan**

SAUCE
250 ml/8 fl oz sweet chilli sauce
3 tablespoons fresh mint, finely chopped
1 teaspoon finely grated lime zest
4 teaspoons fresh lime juice
2 teaspoons peeled fresh ginger, finely chopped
1 large garlic clove, finely chopped or crushed

500 g/1 lb cleaned squid, tubes and tentacles separated,
    thawed if frozen
1 tablespoon vegetable oil
½ teaspoon sea salt
¼ teaspoon freshly ground black pepper
½ cucumber
8 large leaves round lettuce
2 tablespoons fresh mint

1 Whisk the sauce ingredients in a bowl. Transfer 125 ml/
4 fl oz of the sauce to a large bowl. Set aside the
remaining sauce in a bowl for serving.

2 Prepare the grill for grilling/direct cooking over high
heat (230–290°C/450–550°F) and preheat a perforated
grill pan.

3 Pat the squid dry with kitchen paper. To the large bowl,
add the squid, oil, salt and pepper. Stir to coat evenly.

4 Cut the cucumber crossways into thin slices, and then
cut the slices into 1-cm/½-inch-wide strips.

5 Lift the squid from the bowl and place in a single layer
on the grill pan. Discard the sauce in the large bowl.
Grill over *grilling/direct high heat* for 2–4 minutes, with the
lid closed, until the squid pieces are just turning opaque
and no longer look wet, turning once. Remove from the grill
and cut the tubes crossways into 1-cm/½-inch-wide rings.
Leave the tentacles whole.

6 Arrange two lettuce leaves on each of four plates. Divide
the squid equally among the lettuce leaves and top with
the cucumber strips. Drizzle with the reserved sauce from
the bowl and finish with the mint. Serve immediately.

TIP Many supermarkets stock squid that has already
been cleaned. Often sold frozen, with the tubes
and tentacles separated, the squid just needs a little time
to thaw before you prepare it.

SMOKY ONION AND BLUE CHEESE DIP

SERVES: 8–10 | PREP TIME: 15 minutes | GRILLING TIME: 35–45 minutes | CHILLING TIME: 30 minutes–8 hours
SPECIAL EQUIPMENT: 1 large handful hickory wood chips, large disposable foil tray

2 tablespoons vegetable oil
2 large onions, thinly sliced
250 ml/8 fl oz soured cream
125 g/4 oz plain low-fat yogurt or additional soured cream
50 g/2 oz blue cheese, crumbled, at room temperature
Sea salt
Freshly ground black pepper
1 tablespoon finely chopped fresh chives
Crisps

1 Soak the wood chips in water for at least 30 minutes.

2 Prepare the grill for roasting/indirect cooking over medium heat (180–230°C/350–450°F).

3 Pour the oil into a large disposable foil tray and tilt to coat the bottom of the tray. Add the onions and turn to coat in the oil.

4 Drain and add the wood chips to the charcoal or to the smoker box of a gas grill, following manufacturer's instructions, and close the lid. When the wood begins to smoke, cook the tray of onions over *roasting/indirect medium heat* for 35–45 minutes, with the lid closed, until they are rich golden brown and some of their edges are just beginning to char, stirring occasionally. Remove from the grill and let cool completely. Cut the onions into small dice.

5 Combine the soured cream, yogurt and cheese; stir and mash together until the cheese pieces are about half their original size. Add the onions and season the dip with salt and pepper, keeping in mind that the potato crisps are salty, too. Transfer to a serving bowl and top with the chives. Chill the dip for at least 30 minutes or up to 8 hours. Serve with potato crisps.

AVOCADO AND RED ONION QUESADILLAS
WITH SUN-DRIED TOMATO JAM

SERVES: 4–6 | PREP TIME: 20 minutes | GRILLING TIME: 4–6 minutes

JAM
14 sun-dried tomato halves packed in oil, about
   125 g/4 oz total, drained and oil reserved
2 tablespoons oil from the jar of sun-dried tomatoes,
   plus more as needed
1 teaspoon fresh thyme leaves

6 flour tortillas (20 cm/8 inches)
Vegetable oil
375 g/12 oz Monterey Jack or Cheddar cheese, grated
½ red onion, finely chopped
1 large ripe avocado, diced
½ teaspoon sea salt
¼ teaspoon freshly ground black pepper
125 ml/4 fl oz soured cream

1 In a food processor combine the jam ingredients. Process until the mixture has a jam-like consistency, scraping down the sides of the bowl and adding a little more oil, if necessary.

2 Prepare the grill for grilling/direct cooking over medium heat (180–230°C/350–450°F).

3 Lightly brush one side of each tortilla with vegetable oil. Place the tortillas, oiled side down, on a work surface. Assemble the quesadillas by scattering about 4 tablespoons of the cheese on one half of each tortilla. Top the cheese with equal amounts of onion, avocado, salt, pepper and another 4 tablespoons of the cheese. Fold the empty side of each tortilla over the filling and press down.

4 Grill the quesadillas over *grilling/direct medium heat* for 4–6 minutes, with the lid closed, until golden on both sides, turning once. Remove from the grill and cut into wedges. Serve hot with the tomato jam and some soured cream.

TOUR DE TORTILLA

Quesadillas may hail from Mexico, but they're world travellers. Their only necessity is some good melting cheese. Flour tortillas take an Italian turn with pesto, mozzarella and sun-dried tomatoes. Brie and a smear of fruit preserve are a nod to the French. A dollop of chutney and a pinch of curry powder over grilled veggies and mild Cheddar take you to India in an instant. And sliced steak, grilled onions and blue cheese bring you right back home. No passport required.

AUBERGINE CAPRESE
WITH HERB VINAIGRETTE

SERVES: 6 | PREP TIME: 25 minutes | GRILLING TIME: 8–10 minutes

1 large rounded aubergine, 425–500 g/14–16 oz, ends
    trimmed, cut crossways into 12 slices, each about
    8 mm/⅓ inch thick
Extra-virgin olive oil
3 plum tomatoes, each about 75 g/3 oz, chopped
2½ tablespoons white balsamic vinegar
2 tablespoons chopped fresh basil
1 tablespoon chopped fresh chives
1 tablespoon chopped fresh dill
1 garlic clove, finely chopped or crushed
2 beefsteak tomatoes, each about 250 g/8 oz, cut crossways
    into 12 slices total, each about 8 mm/⅓ inch thick
2 balls fresh mozzarella cheese, each about 125 g/
    4 oz, cut into 12 slices total, each about 8 mm/
    ⅓ inch thick
Sea salt
Freshly ground black pepper

1 Prepare the grill for grilling/direct cooking over medium
heat (180–230°C/350–450°F).

2 Brush the aubergine slices on both sides with oil and
season with ¾ teaspoon salt and ½ teaspoon pepper.

3 Grill the aubergine slices over *grilling/direct medium
heat* for 8-10 minutes, with the lid closed, until lightly
charred and tender, turning once or twice. At the same
time, grill the plum tomatoes over *grilling/direct medium
heat* for 5-6 minutes until the skins wrinkle and start to
brown, turning once or twice. Remove from the grill as they
are done. When the tomatoes are cool enough to handle,
remove and discard the skin and seeds and chop them.

4 To make the vinaigrette: in a small bowl whisk the
plum tomatoes, 5 tablespoons oil, the vinegar, basil,
chives, dill, garlic, ½ teaspoon salt and ½ teaspoon pepper.

5 Arrange the aubergine slices, tomato slices and
mozzarella slices on a large serving plate so that they
overlap slightly. Spoon the vinaigrette over and serve.

TIP Keep herbs fresh much longer by storing them in a
jar covered with a plastic bag. Trim off the bottom
of the stems. Fill a jar with 2.5 cm/1 inch of water and place
the stem ends of the herbs in the water. Cover the herbs
with a plastic bag and store in the refrigerator. If the water
discolours after a few days, change it.

ROASTED PEPPERS
WITH MOZZARELLA AND GARLIC OIL

SERVES: 6–8 | PREP TIME: 20 minutes | GRILLING TIME: 13–17 minutes

GARLIC OIL
2 garlic cloves, chopped
½ teaspoon sea salt
4 tablespoons extra-virgin olive oil
2 tablespoons capers, rinsed, drained and finely chopped
1 tablespoon finely chopped fresh flat-leaf parsley
¼ teaspoon freshly ground black pepper

4 large peppers, preferably 2 red and 2 yellow or orange
150 g/5 oz fresh mozzarella cheese, cut into 16 slices,
    each about 5 mm/¼ inch thick, at room temperature
Juice of 1 lemon

1 Prepare the grill for grilling/direct cooking over medium heat (180–230°C/350–450°F).

2 Pound the chopped garlic with the salt, occasionally scraping the mixture against a chopping board with the side of your knife to form a paste. Thoroughly combine the garlic paste with the remaining garlic oil ingredients.

3 Grill the peppers over *grilling/direct medium heat* for 10–12 minutes, with the lid closed, until blackened and blistered all over, turning occasionally. Put the peppers in a bowl and cover with clingfilm to trap the steam. Let stand for about 10 minutes. Remove the peppers from the bowl and peel away and discard the charred skin and remove the stalks. Cut the peppers lengthways into quarters, and scrape away the veins and seeds.

4 Grill the pepper quarters, smooth side up, over *grilling/ direct medium heat* for 1–2 minutes, with the lid closed, just to warm them through. Turn the peppers over, and top each with a slice of mozzarella. Continue grilling for 2–3 minutes, with the lid closed, until the cheese is beginning to soften and run slightly at the edges. Transfer to a large serving plate and top with the garlic oil and fresh lemon juice. Serve warm or at room temperature.

BABY ARTICHOKES
WITH LEMON-PARSLEY AIOLI

SERVES: 4–6 | PREP TIME: 30 minutes | GRILLING TIME: 6–8 minutes

1 lemon
12 baby artichokes
1 tablespoon extra-virgin olive oil
Sea salt
Freshly ground black pepper

AIOLI
125 ml/4 fl oz mayonnaise
1 tablespoon freshly grated
   Parmesan cheese
1 tablespoon finely chopped fresh flat-leaf parsley
1 garlic clove, finely chopped or crushed

1 Finely grate 2 teaspoons zest from the lemon and set aside. Cut the lemon in half. Squeeze the juice of one half into a large bowl of water. Juice the other half and set aside to use in the aioli.

2 Snap off the dark green outer leaves of the artichokes to reveal the yellowish leaves with light green tips. Cut off the stem end and the sharp tip of each artichoke. Cut each artichoke in half lengthways. Pare off the green skin from the base and stalk. After each artichoke is trimmed, place in the lemon water.

3 Prepare the grill for grilling/direct cooking over medium heat (180–230°C/350–450°F).

4 Bring a saucepan of lightly salted water to the boil. Drain the artichokes. Cook them in the boiling water for 5–7 minutes until just tender when pierced with the tip of a knife. Drain and rinse them under cold water. Pat dry, transfer to a bowl, toss with the oil, and season with salt and pepper.

5 Whisk the aioli ingredients, including the 2 teaspoons of lemon zest and 1 tablespoon of the reserved lemon juice.

6 Grill the artichokes over *grilling/direct medium heat* for 6–8 minutes, with the lid closed, until golden brown, turning once or twice. Remove from the grill and serve warm with the aioli.

Unlike mature artichokes, baby artichokes do not have a fully developed choke, so there is no need to remove it.

PROSCIUTTO-WRAPPED SPICED PINEAPPLE SPEARS

SERVES: 8 | PREP TIME: 20 minutes | GRILLING TIME: 8–10 minutes

PASTE

2 spring onions, thinly sliced (white and light green
   parts only)
1 jalapeño chilli, roughly chopped
1 tablespoon groundnut oil
1 tablespoon peeled fresh ginger, finely chopped
1 tablespoon dark brown sugar
½ teaspoon dried thyme
½ teaspoon ground allspice
½ teaspoon ground cinnamon
½ teaspoon sea salt

1 large pineapple, peeled, cored and cut into
   16 spears, each about 2.5 by 12 cm/1 by 5 inches
32 thin slices Parma ham, about 500 g/1 lb total

1 Prepare the grill for grilling/direct cooking over high
heat (230–290°C/450–550°F).

2 In a food processor or blender combine the paste
ingredients. Process until a chunky paste forms,
scraping down the sides of the bowl at least once.

3 Coat each pineapple spear with about 1 teaspoon of the
paste, and then wrap each spear with two slices of the
Parma ham. Grill the spears over *grilling/direct high heat*
for 8–10 minutes, with the lid closed, until the ham is crisp
on all sides, turning occasionally. Serve immediately.

HELPFUL KITCHEN EQUIPMENT

The grill is the star of this show, but it's time for the
'best supporting appliances' to take a bow. Ladies and
gentlemen: the food processor and the blender.

Our favourite kitchen appliances make short work of what
can be tedious grill prep. Yes, there is a difference between
the two gadgets, and yes, having both is worthwhile. The
food processor uniformly minces, chops, grates and grinds
vegetables, herbs, cheese and even meat so fast you'll
wonder why you have knives (OK, you still need knives).
The blender needs some liquid in order to work, which is
why it is a whizz at whirring up velvety smooth sauces
and marinades. Both are speedy, efficient, multitasking
additions to our grilling cast of characters – they're
winners, without a doubt.

ROMAINE LETTUCE HEARTS
WITH CAESAR DRESSING

SERVES: 4 | PREP TIME: 15 minutes | GRILLING TIME: 2–3 minutes

DRESSING

1 anchovy fillet packed in olive oil, drained *or*
    ½ teaspoon anchovy paste
2 tablespoons extra-virgin olive oil
1½ tablespoons mayonnaise
1½ teaspoons fresh lemon juice
1 teaspoon Dijon mustard
½ teaspoon Worcestershire sauce
½ small garlic clove, finely chopped or crushed
¼ teaspoon freshly ground black pepper

1 small baguette, about 15 cm/6 inches long, cut lengthways
    into quarters
1 garlic clove, cut in half
3 hearts of romaine lettuce, about 500 g/1 lb total, each cut
    lengthways into quarters
2 tablespoons extra-virgin olive oil
2 tablespoons freshly grated Parmesan cheese

1 Prepare the grill for grilling/direct cooking over medium heat (180–230°C/350–450°F).

2 Mash the anchovy fillet into a paste. Put all of the dressing ingredients into a bowl and whisk to combine.

3 Grill the bread quarters over *grilling/direct medium heat* for 1–2 minutes, with the lid closed, until lightly toasted, turning three times. Remove from the grill and rub the cut sides of the bread with the cut sides of the garlic clove. Set aside.

4 Brush the lettuce hearts all over with the oil and grill over *grilling/direct medium heat* for about 1 minute, with the lid open, until slightly wilted (you may not need to turn). Remove from the grill. Top the lettuce with the dressing and the cheese, and serve with the toasted bread quarters.

TIP Anchovy paste is a good substitute for anchovy fillets here. Once opened, the tube can be stored in the refrigerator for several months.

RADICCHIO AND WATERCRESS SALAD
WITH SHALLOT VINAIGRETTE

SERVES: 6 | PREP TIME: 25 minutes | MARINATING TIME: 10 minutes | GRILLING TIME: 5–7 minutes

2 heads radicchio, about 625 g/1¼ lb total, each
   cut through the core into quarters

MARINADE/VINAIGRETTE
65 ml/2½ fl oz balsamic vinegar
100 ml/3½ fl oz extra-virgin olive oil
1 large garlic clove, finely chopped or crushed
1½ teaspoons finely chopped fresh rosemary leaves
1 teaspoon sea salt
½ teaspoon freshly ground black pepper
2 shallots, finely chopped

100 g/4 oz watercress leaves and tender stems
1 tablespoon finely grated lemon zest
1 wedge, about 75 g/3 oz, Parmesan cheese
3 tablespoons pine nuts, toasted

1 Prepare the grill for grilling/direct cooking over medium heat (180–230°C/350–450°F).

2 Rinse the radicchio under cold water and then drain briefly, cut side down, on kitchen paper.

3 In a large bowl whisk 4 tablespoons of the vinegar, 75 ml/3 fl oz of the oil, the garlic, rosemary, salt and pepper. Add the radicchio to the bowl and turn to coat evenly. Let stand for 10 minutes.

4 Lift the radicchio from the bowl and transfer to a plate, leaving any excess marinade in the bowl. To make the vinaigrette, whisk the remaining vinegar and oil into the marinade. Stir in the shallots and set aside.

5 Grill the radicchio over *grilling/direct medium heat* for 3–4 minutes, with the lid closed, until slightly charred. Turn the radicchio over and grill for 2–3 minutes more, until the outer layers are browned and crisp and the inside is still tender and purple. Remove from the grill. When cool enough to handle, cut the radicchio crossways into 2.5-cm/1-inch strips. Add to the bowl with the vinaigrette along with the watercress and the lemon zest. Toss to coat evenly. Using a vegetable peeler, shave curls of the Parmesan cheese over the salad and top with the pine nuts. Serve immediately.

PEACH AND BLUE CHEESE BRUSCHETTA
DRIZZLED WITH HONEY

SERVES: 4 | PREP TIME: 10 minutes | GRILLING TIME: about 8 minutes

125 g/4 oz cream cheese, softened
2 tablespoons granulated sugar
1 tablespoon fresh thyme leaves
4 firm but ripe peaches, each cut in half
8 slices Italian or French bread, each about 1 cm/
    ½ inch thick
Extra-virgin olive oil
125 g/4 oz blue cheese, crumbled
3 tablespoons honey

1 Prepare the grill for grilling/direct cooking over medium-low heat (180°C/350°F).

2 Stir the cream cheese, sugar and thyme until blended. Set aside. Lightly brush the peach halves and the bread slices on both sides with oil.

3 Grill the peach halves over *grilling/direct medium-low heat* for about 8 minutes, with the lid closed, until lightly charred and beginning to soften, turning once. During the last minute of grilling time, toast the bread slices over *grilling/direct heat*, turning once or twice. Remove the peaches and the bread from the grill.

4 Spread each bread slice with an equal amount of the cream cheese mixture.

5 Cut the peach halves into 5-mm/¼-inch slices. Divide the peach slices among the bread slices, overlapping them slightly. Top with the blue cheese and drizzle with the honey. Serve right away.

TIP Apricots or nectarines may be substituted for the peaches.

TOASTED BRUSCHETTA
WITH SAUSAGE AND TOMATO

SERVES: 6 | PREP TIME: 45 minutes | GRILLING TIME: about 6 minutes

TOPPING
Extra-virgin olive oil
250 g/8 oz sweet Italian sausages, casings removed
1 onion, finely chopped
2 garlic cloves, finely chopped or crushed
1 450-g/14½-oz can diced plum tomatoes in juice
1½ teaspoons Italian herb seasoning
¼ teaspoon crushed red chilli flakes

1 baguette, about 175 g/6 oz, cut crossways into
   1- to 2.5-cm/½- to 1-inch slices
40 g/1½ oz Parmesan cheese, freshly grated
175 g/6 oz mozzarella cheese, grated

1 In a saucepan over a medium-high heat, warm
1 tablespoon oil. Add the sausages and cook for about
5 minutes until lightly browned, breaking up the meat with
the side of a spoon. Using a slotted spoon, transfer the
sausage to a bowl, leaving the fat in the saucepan.

2 Add the onion to the saucepan and cook for about
3 minutes until softened, stirring occasionally. Add the
garlic and cook for about 1 minute until fragrant, stirring
often. Add the tomatoes and juice, Italian herb seasoning
and chilli flakes and stir to combine. Add the sausage and
bring the mixture to the boil. Reduce the heat to medium-
low and simmer for 10–15 minutes until the liquid is almost
completely evaporated, stirring occasionally. Remove from
the heat.

3 Prepare the grill for grilling/direct cooking over
medium-low heat (180°C/350°F).

4 Lightly brush one side of each baguette slice with oil.
Toast the baguette slices over *grilling/direct medium-
low heat* for about 1 minute, with the lid closed, turning
once or twice. Transfer the slices, oiled side up, to a roasting
tray or a baking sheet. Top with equal amounts of Parmesan
cheese, the topping and the mozzarella. Grill the bruschetta
on the roasting tray over *grilling/direct medium-low heat*
for about 5 minutes, with the lid closed, until the cheese is
melted. Serve warm.

TURKEY MEATBALLS
WITH CHILLI-GINGER SAUCE

SERVES: 8–12 (makes about 28 meatballs) | PREP TIME: 30 minutes | CHILLING TIME: 1 hour | GRILLING TIME: 8–10 minutes

MEATBALLS
750 g/1½ lb minced turkey, preferably thigh meat
4 tablespoons finely chopped fresh coriander
2 spring onions, finely chopped (white and light green parts only)
1 tablespoon soy sauce
1 tablespoon peeled, grated fresh ginger
2 teaspoons hot chilli-garlic sauce
2 garlic cloves, finely chopped or crushed
1 teaspoon ground coriander
1 teaspoon sea salt

SAUCE
125 ml/4 fl oz rice vinegar
4 tablespoons fresh lime juice
50 g/2 oz granulated sugar
1 tablespoon finely chopped fresh coriander
2 teaspoons finely chopped red jalapeño chilli
2 teaspoons peeled, grated fresh ginger
1 teaspoon sea salt
1 garlic clove, finely chopped or crushed
Vegetable oil

1 Combine the meatball ingredients, gently mixing until the ingredients are evenly distributed. With wet hands, form into equal-sized balls, each about 3.5 cm/1½ inches in diameter. Cover with clingfilm and refrigerate for at least 1 hour.

2 In a saucepan over medium-high heat, combine the vinegar, lime juice and sugar. Bring to the boil and cook for about 5 minutes until the sugar dissolves and the liquid is reduced by one-third, stirring occasionally. Transfer the mixture to a bowl and stir in the remaining sauce ingredients. Let cool completely.

3 Prepare the grill for grilling/direct cooking over medium heat (180–230°C/350–450°F).

4 Lightly brush the meatballs with oil. Grill over *grilling/direct medium heat* for 8–10 minutes, with the lid closed, until the meat is cooked through, turning two or three times. Remove from the grill and serve warm with the sauce.

> **TIP** Be sure to purchase minced turkey made from dark meat rather than white meat. Not only is dark meat turkey more flavourful, but it also holds up better to handling, which is important when you're shaping the meatballs.

CHICKEN WINGS
WITH SWEET BALSAMIC GLAZE

SERVES: 4–6 | PREP TIME: 20 minutes | GRILLING TIME: 20–25 minutes
SPECIAL EQUIPMENT: spice mill or pestle and mortar (optional)

GLAZE
225 g/7½ oz seedless raspberry jam
4 tablespoons balsamic vinegar
2 teaspoons finely grated lemon zest
¼ teaspoon crushed red chilli flakes

RUB
1 teaspoon fennel seeds
1 teaspoon garlic powder
1 teaspoon dried basil
1 teaspoon sea salt
½ teaspoon freshly ground black pepper

12 chicken wings, about 1.5 kg/3 lb total, each cut in half at
    the joint and wing tips removed

1 Prepare the grill for grilling/direct and roasting/indirect
cooking over medium heat (180–230°C/350–450°F).

2 Whisk the glaze ingredients.

3 In a spice mill process the fennel seeds until coarsely
ground (or use the bottom of a heavy pan to crush
them). Pour the fennel seeds into a large bowl and add the
remaining rub ingredients. Add the chicken wings and toss
to coat them with the rub.

4 Grill the wings over *grilling/direct medium heat* for
10–15 minutes, with the lid closed, until golden brown,
turning once or twice. Move the wings over *roasting/
indirect medium heat*, brush with half of the glaze, and
continue grilling for about 10 minutes more, until the skin
is crisp at the edges and the meat is no longer pink at the
bone. During the last 5 minutes of grilling time, brush the
wings evenly with the remaining glaze, turning once or
twice (you may not need all of the glaze). Serve warm.

CHICKEN DRUMETTES
WITH BARBECUE SAUCE AND BLUE CHEESE

SERVES: 4–6 | PREP TIME: 30 minutes | GRILLING TIME: about 16 minutes

SAUCE
250 g/8 oz good-quality tomato sauce
1 onion, finely chopped
4 tablespoons tomato purée
3 tablespoons cider vinegar
1½ tablespoons soft light brown sugar
1½ teaspoons Worcestershire sauce
1 teaspoon fresh lemon juice
¾ teaspoon mustard powder
½ teaspoon celery salt
½ teaspoon sea salt
1 garlic clove, finely chopped or crushed
¼ teaspoon prepared chilli seasoning
⅛ teaspoon freshly ground black pepper
2 drops hot pepper sauce, or to taste

18 chicken drumsticks, about 1 kg/2 lb total
Extra-virgin olive oil
½ teaspoon sea salt
¼ teaspoon freshly ground black pepper
50 g/2 oz blue cheese, crumbled

1 In a saucepan combine the sauce ingredients. Cover and simmer gently over a medium heat for about 15 minutes until thickened, stirring occasionally. Remove from the heat and let cool. Pour the sauce through a fine sieve, and then use the back of a spoon to press on the solids to extract the liquid. Discard the solids. Put about one-third of the sauce in a small bowl for brushing on the chicken while grilling. Reserve the remaining sauce for serving.

2 Prepare the grill for grilling/direct cooking over low heat (130–180°C/250–350°F).

3 Lightly brush the chicken drumsticks on both sides with oil and season evenly with the salt and pepper.

4 Grill the chicken pieces over *grilling/direct low heat* for about 8 minutes, with the lid closed, until sizzling and nicely marked, turning once. Brush the chicken with some of the sauce in the small bowl and continue cooking for about 8 minutes more, until the juices run clear and the meat is no longer pink at the bone, turning and brushing with sauce once. Remove from the grill. Brush the drumsticks with some of the reserved sauce and top with blue cheese. Serve with any remaining reserved sauce.

RED MEAT

GRILLING BEEF

CUT	THICKNESS / WEIGHT	APPROXIMATE GRILLING TIME
Steak: sirloin, porterhouse, rib-eye, T-bone, rump and fillet	1.5 cm / ¾ inch thick	**4–6 minutes** grilling/direct high heat
	2.5 cm/1 inch thick	**6–8 minutes** grilling/direct high heat
	3 cm/1¼ inches thick	**8–10 minutes** grilling/direct high heat
	3.5 cm/1½ inches thick	**10–14 minutes:** sear 6–8 minutes grilling/direct high heat, grill 4–6 minutes roasting/indirect high heat
Beef, minced	1.5 cm/¾ inch thick	**8–10 minutes** grilling/direct medium-high heat
Flank steak	750 g–1 kg/1½ –2 lb, 1.5 cm/¾ inch thick	**8–10 minutes** grilling/direct medium heat
Blade steak	2.5 cm/1 inch thick	**8–10 minutes** grilling/direct medium heat
Onglet steak	2.5 cm/1 inch thick	**8–10 minutes** grilling/direct medium heat
Kebab	2.5-cm/1-inch cubes	**4–6 minutes** grilling/direct high heat
	3.5-cm/1½-inch cubes	**6–7 minutes** grilling/direct high heat
Fore rib, boneless	2.5–3 kg/5–6 lb	**1¼–1¾ hours** roasting/indirect medium heat
Fore rib, with bone	4 kg/8 lb	**2–3 hours:** sear 10 minutes grilling/direct medium heat, grill 2–3 hours roasting/indirect low heat
Skirt steak	5 mm–1 cm/¼ –½ inch thick	**4–6 minutes** grilling/direct high heat
Sirloin roast, boneless	2–2.5 kg/4–5 lb	**50 minutes–1 hour:** sear 10 minutes grilling/direct medium heat, grill 40–50 minutes roasting/indirect medium heat
Fillet, whole	1.75–2 kg/3½–4 lb	**35–45 minutes:** sear 15 minutes grilling/direct medium heat, grill 20–30 minutes roasting/indirect medium heat
Top sirloin	3.5 cm/1½ inches thick	**10–14 minutes:** sear 6–8 minutes grilling/direct high heat, grill 4–6 minutes roasting/indirect high heat
Top rump	1–1.25 kg/2–2½ lb	**30–40 minutes:** sear 10 minutes grilling/direct medium heat, grill 20–30 minutes roasting/indirect medium heat
Veal loin chop	1 inch thick	**6–8 minutes** direct high heat

All cooking times are for medium-rare doneness, except minced beef (medium).

TYPES OF RED MEAT FOR THE GRILL

TENDER CUTS FOR GRILLING

▸ *Beef sirloin steak*
▸ *Beef porterhouse steak*
▸ *Beef rib-eye steak*
▸ *Beef T-bone steak*
▸ *Beef fillet steak*
▸ *Lamb loin chop*
▸ *Lamb cutlet*
▸ *Veal loin chop*

MODERATELY TENDER CUTS FOR GRILLING

▸ *Beef blade steak*
▸ *Beef onglet steak*
▸ *Beef skirt steak*
▸ *Lamb shoulder blade chop*
▸ *Lamb chump chop*
▸ *Veal shoulder blade chop*

BIGGER CUTS FOR SEARING AND GRILL-ROASTING

▸ *Beef fore rib*
▸ *Beef sirloin roast*
▸ *Beef top rump roast*
▸ *Beef whole fillet*
▸ *Leg of lamb*
▸ *Rack of lamb*
▸ *Rack of veal*

TOUGHER CUTS FOR BARBECUING

▸ *Beef ribs*
▸ *Brisket*

RED MEAT DONENESS

DONENESS	CHEF STANDARDS	OFFICIAL GUIDE
Rare	49–52°C/120–125°F	n/a
Medium rare	52–57°C/125–135°F	63°C/145°F
Medium	57–63°C/135–145°F	70°C/160°F
Medium well	63–68°C/145–155°F	n/a
Well done	68°C/155°F +	77°C/170°F

GRILLING LAMB

CUT	THICKNESS/ WEIGHT	APPROXIMATE GRILLING TIME
Chop: loin or cutlet	1.5 cm/³⁄₄ inch thick	**4–6 minutes** grilling/direct high heat
	2.5 cm/1 inch thick	**6–8 minutes** grilling/direct high heat
	3.5 cm/1½ inches thick	**8–10 minutes** grilling/direct high heat
Lamb, minced	1.5 cm/³⁄₄ inch thick	**8–10 minutes** grilling/direct medium-high heat
Leg of lamb, boneless, rolled	1.25–1.5 kg/ 2½–3 lb	**30–45 minutes:** sear 10–15 minutes grilling/direct medium heat, grill 20–30 minutes roasting/indirect medium heat
Leg of lamb, butterflied	1.5–1.75 kg/ 3–3½ lb	**30–45 minutes:** sear 10–15 minutes grilling/direct medium heat, grill 20–30 minutes roasting/indirect medium heat
Rack of lamb	500–750 g/ 1–1½ lb	**15–20 minutes:** sear 5 minutes grilling/ direct medium heat, grill 10–15 minutes roasting/indirect medium heat
Rib crown roast	1.5–2 kg/3–4 lb	**1–1¼ hours** indirect medium heat

All cooking times are for medium-rare doneness, except minced lamb (medium). The cuts, thicknesses, weights and grilling times are meant to be guidelines rather than hard and fast rules. Cooking times are affected by such factors as altitude, wind, outside temperature and desired doneness. Two rules of thumb: grill steaks, chops and kebabs using the direct method for the time given on the chart or to your desired doneness, turning once. Grill roasts and thicker cuts using the indirect method for the time given on the chart or until an instant-read meat thermometer reaches the desired internal temperature. Let roasts, larger cuts of meat and thick steaks rest for 5–10 minutes before carving. The internal temperature of the meat will rise 5–10 degrees during this time.

GRILL SKILLS
PERFECT BURGERS

CHOOSE WISELY

Hamburgers need some fat to be delicious – about 20 per cent, actually. Hamburgers with less fat are destined to be dry and crumbly; however, when the meat has enough milky white fat speckled throughout it, the fat dissolves into mouthwatering moisture that not only feels good on your tongue, but also tastes good. Fat has its own beefy flavours, and it carries other flavours, too, including the seasonings in the burgers and the smokiness of the grill.

Most people get their mince from a supermarket, where it has been packed into a foam tray. You can make some very good burgers with this meat, but if you are in search of perfection, ask a butcher to mince the meat for you so that the meat is loosely packed. This type of texture, where you can see long strands of beef just as they came out of the mincer (see photo left), leads to the plumpest, juiciest burgers, assuming the meat has enough fat. This also allows you to choose the best cut. An excellent choice is chuck steak, a well-exercised, flavourful shoulder cut. Rump, a cut from close to the hardworking hip, is another good choice.

BUILDING A BETTER BURGER

1 Put the meat in a bowl and season with salt and pepper before you make the burgers.

2 Divide the meat into equal portions before you shape the burgers. This step avoids the problem of having too much or too little meat left over for that last burger.

3 With wet hands, gently shape each portion into a loose, round ball. Then flatten each ball into a burger with a thickness between 1.5 and 2.5 cm/^{3}/4 and 1 inch.

4 Use a spoon or your thumb to create a shallow well in the middle of each burger. This will prevent 'the meatball effect', where the burger develops a domed top.

BUTTER UP

A trick for making really juicy burgers is to nestle a small pat of cold butter in the centre of each burger. Just be sure to seal the butter well inside so that it doesn't cause flare-ups.

GRILLING PERFECT BURGERS

A perfect burger is a study in contrasts. The top and bottom of each burger is lightly charred with crispy brown bits all over. Inside each burger the meat is soft, tender and dripping with juices. The key to this kind of contrast is the magic combination of the burger's thickness (1.5–2.5 cm/¾–1 inch) and the grill's temperature (200–260°C/400–500°F). Over the course of 8–10 minutes, the surface has just enough time to turn dark brown and delicious while the inside cooks fully without losing much of its juices, assuming the lid is closed.

Cooking with the lid closed reflects heat on to the top of each burger, meaning the burgers are cooking on both sides. This speeds up the overall cooking time. Also, closing the lid restricts the amount of air getting to the fire and eliminates a lot of potential flare-ups. And finally, the lid also keeps the cooking grate hot enough to sear the surface of each burger properly.

NO FLIPPING OUT. You should only turn burgers once or twice. If you try to turn a burger during the first few minutes, you are bound to leave some meat sticking to the grate. If you can manage to wait 4 minutes or so, the meat will develop a lightly charred crust that releases naturally from the grate.

NO SMASHING. One of the worst things you can do to a burger is to press or smash it with a spatula. The juices run out quickly, causing flare-ups and drying out your burger.

CHEESEBURGERS
WITH MANGO-CHILLI SALSA

SERVES: 4 | PREP TIME: 20 minutes | CHILLING TIME: 30 minutes–1 hour | GRILLING TIME: 8–10 minutes

BURGERS
750 g/1½ lb minced beef (80% lean)
½ teaspoon garlic powder
½ teaspoon sea salt
½ teaspoon freshly ground black pepper

SALSA
1 large mango, cut into 1-cm/½-inch dice
2 tablespoons roughly chopped fresh coriander
1 tablespoon fresh lime juice
1 serrano chilli, deseeded and finely chopped
¼ teaspoon sea salt

4 thin slices pepper jack or Cheddar cheese
4 hamburger buns, split
Dijon mustard

1 Combine the burger ingredients, keeping the mixture crumbly rather than compressed. With wet hands, gently form four loosely packed burgers of equal size, each about 1.5 cm/¾ inch thick. Don't compact the meat too much or the burgers will be tough. Using your thumb or the back of a spoon, make a shallow indentation about 2.5 cm/1 inch wide in the centre of each burger. This will help the burgers cook evenly and prevent them from puffing on the grill.

2 Combine the salsa ingredients in a non-reactive bowl. Toss gently and then refrigerate for at least 30 minutes or up to 1 hour. (After an hour, the fruit starts to become mushy.)

3 Prepare the grill for grilling/direct cooking over medium-high heat (200–260°C/400–500°F).

4 Grill the burgers over *grilling/direct medium-high heat* for 8–10 minutes, with the lid closed, until cooked to medium doneness, turning once when the burgers release easily from the grate without sticking. During the last minute of grilling time, place a slice of cheese on each burger to melt, and toast the buns, cut side down, over grilling/direct heat.

5 Spread the bottom half of each bun with mustard, and serve the burgers warm on the buns topped with salsa.

A TOURIST FROM THE TROPICS THAT IS HERE TO STAY

Once upon a time, a couple of decades ago, the exotic mango was little known, except in stories about shipwrecks on tropical islands.

Nowadays, you can't swing a palm frond without knocking one off a supermarket shelf.

A mainstay of the South Asian diet for centuries, this nutrient-packed stone fruit is becoming ever more common on shopping lists, thanks to expanding tastes in food and travel – as well as improvements in cultivation and distribution that make mangoes hardier and easier to ship. Most common in stores is the greenish orange, oblong variety, which is grown for its disease-resistance, portability and good size. Elsewhere in the frost-free world, the abundant mango crop is much more varied.

Sweet mango is a great match with spicy foods as a cool, juicy side dish, a dessert, or right in the thick of things, mixed into a salsa with fiery chillies, as in the accompanying cheeseburger recipe.

Pick blemish-free, heavy mangoes that give slightly when pressed. And leave the high seas travel to the pros.

BRIE BURGERS
WITH GRILLED TOMATO

SERVES: 4 | PREP TIME: 20 minutes | GRILLING TIME: 10–12 minutes

SAUCE
100 ml/3½ fl oz mayonnaise
1½ tablespoons Dijon mustard
1 teaspoon fresh lemon juice

750 g/1½ lb minced beef (80% lean)
1 teaspoon dried tarragon
½ teaspoon freshly ground black pepper
125 g/4 oz Brie cheese, cut into 8 wedges
4 hamburger buns, split
1 beefsteak tomato, about 250 g/8 oz, cut crossways into
    4 slices, each about 1 cm/½ inch thick
1 tablespoon extra-virgin olive oil
4 lettuce leaves
Sea salt

1 Whisk the sauce ingredients.

2 Prepare the grill for grilling/direct cooking over medium-high heat (200–260°C/400–500°F).

3 Gently combine the minced beef, tarragon, 1 teaspoon salt and the pepper. With wet hands, form four loosely packed burgers of equal size, each about 1.5 cm/¾ inch thick. Don't compact the meat too much or the burgers will be tough. Using your thumb or the back of a spoon, make a shallow indentation about 2.5 cm/1 inch wide in the centre of each burger. This will help the burgers cook evenly and prevent them from puffing on the grill.

4 Grill the burgers over *grilling/direct medium-high heat* for 8–10 minutes, with the lid closed, until cooked to medium doneness, turning once when the burgers release easily from the grate without sticking. During the last minute of grilling time, place two pieces of the Brie on each burger to melt, and toast the buns, cut side down, over grilling/direct heat. Remove from the grill.

5 Brush the tomato slices on both sides with the oil and season with ½ teaspoon salt. Grill over *grilling/direct medium-high heat* for about 2 minutes, with the lid closed, until they are tender and nicely marked, turning once. Spread the sauce on the cut sides of each bun. Build each burger with a bun, lettuce and tomato. Serve warm.

KOREAN-STYLE BEEF BURGERS
WITH FRESH SPINACH

SERVES: 4 | PREP TIME: **20 minutes** | GRILLING TIME: **8–10 minutes**

BURGERS
750 g/1½ lb minced beef (80% lean)
6 spring onions, thinly sliced (white and light
    green parts only)
1½ tablespoons toasted sesame seeds
1½ tablespoons soy sauce
1 tablespoon freshly ground black pepper

2 tablespoons toasted sesame oil
2 tablespoons dark brown sugar
4 onion rolls or burger buns, split
50 g/2 oz baby spinach

1 Prepare the grill for grilling/direct cooking over
medium-high heat (200–260°C/400–500°F).

2 Gently combine the burger ingredients. With wet hands,
form four loosely packed burgers of equal size, each
about 1.5 cm/¾ inch thick. Don't compact the meat too
much or the burgers will be tough. Using your thumb or the
back of a spoon, make a shallow indentation about 2.5 cm/
1 inch wide in the centre of each burger. This will help the
burgers cook evenly and prevent them puffing on the grill.

3 Mix the oil and the brown sugar to form a paste.

4 Grill the burgers over *grilling/direct medium-high heat*
for 4–5 minutes, with the lid closed. Brush half of the
paste over the burgers, turn them, and brush with the
remaining paste. Continue grilling for 4–5 minutes more
until cooked to medium doneness. During the last minute
of grilling time, toast the rolls, cut side down, over direct
heat. Serve the burgers on the toasted rolls with a handful of
the spinach on top.

ITALIAN MEATBALLS
WITH TWO CHEESES AND MARINARA SAUCE

SERVES: 6 | PREP TIME: 30 minutes, plus 35 minutes for the sauce | CHILLING TIME: 1–5 hours | GRILLING TIME: 11–15 minutes

MEATBALLS
500 g/1 lb minced beef (80% lean)
500 g/1 lb lean minced pork
100 g/3½ oz dried breadcrumbs
2 large eggs, lightly beaten
50 g/2 oz pecorino romano cheese, grated
50 g/2 oz Parmesan cheese, grated
½ onion, finely chopped
4 tablespoons fresh flat-leaf parsley, finely chopped
2 large garlic cloves, minced or crushed

Sea salt
Freshly ground black pepper

SAUCE
1 tablespoon extra-virgin olive oil
1 onion, finely chopped
2 garlic cloves, finely chopped or crushed
875 g/1¾ lb canned crushed Italian plum tomatoes
1 bay leaf
1 teaspoon dried oregano, crumbled
⅛ teaspoon crushed red chilli flakes

Extra-virgin olive oil
6 slices French bread, about 1 cm/½ inch thick (optional)

1 Thoroughly combine the meatball ingredients, including 1 teaspoon salt and ½ teaspoon pepper, keeping the mixture crumbly rather than compressed. With wet hands, form into equal-sized balls, each about 3.5 cm/1½ inches in diameter (yield: about 30 meatballs). Cover with clingfilm and refrigerate for at least 1 hour or up to 5 hours.

2 In a medium saucepan over medium heat, warm the oil. Add the onion and sauté for 3–4 minutes until tender. Add the garlic and sauté for 1 minute more. Add the remaining sauce ingredients, including ½ teaspoon salt and ¼ teaspoon pepper, and simmer for about 30 minutes, uncovered, until thickened. Discard the bay leaf. Keep warm.

3 Prepare the grill for grilling/direct cooking over medium heat (180–230°C/350–450°F).

4 Brush the meatballs all over with oil. Grill over *grilling/direct medium heat* for 11–15 minutes, with the lid closed, until the meatballs are thoroughly cooked but not dry, turning occasionally. Serve warm on grilled French bread, if liked, with the sauce spooned on top.

HOT DOGS
WITH SPICY PICKLED VEGETABLES

SERVES: 6 | PREP TIME: 20 minutes | DRAINING/COOLING/PICKLING TIME: 5 hours–3 days | GRILLING TIME: 5–7 minutes

500 g/1 lb green cabbage, roughly chopped
2 pickling or ridge cucumbers, deseeded and cut into
   1-cm/½-inch dice
1 onion, chopped
½ red pepper, cut into 1-cm/½-inch dice
2 jalapeño chillies, deseeded and finely chopped
1 tablespoon sea salt
250 ml/8 fl oz cider vinegar
175/6 oz light brown sugar
1 teaspoon mustard powder
½ teaspoon celery seeds
¼ teaspoon ground turmeric
12 all-beef hot dog sausages
12 hot dog buns, split

1 In a large colander toss the cabbage, cucumbers, onion, red pepper, jalapeños and salt. Place a dinner plate on top of the vegetables to weigh them down. Let stand in the sink to drain for 1 hour.

2 In a large saucepan over a medium heat, combine the vinegar, brown sugar, mustard powder, celery seeds and turmeric. Bring to a simmer, stirring to dissolve the sugar. Add the cabbage mixture (do not rinse) to the saucepan and cook for 4–6 minutes until the cabbage is crisp-tender, stirring occasionally. Transfer to a bowl and let cool for 2 hours at room temperature. Cover and refrigerate for at least 2 hours or up to 3 days.

3 Prepare the grill for grilling/direct cooking over medium heat (180–230°C/350–450°F).

4 Cut a few shallow slashes in each sausage. Grill the sausages over *grilling/direct medium heat* for 5–7 minutes, with the lid closed, until lightly marked on the outside and hot all the way through, turning occasionally. During the last minute of grilling time, toast the buns, cut side down, over grilling/direct heat.

5 Place the sausages in the buns. Using a slotted spoon to drain the excess liquid, spoon about 4 tablespoons of the vegetables on top of each hot dog. Serve immediately.

GRILL SKILLS
PERFECT STEAKS

CHOOSE WISELY

The main thing to look for in steaks is marbling, those visible lines of fat running throughout the meat. This fat is essential to great steaks because, as it melts on the grill, it fills the meat with juice and flavour. On the other hand, wide streaks or hunks of fat, particularly around the outer edges of steaks, can melt and drip so much flammable fat into the fire that you get unwanted flare-ups and risk burning the meat. So choose your steaks well and trim any excess perimeter fat.

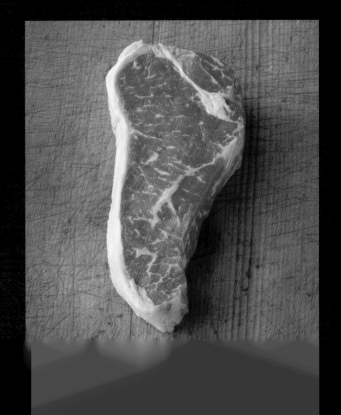

PREPPING STEAKS

1 Pull your steaks out of the refrigerator 15–30 minutes before you plan to grill them, and trim the fat around the edges to 5 mm/¼ inch or less to prevent flare-ups.

2 Lightly coat trimmed steaks with extra-virgin olive oil. This adds flavour and prevents sticking.

3 Rub the oil evenly all over the steaks to prevent them from sticking to the cooking grate. The oil also helps the seasonings to adhere to the meat.

4 Season with sea salt. Within 15–30 minutes, the salt seasons the meat deeply, amplifying the steak flavour below the surface. Don't be timid with the salt.

5 Generously season with freshly ground black pepper for a kick of flavour.

GRILLING PERFECT STEAKS

1 Brush the cooking grates clean and place your steaks over direct high heat. A good hot grill won't 'seal in the juices', as you may have heard, but it will add tremendous flavour and texture.

2 Leave the steaks alone for at least 2 minutes, preferably 3 minutes. Resist the urge to fiddle with them, unless:
A. You want cross-hatch marks. In this case, rotate each steak 90 degrees after about 1½ minutes.
B. You're fighting a flare-up. Move the steaks over indirect heat temporarily, until the flames subside, and then move them back over direct heat.

3 Once you have a deep, delicious sear on the first side, turn the steaks over and sear them on the second side for 2–3 minutes.

4 If your steaks are thinner than 3.5 cm/1½ inches, finish them over direct heat. If they are 3.5 cm/1½ inches or thicker, finish them over indirect heat so that the inside has a chance to cook before the outside burns. Use the handy doneness tests below to help determine when the steaks are ready to come off the grill.

5 Let steaks rest at room temperature for just a few minutes before anyone cuts into them. This does so much to help each steak hold on to its juices.

WHEN IS IT DONE?

TOUCH TEST. Press the meat surface with your fingertip. When it has the same firmness as the base of your thumb, take the steak off.

HAND TEST: RARE. If you touch your index finger and thumb together and then press the base of your thumb, that's how most steaks feel when they are rare.

HAND TEST: MEDIUM RARE. If you touch your middle finger and thumb together and then press the base of your thumb, that's how most steaks feel when they are medium rare.

HORSERADISH-CRUSTED SIRLOIN STEAKS
WITH TOMATO AND BACON SALAD

SERVES: 4 | PREP TIME: 25 minutes | GRILLING TIME: 6–8 minutes

TOPPING
100 ml/3½ fl oz mayonnaise
4 tablespoons Parmesan cheese, finely grated
2 tablespoons prepared horseradish

4 sirloin steaks, each 250–300 g/8–10 oz and 2.5 cm/1 inch
    thick, trimmed of excess fat
Extra-virgin olive oil
1 tablespoon balsamic vinegar
4 rashers apple-wood smoked bacon, cut crossways into
    8-mm/⅓-inch strips
1 large bunch watercress, thick stems trimmed
375 g/12 oz mixed red and yellow cherry tomatoes,
    each cut in half
Sea salt
Freshly ground black pepper

1 Whisk the topping ingredients.

2 Lightly brush the steaks on both sides with oil and
season evenly with 1 teaspoon salt and 1 teaspoon
pepper. Allow the steaks to stand at room temperature
for 15–30 minutes before grilling.

3 Prepare the grill for grilling/direct cooking over high
heat (230–290°C/450–550°F).

4 In a large salad bowl whisk 3 tablespoons oil, the
balsamic vinegar, ¼ teaspoon salt and ¼ teaspoon
black pepper.

5 In a medium frying pan over a medium heat, cook the
bacon for 8–10 minutes until crisp. Using a slotted spoon,
transfer the bacon to kitchen paper to drain.

6 Add the watercress and the tomatoes to the salad bowl,
but do not toss.

7 Sear the steaks over *grilling/direct high heat* for
2–3 minutes, with the lid closed. Turn the steaks over
and spread the top of each steak with an equal amount of
the topping. Close the lid and continue grilling until the
topping is golden and slightly browned in spots and the
steaks are cooked to your desired doneness, 4–5 minutes
more for medium rare. Remove from the grill and let rest
for 3–5 minutes.

8 Toss the salad and top with the bacon. Serve the steak
warm with the salad.

ALWAYS A KICK

Pungent, assertive horseradish has jumped out of the
Bloody Mary and into our spotlight.

This perennial plant, cousin to wasabi, mustard and
broccoli, was long valued for its medicinal as well as
its culinary qualities, thanks to that distinct chemical
compound – the one that makes you blink and go 'whoa!'.
The grated root mixed with vinegar (as it's found in
'prepared horseradish'), however, adds a smack of spicy,
inimitable flavour to sauces, spreads and dressings.

Use it in sandwiches and sauces, potatoes or dips.
We top grilled meat with it and love how horseradish's
eye-watering potency mellows a bit under the grill lid.
And yes, it's still great in the Bloody Mary.

Long live horseradish, in all its sinus-clearing glory.

SIRLOIN STEAKS
WITH PARMESAN-BASIL CRUST AND GARLIC BUTTER

SERVES: 4 | PREP TIME: 10 minutes | GRILLING TIME: 6–8 minutes

4 sirloin steaks, each 300–375 g/10–12 oz and about 2.5 cm/
   1 inch thick, trimmed of excess fat
1 tablespoon extra-virgin olive oil
1½ teaspoons sea salt
1 teaspoon freshly ground black pepper
100 g/3½ oz Parmesan cheese, freshly grated
2 tablespoons finely chopped fresh basil
50 g/2 oz unsalted butter
2 garlic cloves, finely chopped or crushed

1 Lightly brush the steaks on both sides with the oil and season evenly with the salt and pepper. Allow the steaks to stand at room temperature for 15–30 minutes before grilling.

2 Prepare the grill for grilling/direct cooking over high heat (230–290°C/450–550°F).

3 Combine the cheese and the basil.

4 Sear the steaks over *grilling/direct high heat* for 3–4 minutes, with the lid closed. Turn the steaks over and generously coat the top of each steak with the cheese and basil mixture. Close the lid and continue grilling until the cheese is melted and the steaks are cooked to your desired doneness, 3–4 minutes more for medium rare. Remove from the grill and let rest for 3–5 minutes.

5 Meanwhile, in a saucepan over a medium heat, combine the butter and the garlic and heat for about 3 minutes until the butter is melted and the garlic is sizzling. Remove from the heat. Spoon the garlic butter over the steaks and serve right away.

CHEESESTEAKS
WITH THE WORKS

SERVES: 4 | PREP TIME: 20 minutes | GRILLING TIME: 16–17 minutes | SPECIAL EQUIPMENT: grill-proof griddle or cast-iron frying pan

4 sirloin steaks, each about 150 g/5 oz and
   5 mm/¼ inch thick, trimmed of excess fat
4 tablespoons extra-virgin olive oil
1 large onion, cut into 5-mm/¼-inch half-moons
1 small green pepper, cut into 5-mm/¼-inch strips
250 g/8 oz button mushrooms, thinly sliced
4 mini baguettes, split
8 slices gruyere cheese
Sea salt
Freshly ground black pepper

1 Brush the steaks on both sides with 2 tablespoons oil. Season evenly with 1½ teaspoons salt and ¾ teaspoon pepper. Allow the steaks to stand at room temperature for 15–30 minutes before grilling.

2 Prepare the grill for grilling/direct cooking over high heat (230–290°C/450–550°F) and preheat a grill-proof griddle for 10 minutes.

3 In a bowl mix the onion and green pepper with 1 tablespoon oil. In another bowl mix the mushrooms with 1 tablespoon oil. Spread the onion and pepper in a single layer on the griddle and cook for about 8 minutes until softened, stirring occasionally. Push the onion and

pepper to one side of the griddle. Add the mushrooms to the griddle and cook them for about 8 minutes, until the juices evaporate and the mushrooms are beginning to brown, stirring occasionally. Remove the vegetables from the griddle, season with salt and pepper and keep warm.

4 Grill the steaks on the cooking grate over *grilling/direct high heat* for 2 minutes, with the lid closed, turning when the first side is nicely marked. The second side will only take about 30 seconds to reach medium-rare doneness. Remove from the grill. Toast the rolls, cut side down, over *grilling/direct high heat*, for about 1 minute. Remove from the grill and fill each roll with two slices of cheese.

5 To assemble, place a steak in each roll and top with an equal amount of the vegetables. Warm the sandwiches on the griddle until the outsides are crusty. If desired, flatten the sandwiches with a grill press. Serve warm.

TIP Your butcher should be able to cut the steaks for you. Or buy a 625-g/1¼-lb sirloin roast, freeze it for a few hours until it is somewhat firm, and cut it crossways into 5-mm/¼-inch-thick steaks.

T-BONE STEAKS
WITH MOROCCAN SPICE PASTE

SERVES: 4 | PREP TIME: 15 minutes | GRILLING TIME: 6–8 minutes

PASTE
3 medjool dates, each cut into quarters
2 tablespoons red wine vinegar
4 tablespoons extra-virgin olive oil
1½ teaspoons sea salt
1 teaspoon ground cumin
½ teaspoon smoked paprika
½ teaspoon ground ginger
½ teaspoon freshly ground black pepper

4 T-bone steaks, each about 375 g/12 oz and 2.5 cm/1 inch
   thick, trimmed of excess fat
Vegetables, to serve

1 In a small bowl combine the dates and the vinegar. Add just enough hot water to cover, and let stand for about 10 minutes until the dates are softened. Transfer the mixture to a food processor, add the remaining paste ingredients and process until smooth.

2 Set aside 3 tablespoons of the paste in a small bowl. Spread the remaining paste evenly on both sides of each steak. Allow the steaks to stand at room temperature for 15–30 minutes before grilling.

3 Prepare the grill for grilling/direct cooking over high heat (230–290°C/450–550°F).

4 Grill the steaks over *grilling/direct high heat*, with the lid closed, until cooked to your desired doneness, 6–8 minutes for medium rare, turning once or twice. Remove from the grill and brush the top of the steaks with the reserved paste. Let rest for 3–5 minutes. Serve warm with vegetables of your choice on the side.

TIP For Moroccan-spiced burgers, gently mix 2–3 tablespoons of the paste into 500 g/1 lb of minced beef.

SPICE-CRUSTED T-BONE STEAKS
WITH COGNAC CREAM SAUCE

SERVES: 4 | PREP TIME: 10 minutes, plus about 25 minutes for the sauce | GRILLING TIME: 6–8 minutes

RUB
2 tablespoons four-peppercorn blend
1½ teaspoons mustard seeds

4 T-bone steaks, each about 375 g/12 oz and 2.5 cm/1 inch
   thick, trimmed of excess fat
Extra-virgin olive oil

SAUCE
15 g/½ oz unsalted butter
2 tablespoons finely chopped shallots
4 tablespoons cognac or brandy
250 ml/8 fl oz beef stock
250 ml/8 fl oz whipping cream
1 teaspoon Dijon mustard
Sea salt
Freshly ground black pepper
Grilled vegetables, to serve (optional)

1 Coarsely crush the peppercorns and the mustard seeds in a spice mill. Pour into a bowl and mix in 1½ teaspoons salt. Brush the steaks on both sides with oil and season evenly with the rub, pressing the spices into the meat. Allow the steaks to stand at room temperature for 15–30 minutes. Meanwhile, prepare the grill and make the sauce.

2 Prepare the grill for grilling/direct cooking over high heat (230–290°C/450–550°F).

3 In a saucepan (with a lid) over a medium heat, melt the butter. Add the shallots and cook for about 1 minute until softened, stirring often. Remove from the heat and add the cognac. Using a long match, carefully ignite the cognac (the flames will rise high above the pan, so be careful) and let it burn for 30 seconds. If the cognac does not extinguish itself, cover the pan tightly with the lid. Place the saucepan over a high heat and add the stock; bring to the boil. Cook for about 12 minutes until reduced to about 2 tablespoons. Add the cream and boil for 8–10 minutes until reduced to about 175 ml/6 fl oz, reducing the heat if the sauce starts to boil over. Remove from the heat, season with salt and pepper, and whisk in the mustard. Cover partially to keep warm.

4 Grill the steaks over *grilling/direct high heat*, with the lid closed, until cooked to your desired doneness, 6–8 minutes for medium rare, turning once or twice. Remove from the grill and let rest for 3–5 minutes. Spoon the sauce over the steaks and serve warm with grilled vegetables, if desired.

PORTERHOUSE STEAKS AND SMASHED POTATOES
WITH GARLIC BUTTER

SERVES: 4 | PREP TIME: 25 minutes | CHILLING TIME: about 1 hour | GRILLING TIME: 36–48 minutes

GARLIC BUTTER
125 g/4 oz unsalted butter, softened
4 tablespoons fresh flat-leaf parsley, finely chopped
1½ teaspoons finely grated lemon zest
2 teaspoons fresh lemon juice
2 large garlic cloves, finely chopped or crushed
1 teaspoon freshly ground four-peppercorn blend

4 rashers apple-wood smoked bacon, cut crossways into
    8-mm/⅓-inch strips
750 g/1½ lb waxy potatoes, unpeeled, each about
    6 cm/2½ inches in diameter, cut in half
2 porterhouse steaks, each 500–625 g/1–1¼ lb and about
    2.5 cm/1 inch thick, trimmed of excess fat
2 tablespoons extra-virgin olive oil
2 teaspoons coarsely crushed mixed peppercorns
Sea salt
Freshly ground black pepper

1 Combine the garlic butter ingredients, including ¾ teaspoon salt, and mash with a fork until well blended. Transfer to a small sheet of clingfilm and roll into a log 3-3.5 cm/1¼-1½ inches in diameter, enclosing the butter completely in the clingfilm. Refrigerate for about 1 hour until cold. (The butter can be prepared up to a day in advance and kept, wrapped, in the refrigerator. Let stand at room temperature for 30 minutes–1 hour before using.)

2 In a medium frying pan over a medium heat, cook the bacon for 8-10 minutes until crisp. Using a slotted spoon, transfer the bacon to kitchen paper to drain.

3 Prepare the grill for grilling/direct cooking over medium heat (180-230°C/350-450°F). Place a sheet of heavy-duty aluminium foil (large enough to enclose the potatoes in a single layer) on a work surface. Place the potatoes, cut side up, on the foil. Lightly season with salt and pepper. Wrap the foil around the potatoes and crimp the edges to seal the parcel completely. Place the parcel over *grilling/direct medium heat*, close the lid, and cook until the potatoes are tender when pierced with a fork, 30-40 minutes. Transfer the potatoes to a heatproof bowl and add the cooked bacon. Add half of the garlic butter and coarsely smash the potatoes with a potato masher or a fork, leaving the potatoes chunky. Cover to keep warm.

4 Brush the steaks on both sides with the oil and season evenly with 2 teaspoons salt and the crushed peppercorns. Allow the steaks to stand at room temperature for 15-30 minutes before grilling.

5 Increase the temperature of the grill to high heat (230-290°C/450-550°F).

6 Grill the steaks over *grilling/direct high heat,* with the lid closed, until cooked to your desired doneness, 6-8 minutes for medium rare, turning once or twice. Remove from the grill and let rest for 3-5 minutes. Cut the steaks across the grain and divide the slices among four plates. Dot the slices with the remaining garlic butter. Reheat the smashed potatoes, if necessary. Serve the steaks warm with the potatoes.

TIP A simple and flavourful version of the classic compound butter known as maître d'hôtel butter serves as the topping for both the steaks and the potatoes. If you like, add a few tablespoons of chopped fresh chives to the butter mixture to give it a slightly more assertive flavour. Grill some asparagus or sauté some sugar snap peas to serve alongside for a complete meal. If you make the compound butter the day before and refrigerate it, you'll have a delicious and effortless dinner in less than an hour. If you don't have four-peppercorn blend on hand, black peppercorns will do.

FILLET STEAKS
WITH BÉARNAISE BUTTER

SERVES: 4 | PREP TIME: 25 minutes | CHILLING TIME: about 1 hour | GRILLING TIME: 8–10 minutes

4 tablespoons white wine vinegar
2 tablespoons finely chopped shallots
3 tablespoons chopped fresh tarragon
1 tablespoon chopped fresh flat-leaf parsley
75 g/3 oz unsalted butter, softened
½ teaspoon finely grated lemon zest
4 fillet steaks, each 175–250 g/6–8 oz and about
    3 cm/1¼ inches thick
1 tablespoon extra-virgin olive oil
Sea salt
Freshly ground black pepper
Vegetables, to serve

1 In a small saucepan over a medium-high heat, combine the vinegar, shallots, 1 tablespoon of the tarragon and the parsley and bring to the boil. Reduce the heat to medium and continue to boil for 2–4 minutes until only a scant tablespoon of the vinegar remains in the saucepan, stirring occasionally. Transfer the mixture to a fine sieve set over a bowl and press on the solids to extract as much of the vinegar as possible. Reserve the vinegar and transfer the solids to a bowl and let cool.

2 To the bowl with the solids add the butter, lemon zest, ¼ teaspoon salt, ¼ teaspoon pepper, the remaining 2 tablespoons tarragon and 1 scant teaspoon of the reserved vinegar. Thoroughly blend with a fork. Transfer to a sheet of clingfilm and roll the mixture into a log about 12 cm/5 inches long, enclosing the butter completely in the clingfilm. Refrigerate for about 1 hour until cold.

3 Brush the steaks on both sides with the oil and season evenly with 1 teaspoon salt and 1 teaspoon pepper. Allow the steaks to stand at room temperature for 15–30 minutes before grilling.

4 Prepare the grill for grilling/direct cooking over high heat (230–290°C/450–550°F).

5 Grill the steaks over *grilling/direct high heat*, with the lid closed, until cooked to your desired doneness, 8–10 minutes for medium rare, turning once or twice. Remove from the grill and let rest for 3–5 minutes. Cut the butter log crossways into 1-cm/½-inch slices. (Rewrap and refrigerate or freeze the leftover butter for another use.) Immediately top each steak with a slice of the butter. Serve warm with vegetables of your choice.

HERB-CRUSTED BEEF FILLET
WITH CHIMICHURRI SAUCE

SERVES: 4–6 | PREP TIME: 25 minutes | DRY BRINING TIME: 4–8 hours | GRILLING TIME: 30–35 minutes
SPECIAL EQUIPMENT: kitchen string (optional), instant-read meat thermometer

1 fillet beef, about 1 kg/2 lb
2 tablespoons sea salt

SAUCE
125 g/4 oz fresh flat-leaf parsley
125 ml/4 fl oz extra-virgin olive oil
4 tablespoons fresh lemon juice
2 large garlic cloves
1 teaspoon sea salt
½ teaspoon freshly ground black pepper
¼ teaspoon crushed red chilli flakes

RUB
2 tablespoons finely chopped fresh thyme
2 tablespoons finely chopped fresh rosemary
3 garlic cloves, finely chopped or crushed
2 tablespoons extra-virgin olive oil
2½ teaspoons freshly ground black pepper

1 At least 4 hours or up to 8 hours before serving, season the beef all over with the salt. This gives the salt enough time to seep into the meat and season more than just the surface. If desired, for a perfectly round appearance, tie the joint with kitchen string every 5 cm/2 inches.

Wrap in clingfilm and refrigerate. Allow the meat to stand at room temperature for 30 minutes before grilling.

2 Prepare the grill for grilling/direct cooking over medium heat (180–230°C/350–450°F).

3 In a food processor combine the sauce ingredients and process until thoroughly combined. Transfer to a bowl, cover and refrigerate until ready to serve.

4 Combine the rub ingredients, rubbing the herbs between your fingertips to release their oils. Brush the beef all over with the oil and season evenly with the rub, pressing it into the meat.

5 Grill the beef over *grilling/direct medium heat* for 30–35 minutes, with the lid closed, until an instant-read thermometer inserted into the thickest part of the joint registers 52°C/125°F for medium rare, turning four times. Remove from the grill and let rest for about 10 minutes (the internal temperature will rise 5–10 degrees during this time). Cut the beef into 1-cm/½-inch slices. Serve warm with the sauce.

RIB-EYE STEAK SANDWICHES
WITH SWISS CHEESE AND HAM

SERVES: 4 | PREP TIME: 15 minutes | GRILLING TIME: 4–5 minutes

RUB
1½ teaspoons dried oregano
2 teaspoons sea salt
1 teaspoon freshly ground black pepper

4 boneless rib-eye steaks, each about 175 g/6 oz and
   1 cm/½ inch thick, trimmed of all exterior fat
1 tablespoon extra-virgin olive oil
125 ml/4 fl oz mayonnaise
2 large garlic cloves, finely chopped or crushed
8 slices ciabatta bread
8 thin slices Emmenthal cheese
4 leaves crisp lettuce
8 thin slices smoked ham

1 Combine the rub ingredients. Place each steak between two pieces of clingfilm and pound to an even 5-mm/ ¼-inch thickness. Lightly brush the steaks on both sides with the oil and season evenly with the rub, pressing the spices into the meat. Allow the steaks to stand at room temperature for 15–30 minutes before grilling.

2 Whisk the mayonnaise and garlic and set aside at room temperature for 15–30 minutes before serving.

3 Prepare the grill for grilling/direct and roasting/indirect cooking over high heat (230–290°C/450–550°F).

4 Grill the steaks over *grilling/direct high heat* for 2–3 minutes, with the lid closed, until the first side is nicely marked, turning once. The second side will only take about 30 seconds to reach medium-rare doneness. Remove from the grill and let rest for 3–5 minutes.

5 Grill the bread over *grilling/direct high heat* for about 30 seconds, with the lid open, until lightly toasted. Turn the bread over and move to *roasting/indirect high heat*. Top each of four slices of the bread with two slices of cheese. Grill for about 1 minute, with the lid closed, just until the cheese begins to melt. Remove from the grill. Spread the plain bread slices with the garlic mayonnaise. Top with lettuce, ham slices, a steak and a cheese-topped bread slice. Serve warm.

RIB STEAKS
WITH SHAVED FENNEL, LEMON AND PARSLEY SALAD

SERVES: 2–4 | PREP TIME: 15 minutes | GRILLING TIME: 12–13 minutes | SPECIAL EQUIPMENT: instant-read meat thermometer

2 bone-in rib steaks, each about 625 g/1¼ lb and
   3 cm/1¼ inches thick, trimmed of excess fat
Extra-virgin olive oil

DRESSING
1½ teaspoons finely grated lemon zest
2 tablespoons fresh lemon juice
1 tablespoon red wine vinegar
1 teaspoon Dijon mustard
2 garlic cloves, finely chopped or crushed

2 fennel bulbs, trimmed, quartered, cored and very
   thinly sliced
75 g/3 oz fresh flat-leaf parsley, roughly chopped
Sea salt
Freshly ground black pepper

1 Brush the steaks on both sides with oil. Allow them to stand at room temperature for 15–30 minutes.

2 Prepare the grill for roasting/indirect cooking over low heat (130–180°C/250–350°F) and grilling/direct cooking over high heat (230–290°C/450–550°F).

3 Whisk the dressing ingredients in a large bowl. Then slowly drizzle and whisk in 100 ml/3½ fl oz oil until it is emulsified. Add the fennel and parsley and toss to combine. Season with ½ teaspoon salt and ¼ teaspoon pepper.

4 Generously season the steaks on both sides with salt. Grill the steaks over *roasting/indirect low heat* for 5 minutes, without disturbing them. Turn them over and continue cooking for about 5 minutes more, until an instant-read thermometer inserted into the centre of the thickest steak (not touching the bone) registers 43–46°C/110–115°F. Move the steaks over *grilling/direct high heat* and continue cooking for 2–3 minutes more, until the internal temperature reaches 55°C/130°F (medium rare) or 57°C/135°F (medium), turning once. Keep the lid closed as much as possible during grilling. Remove the steaks from the grill and let them rest for 3–5 minutes. Season the steaks generously with pepper, and serve warm with some of the fennel salad mounded on top.

> **TIP** The 'reverse sear' used here is a clever technique that involves warming thick steaks first over indirect heat and then finishing them with a strong sear over direct heat. Try it. It looks great!

COFFEE-RUBBED RIB-EYE STEAKS
WITH STOUT GLAZE

SERVES: 4 | PREP TIME: 20 minutes, plus about 20 minutes for the glaze | GRILLING TIME: 6–8 minutes

RUB
1 tablespoon finely ground dark roast coffee
1 tablespoon light brown sugar
1 tablespoon paprika
2 teaspoons ground cumin
2 teaspoons sea salt
1 teaspoon freshly ground black pepper

4 boneless or bone-in rib-eye steaks, each about
    375 g/12 oz and 2.5 cm/1 inch thick, trimmed of
    excess fat
Extra-virgin olive oil

GLAZE
2 tablespoons finely chopped shallots
1 garlic clove, finely chopped or crushed
250 ml/8 fl oz beef stock
125 ml/4 fl oz stout or porter
1 tablespoon black treacle
1 tablespoon Dijon mustard
1 teaspoon sea salt
1 teaspoon freshly ground black pepper

Cooked potato wedges, to serve (optional)

1 Combine the rub ingredients. Lightly brush the steaks on both sides with oil and season evenly with the rub, gently pressing the rub into the meat. Allow the steaks to stand at room temperature for 15–30 minutes before grilling.

2 Prepare the grill for grilling/direct cooking over high heat (230–290°C/450–550°F). Meanwhile, make the glaze.

3 In a saucepan over a medium heat, warm 1 tablespoon oil. Add the shallots and garlic and sauté for about 2 minutes until the shallots are tender but not browned. Add the remaining glaze ingredients, bring to the boil, and cook for 15–20 minutes until the glaze is reduced by half and has the consistency of maple syrup. Keep warm.

4 Grill the steaks over *grilling/direct high heat*, with the lid closed, until cooked to your desired doneness, 6–8 minutes for medium rare, turning once or twice. Remove from the grill and let rest for 3–5 minutes. Serve warm with the glaze and potato wedges, if desired.

WHO PUT COFFEE ON MY STEAK?

A steak in its simplest form is iconic. If the meat is well marbled and the griller has adequate skills, this classic stands proudly at any barbecue, and yet it is also confident enough that it can run with the times. These days, spiced rubs with strong ground coffee beans are all the rage – and why not? The coffee brings a nice touch of bitterness that balances well with the sweetness that you usually find in these rubs. The glaze in this recipe plays with the same sort of flavour balance. You get a little edge of bitterness from the stout that is mellowed by the sweetness of the treacle, and underlying all of that is the richness of concentrated beef stock. Are all of these elements necessary for enjoying a fine steak? No. But occasionally we like to dress our icons in the latest styles.

ESPRESSO-RUBBED RUMP ROAST
WITH CORN AND BEAN SALAD

SERVES: 6–8 | PREP TIME: 20 minutes | GRILLING TIME: 40–48 minutes

3 corn cobs, outer leaves and silk removed
Extra-virgin olive oil
3 tablespoons fresh lime juice
1 garlic clove, finely chopped or crushed
1 teaspoon dried oregano
475-g/15-oz can pinto beans, rinsed and drained
2 spring onions, ends trimmed and finely chopped
½ red pepper, cut into 1-cm/½-inch dice
1 jalapeño chilli, deseeded and finely chopped

RUB

1 tablespoon coarsely ground espresso powder
2 teaspoons prepared chilli seasoning
2 teaspoons light brown sugar
1 teaspoon dried oregano
¼ teaspoon garlic granules
¼ teaspoon onion flakes

1.4 kg/2¾ lb top rump, 5 cm/2 inches thick, trimmed of skin
    and any excess fat
Sea salt
Freshly ground black pepper

1 Prepare the grill for grilling/direct and roasting/indirect
  cooking over medium heat (180–230°C/350–450°F).

2 Brush the corn cobs with oil. Grill over *grilling/direct medium heat* for 8–10 minutes, with the lid closed, until browned in spots and tender, turning occasionally. Remove from the grill, and let cool. In a large bowl whisk the lime juice, garlic, oregano, ½ teaspoon salt and ½ teaspoon pepper. Slowly whisk in 75 ml/3 fl oz oil. Add the pinto beans, spring onions, red pepper and jalapeño. Cut off the corn kernels and add them to the salad.

3 Combine the rub ingredients, including 1 teaspoon salt and ½ teaspoon pepper. Brush the meat on both sides with oil and season evenly with the rub. Allow the joint to stand at room temperature for 15–30 minutes. Grill the meat over *grilling/direct medium heat* for 8–10 minutes, with the lid closed, until well marked on both sides, turning once or twice. Move the meat over *roasting/indirect medium heat* and cook to your desired doneness, 24–28 minutes for medium rare, turning every 5 minutes. Remove from the grill and let rest for 5–10 minutes. Carve the joint across the grain into thin slices and serve with the salad.

FIVE-MINUTE PEPPER STEAK STIR-FRY

SERVES: 6 | PREP TIME: 25 minutes | GRILLING TIME: about 5 minutes
SPECIAL EQUIPMENT: grill-proof wok or 30-cm/12-inch cast-iron frying pan

SAUCE
125 ml/4 fl oz beef stock
4 tablespoons oyster sauce
2 tablespoons soy sauce
1 tablespoon granulated sugar
2 teaspoons cornflour

1 tablespoon vegetable oil
1 tablespoon toasted sesame oil
1 tablespoon peeled, finely grated fresh ginger
2 large garlic cloves, finely chopped or crushed
500 g/1 lb top sirloin steak, cut into strips about
    7 cm/3 inches by 5 mm/¼ inch by 5 mm/¼ inch
3 large peppers, 1 red, 1 green, 1 orange, each cut into
    5-mm/¼-inch strips
1 onion, cut vertically in half and thinly sliced
4 tablespoons fresh coriander
375 g/12 oz warm cooked rice, to serve

1 Whisk the sauce ingredients together.

2 Whisk the vegetable oil, sesame oil, ginger and garlic. Add the sirloin strips and turn to coat.

3 Prepare the grill for grilling/direct cooking over high heat (230–290°C/450–550°F).

4 Place a grill-proof wok on the cooking grate, close the lid, and preheat it for about 10 minutes. Bring the sauce, meat mixture, peppers, onion and coriander to the grill.

5 When the wok is smoking hot, add the meat mixture, separating the meat as you add it to the wok. Grill over *grilling/direct high heat* for about 1 minute, with the lid open, until the meat starts to brown and releases easily from the wok, stirring once after 30 seconds. Add the peppers and the onion all at once. Stir to combine and cook for about 2 minutes until the vegetables turn a shade brighter, stirring frequently. Add the sauce, stir for 10 seconds, close the lid, and cook for about 1 minute until the sauce comes to the boil. Simmer for about 1 minute more, until the sauce is thick enough to coat the vegetables. Stir in the coriander. Remove the wok from the grill and serve the stir-fry immediately over warm rice.

SIRLOIN BEEF KEBABS
WITH TOMATO TABBOULEH

SERVES: 4 | PREP TIME: 20 minutes | MARINATING TIME: 15–30 minutes | GRILLING TIME: 6–8 minutes
SPECIAL EQUIPMENT: metal or bamboo skewers

1.2 litres/2 pints water
150 g/5 oz bulgar wheat

RUB
1½ teaspoons sea salt
1½ teaspoons ground cumin
½ teaspoon Aleppo chilli flakes *or* ¼ teaspoon ground
   cayenne pepper plus ¼ teaspoon freshly ground
   black pepper

1 kg/2 lb sirloin steak, about 3 cm/1¼ inches thick, trimmed
   of excess fat, cut into 3-cm/1¼-inch cubes
Extra-virgin olive oil
3 tablespoons fresh lemon juice
3 plum tomatoes, deseeded and diced
40 g/1½ oz fresh flat-leaf parsley, finely chopped
2 spring onions, finely chopped (white and light green
   parts only)
½ teaspoon sea salt
¼ teaspoon freshly ground black pepper

1 If using bamboo skewers, soak in water for at least
   30 minutes.

2 In a saucepan over a high heat, bring the water to the
   boil. Stir in the bulgar wheat and remove from the heat.
Let stand for about 30 minutes until the bulgar is tender.

3 Combine the rub ingredients. Place the meat cubes in
   a large bowl and add enough oil to coat the meat lightly.
Add the rub and turn to coat evenly. Thread the meat on to
skewers and allow to stand at room temperature for 15–30
minutes before grilling.

4 Prepare the grill for grilling/direct cooking over high
   heat (230–290°C/450–550°F).

5 In a large bowl whisk the lemon juice with 3 tablespoons
   oil. Drain the softened bulgar in a fine sieve. Using your
hands, squeeze the excess water from the bulgar. Add the
bulgar, tomatoes, parsley and spring onions to the lemon-oil
mixture and stir to combine. Season with salt and pepper.

6 Grill the kebabs over *grilling/direct high heat*,
   with the lid closed, until the meat is cooked to your
desired doneness, 6–8 minutes for medium rare, turning
occasionally. Remove the kebabs from the grill and serve
warm with the tabbouleh.

JERK BEEF KEBABS
WITH PINEAPPLE SALSA

SERVES: 4 | PREP TIME: 20 minutes | MARINATING TIME: 2–4 hours | GRILLING TIME: 6–8 minutes
SPECIAL EQUIPMENT: metal or bamboo skewers, rubber gloves

MARINADE

1 Scotch bonnet or habanero chilli
3 spring onions, chopped (white and green parts only)
5 tablespoons roughly chopped fresh basil
4 tablespoons rapeseed oil
2 tablespoons cider vinegar
2 tablespoons dark brown sugar
1 tablespoon finely chopped fresh ginger
1 teaspoon finely chopped garlic
1 teaspoon ground allspice
1 teaspoon sea salt

1 kg/2 lb top sirloin steak, about 3 cm/1¼ inches thick,
    trimmed of excess fat, cut into 3-cm/1¼-inch cubes

SALSA

½ pineapple, cut into 5-mm/¼-inch cubes
1 red pepper, finely chopped
1 spring onion, finely chopped (white and light green parts only)
2 tablespoons finely chopped fresh basil
1 teaspoon cider vinegar
¼ teaspoon sea salt

1 If using bamboo skewers, soak in water for at least 30 minutes.

2 Wearing rubber gloves (to avoid burning your skin), remove and discard the stem and seeds from the chilli. Put the chilli in a food processor along with the remaining marinade ingredients, and process until smooth.

3 Place the meat cubes in a large, resealable plastic bag and pour in the marinade. Press the air out of the bag and seal tightly. Turn the bag to distribute the marinade, place in a bowl, and refrigerate for 2–4 hours.

4 Wearing rubber gloves, thread the meat on to skewers and allow to stand at room temperature for 15–30 minutes before grilling. Discard the marinade.

5 Prepare the grill for grilling/direct cooking over high heat (230–290°C/450–550°F).

6 Combine the salsa ingredients.

7 Grill the kebabs over *grilling/direct high heat*, with the lid closed, until the meat is cooked to your desired doneness, 6–8 minutes for medium rare, turning occasionally. Remove the kebabs from the grill and serve warm with the salsa.

SPINACH- AND MOZZARELLA-STUFFED FLANK STEAK

SERVES: 4 | PREP TIME: 40 minutes | GRILLING TIME: 38–48 minutes | SPECIAL EQUIPMENT: kitchen string

STUFFING
50 g/2 oz baby spinach, roughly chopped
175 g/6 oz kalamata olives, roughly chopped
50 g/2 oz dried seasoned breadcrumbs
2 tablespoons currants
1 tablespoon red wine vinegar
1 tablespoon extra-virgin olive oil
2 garlic cloves, finely chopped or crushed

750–875-g/1½–1¾-lb piece of flank steak, about
   1.5 cm/¾ inch thick
125 g/4 oz low-moisture or smoked mozzarella cheese,
   cut into long, thin rectangles
1 tablespoon extra-virgin olive oil
Sea salt
Freshly ground black pepper

1 Combine the stuffing ingredients.

2 Prepare the grill for grilling/direct and roasting/indirect cooking over medium heat (180–230°C/350–450°F).

3 Using a long, flexible knife and keeping the knife parallel to your work surface, split the steak horizontally as shown in photos 1 and 2 below, opening the two halves as you cut and making sure that they are fairly even in thickness.

4 Pound the butterflied (and unfolded) steak to an even thickness. Ideally you want the steak to be roughly square and 30–37 cm/12–15 inches long on each side.

5 Arrange the steak so that the grain runs parallel to the edge of your work surface. Place the cheese slices in a single layer on top of the steak, beginning at the bottom and working towards the top. The cheese will not cover the entire surface. Spread the stuffing evenly over the cheese layer and onto the steak, leaving the top 7 cm/3 inches of the steak uncovered.

6 Starting at the lower edge, roll the steak and stuffing to make a compact roll. Tuck in any stuffing that falls out. Using kitchen string, snugly tie the roll crossways every 3.5 cm/1½ inches. The roll should be about 10 cm/4 inches in diameter.

7 Rub the surface of the roll with the oil and season evenly with salt and pepper. Sear over *grilling/direct medium heat* for about 8 minutes, with the lid open, until well marked, turning every 2 minutes. Move over *roasting/indirect medium heat* and continue grilling, with the lid closed, until cooked to your desired doneness, 30–40 minutes more for medium rare. Transfer to a carving board, cover loosely with foil and let rest for about 10 minutes. Carve crossways into thick slices and serve immediately.

1 Using a long, flexible knife that is very sharp, slowly cut the steak open from the top to the bottom.

2 Continue cutting with shallow strokes until you come to within about 1 cm/½ inch from the opposite edge. Then open the steak like a book.

3 Position the butterflied steak so that the grain of the meat runs parallel to the front and back edges of your work surface.

4 Arrange the cheese and stuffing over the meat, leaving a 7-cm/3-inch space at the top, and roll the steak snugly.

THYME-RUBBED FLANK STEAK
WITH BALSAMIC ONIONS

SERVES: 4 | PREP TIME: 15 minutes | GRILLING TIME: 8–10 minutes

175 ml/6 fl oz water
125 ml/4 fl oz balsamic vinegar
2 tablespoons honey
1½ teaspoons tomato purée
1 large bay leaf
425 g/14 oz silver skin pickled onions
3½ teaspoons finely chopped fresh thyme
2 teaspoons sea salt
1 teaspoon freshly ground black pepper
750-g/1½-lb piece of flank steak, about 1.5 cm/¾ inch thick
1 tablespoon extra-virgin olive oil
Fresh thyme sprigs (optional)

1 In a large frying pan combine the water, vinegar, honey, tomato purée and bay leaf. Add the onions and bring to a simmer over a medium-low heat. Cover and simmer for 10 minutes, stirring occasionally. Uncover the pan and increase the heat to high. Boil for about 5 minutes until the liquid starts to thicken and is reduced to 4–5 tablespoons. Remove from the heat and stir in 1½ teaspoons of the thyme, 1 teaspoon of the salt and ½ teaspoon of the pepper. The sauce will continue to thicken as it cools. If necessary, add water, 1 tablespoon at a time, to thin the mixture to your desired consistency.

2 Combine the remaining 2 teaspoons thyme, 1 teaspoon salt and ½ teaspoon pepper. Brush the steak on both sides with the oil and season evenly with the spice mixture, pressing the spices into the meat. Allow the steak to stand at room temperature for 15–30 minutes before grilling.

3 Prepare the grill for grilling/direct cooking over medium heat (180–230°C/350–450°F).

4 Grill the steak over *grilling/direct medium heat*, with the lid closed, until cooked to your desired doneness, 8–10 minutes for medium rare, turning once or twice. Remove from the grill and let rest for 3–5 minutes. Cut the steak across the grain into thin slices. Serve immediately with the onions and their sauce. Garnish with thyme, if using.

FLANK STEAK
WITH CREAMY POBLANOS AND MUSHROOMS

SERVES: 4 | PREP TIME: 20 minutes | GRILLING TIME: 18–22 minutes

RUB
1 teaspoon paprika
1 teaspoon ground cumin
1 teaspoon garlic granules
1 teaspoon sea salt
¾ teaspoon freshly ground black pepper

750-g/1½-lb piece of flank steak, about 1.5 cm/¾ inch thick
2 tablespoons extra-virgin olive oil
2 poblano or green chillies
250 g/8 oz button mushrooms, cut into 5-mm/¼-inch slices
½ onion, finely chopped
2 garlic cloves, finely chopped or crushed
125 ml/4 fl oz heavy whipping cream
¼ teaspoon sea salt

1 Combine the rub ingredients. Brush the steak on both sides with 1 tablespoon of the oil and season evenly with the rub. Allow the steak to stand at room temperature for 15–30 minutes before grilling.

2 Prepare the grill for grilling/direct cooking over medium heat (180–230°C/350–450°F).

3 Grill the chillies over *grilling/direct medium heat* for 10–12 minutes, with the lid closed, until blackened and blistered all over, turning occasionally. Put the chillies in a bowl and cover with clingfilm to trap the steam. Let stand for about 10 minutes. Remove the chillies from the bowl and peel away and discard the charred skin. Cut off and discard the stems and seeds and then cut each chilli lengthways into 1-cm/½-inch strips.

4 In a large frying pan over medium-high heat, warm the remaining 1 tablespoon oil. Add the mushrooms and onion and cook for about 5 minutes until the mushrooms are lightly browned, stirring occasionally. Stir in the garlic and cook for about 1 minute until fragrant. Add the chillies and cream and increase the heat to high. Cook for 2–3 minutes until the cream is thickened and coats the mushrooms, stirring occasionally. Season with the salt. Remove from the heat and cover to keep warm.

5 Grill the steak over *grilling/direct medium heat*, with the lid closed, until cooked to your desired doneness, 8–10 minutes for medium rare, turning once or twice. Remove from the grill and let rest for 3–5 minutes. Cut the steak across the grain into thin slices. Serve immediately topped with the creamy poblano and mushroom mixture.

MARINATED SKIRT STEAKS
WITH CITRUS AND GARLIC

SERVES: 4–6 | PREP TIME: **15 minutes** | MARINATING TIME: **2–3 hours** | GRILLING TIME: **4–6 minutes**

MARINADE
125 ml/4 fl oz extra-virgin olive oil
4 tablespoons finely chopped fresh coriander
1 teaspoon finely grated lemon zest
3 tablespoons fresh lemon juice
2 tablespoons fresh lime juice
2 teaspoons finely chopped garlic
1 teaspoon ground coriander
1¼ teaspoons sea salt
½ teaspoon freshly ground black pepper

1 kg/2 lb skirt steak, about 1 cm/½ inch thick, trimmed
    of excess surface fat, cut crossways into 15-cm/
    6-inch pieces

1 Combine the marinade ingredients. Pour 6 tablespoons of the marinade into a bowl to serve with the steak.

2 Place the steak pieces in a large, resealable plastic bag and pour in the remaining marinade. Press the air out of the bag and seal tightly. Turn the bag to distribute the marinade, place in a bowl and refrigerate for 2–3 hours, turning occasionally. Allow the steaks to stand at room temperature for 15–30 minutes.

3 Prepare the grill for grilling/direct cooking over high heat (230–290°C/450–550°F).

4 Remove the steaks from the bag and discard the marinade. Grill over *grilling/direct high heat*, with the lid closed, until cooked to your desired doneness, 4–6 minutes for medium rare, turning once or twice. Remove from the grill and let rest for 3–5 minutes. Cut the meat across the grain into thin slices and serve warm with the reserved marinade.

SPICED SKIRT STEAK
WITH TANGERINE AND RED ONION SALSA

SERVES: 4 | PREP TIME: 25 minutes | GRILLING TIME: 4–6 minutes

SALSA
750 g/1½ lb tangerines
1 red onion, finely chopped
2 tablespoons roughly chopped fresh coriander
1 tablespoon vegetable oil
1 tablespoon fresh lime juice
1 red jalapeño or serrano chilli, deseeded and finely chopped
½ teaspoon sea salt

RUB
2 teaspoons ancho chilli powder
1½ teaspoons ground cumin
1 teaspoon sea salt
¾ teaspoon freshly ground black pepper

875 g/1¾ lb skirt steak, about 1 cm/½ inch thick, trimmed of excess surface fat, cut crossways into 15-cm/6-inch pieces
Vegetable oil
Naan (optional)

1 Cut the peel and white pith from each tangerine. Cut the tangerines crossways into 1-cm/½-inch slices, and then cut the slices into ½-inch pieces. Transfer to a bowl and add the remaining salsa ingredients. Stir gently. Cover and refrigerate.

2 Combine the rub ingredients. Lightly brush the steak pieces on both sides with oil and season evenly with the rub. Allow the steaks to stand at room temperature for 15–30 minutes.

3 Prepare the grill for grilling/direct cooking over high heat (230–290°C/450–550°F).

4 Grill the steaks over *grilling/direct high heat*, with the lid closed, until cooked to your desired doneness, 4–6 minutes for medium rare, turning once or twice. Remove from the grill and let rest for 3–5 minutes. Cut the meat across the grain into thin slices and serve warm with the salsa and the naan, if liked.

BEER-MARINATED SKIRT STEAK SKEWERS
WITH GREEN CHILLI SAUCE

SERVES: 4 | PREP TIME: 40 minutes | MARINATING TIME: 4–6 hours | GRILLING TIME: 14–18 minutes
SPECIAL EQUIPMENT: 8 metal or bamboo skewers

MARINADE
125 ml/4 fl oz stout
2 tablespoons fresh lime juice
2 tablespoons dark brown sugar
1 tablespoon hot chilli-garlic sauce
1 tablespoon Dijon mustard
1 tablespoon vegetable oil
2 teaspoons ground cumin
2 garlic cloves, finely chopped or crushed
1 teaspoon paprika
1 teaspoon sea salt

750-g/1½-lb piece of skirt steak, about 1 cm/½ inch thick, trimmed of excess surface fat

SAUCE
1 large green pepper
2 garlic cloves
25 g/1oz fresh coriander leaves and tender stems
1 jalapeño chilli, deseeded and roughly chopped
½ poblano or pasilla chilli, deseeded and roughly chopped
2 tablespoons extra-virgin olive oil
1 tablespoon fresh lime juice
½ teaspoon ground cumin
1 teaspoon sea salt
½ teaspoon freshly ground black pepper

1 Whisk the marinade ingredients together.

2 Cut the steak crossways into four equal pieces. Then cut each piece lengthways in half (against the grain). Place the steak pieces in a large, resealable plastic bag and pour in the marinade. Press the air out of the bag and seal tightly. Turn the bag to distribute the marinade, place in a bowl and refrigerate for 4–6 hours, turning occasionally.

3 If using bamboo skewers, soak in water for at least 30 minutes.

4 Prepare the grill for grilling/direct cooking over medium heat (180–230°C/350–450°F).

5 Grill the green pepper over *grilling/direct medium heat* for 10–12 minutes, with the lid closed, until blackened and blistered all over, turning occasionally. Put the pepper in a bowl and cover with plastic wrap to trap the steam. Let stand for about 10 minutes. Remove the pepper from the bowl and peel away and discard the charred skin. Cut off and discard the stem and seeds, and then roughly chop the pepper. Place the pepper and the garlic in a food processor and pulse until finely chopped. Add the remaining sauce ingredients and process to a chunky paste. Transfer to a bowl. Stir the sauce just before serving.

6 Increase the temperature of the grill to high heat (230–290°C/450–550°F).

7 Remove the steak from the bag and discard the marinade. Thread the steak pieces on to skewers.

8 Grill the skewers over *grilling/direct high heat*, with the lid closed, until cooked to your desired doneness, 4–6 minutes for medium rare, turning once. Remove from the grill and serve warm with the sauce.

> TIP When cutting the skirt steak, remember to cut against the grain to ensure tender results. When making the sauce, be sure to taste a small piece of the jalapeño and the poblano to check their heat. If they are too hot, adjust the quantities to taste and remove the white pithy ribs for less heat.

LAMB LOIN CHOPS
WITH LEMON-MINT SALSA VERDE

SERVES: 4 | PREP TIME: 20 minutes | GRILLING TIME: 8–10 minutes

SALSA
75 g/3 oz fresh mint
50 g/2 oz fresh flat-leaf parsley leaves and tender stems
1 teaspoon finely grated lemon zest
2 tablespoons fresh lemon juice
1 tablespoon roughly chopped shallots
1 tablespoon capers, rinsed and drained
1 garlic clove, roughly chopped
½ teaspoon sea salt
¼ teaspoon crushed red chilli flakes
4 tablespoons extra-virgin olive oil

8 lamb loin chops, each about 3 cm/1¼ inches thick, trimmed of excess fat
Extra-virgin olive oil
Sea salt
Freshly ground black pepper
Cooked potato wedges, to serve (optional)

1 In a food processor or a blender combine all of the salsa ingredients except the oil. Pulse to roughly chop. With the motor running, add the oil to form a chunky salsa. Transfer to a bowl. Cover the surface with clingfilm to prevent discoloration and set aside at room temperature. (The salsa can be made up to 4 hours in advance. Cover and refrigerate. Bring to room temperature before serving and stir to combine.)

2 Lightly brush the lamb chops on both sides with oil and season evenly with salt and pepper. Allow the chops to stand at room temperature for 15–30 minutes before grilling.

3 Prepare the grill for grilling/direct cooking over high heat (230–290°C/450–550°F).

4 Grill the chops over *grilling/direct high heat*, with the lid closed, until cooked to your desired doneness, 8–10 minutes for medium rare, turning once. Remove from the grill and let rest for 3–5 minutes. Serve the chops warm with the salsa spooned on top.

ROSEMARY-DIJON LAMB CHOPS
WITH BALSAMIC RED ONIONS

SERVES: 4 | PREP TIME: 20 minutes | MARINATING TIME: 20–30 minutes | GRILLING TIME: 19–26 minutes

MARINADE
4 tablespoons Dijon mustard
4 tablespoons extra-virgin olive oil
1 tablespoon chopped fresh rosemary
3 garlic cloves, finely chopped or crushed
1½ teaspoons freshly ground black pepper

12 lamb cutlets, each about 1.5 cm/¾ inch thick,
    trimmed of excess fat
2 red onions, each about 175 g/6 oz, quartered through the
    stem and peeled
1 tablespoon extra-virgin olive oil
¼ teaspoon freshly ground black pepper
125 ml/4 fl oz balsamic vinegar
1 tablespoon granulated sugar
Sea salt
Grilled asparagus spears, to serve (optional)

1 In a large bowl whisk together the marinade ingredients. Put the lamb cutlets in the bowl and spread the marinade all over them. Marinate at room temperature for 20–30 minutes.

2 Prepare the grill for grilling/direct cooking over medium heat (180–230°C/350–450°F).

3 Brush the onion wedges all over with the oil and season with ½ teaspoon salt and the pepper. Grill the onions over *grilling/direct medium heat* for 15–20 minutes, with the lid closed, until tender and slightly charred in spots, turning occasionally.

4 In a small saucepan combine the vinegar and sugar and bring to the boil over a medium-high heat. Reduce the heat to medium-low and simmer for 5–7 minutes until syrupy. Remove from the heat. Increase the grill's temperature to high heat (230–290°C/450–550°F).

5 Remove the chops from the bowl and discard the marinade. Lightly season the chops with salt, and grill over *grilling/direct high heat*, with the lid closed, until cooked to your desired doneness, 4-6 minutes for medium rare, turning once or twice. Remove from the grill and let rest for 3–5 minutes. Divide the chops and onions among four serving plates. Drizzle the balsamic syrup over the onions and serve warm.

VEAL CHOPS
WITH ROCKET AND TOMATO SALAD

SERVES: 4 | PREP TIME: 20 minutes | GRILLING TIME: 4–6 minutes

150 g/5 oz baby rocket
500 g/1 lb cherry tomatoes, each cut in half
1 cucumber, cut lengthways in half and thinly sliced
40 g/1½ oz Parmesan cheese, shaved into strips with a
    vegetable peeler
½ sweet onion, thinly sliced
2 tablespoons fresh lemon juice
Extra-virgin olive oil
4 veal chops, each about 250 g/8 oz and 1.5 cm/¾ inch thick
Sea salt
Freshly ground black pepper

1 In a large bowl combine the rocket, tomatoes, cucumber, cheese and onion. In a small bowl whisk the lemon juice, 2 tablespoons oil, ½ teaspoon salt and ¼ teaspoon pepper. Set aside.

2 Brush the veal chops on both sides with oil and season evenly with salt and pepper. Allow the chops to stand at room temperature for 15–30 minutes before grilling.

3 Prepare the grill for grilling/direct cooking over high heat (230–290°C/450–550°F).

4 Grill the chops over *grilling/direct high heat*, with the lid closed, until cooked to your desired doneness, 4–6 minutes for medium rare, turning once. Remove from the grill and let rest for 3–5 minutes.

5 Give the dressing another whisk and toss with the salad. Serve the chops warm with the salad.

ROSEMARY VEAL CHOPS
WITH RED PEPPER AND BROWN BUTTER SAUCE

SERVES: 4 | PREP TIME: 20 minutes | GRILLING TIME: 6–8 minutes

2 tablespoons extra-virgin olive oil
2 teaspoons finely chopped fresh rosemary
1 teaspoon finely chopped garlic
¾ teaspoon sea salt
¼ teaspoon freshly ground black pepper
4 veal chops, each about 375 g/12 oz and 2.5 cm/1 inch thick

SAUCE
50 g/2 oz unsalted butter
¾ teaspoon finely chopped fresh rosemary leaves
2 small red peppers, thinly sliced
2 tablespoons capers, drained
1½ tablespoons fresh lemon juice
¼ teaspoon sea salt

Cooked potato wedges, to serve (optional)

1 Combine the oil, rosemary, garlic, salt and pepper. Brush the veal chops on both sides with the oil mixture. Allow the chops to stand at room temperature for 15–30 minutes before grilling.

2 Prepare the grill for grilling/direct cooking over high heat (230–290°C/450–550°F).

3 Grill the chops over *grilling/direct high heat*, with the lid closed, until cooked to your desired doneness, 6–8 minutes for medium rare, turning once. Remove from the grill and let rest while you make the sauce.

4 In a small frying pan over a medium-high heat, melt the butter and then add the rosemary. Cook for 2–4 minutes until the milk solids are toasted and the butter has a nutty smell, stirring occasionally. Add the red peppers and cook for about 2 minutes until slightly softened, stirring once or twice. Add the capers and lemon juice and cook for 1 minute. Remove the pan from the heat and stir in the salt.

5 Serve the chops warm with the sauce and potato wedges if desired.

HERB-CRUSTED RIB ROAST AU JUS

SERVES: 10–12 | PREP TIME: 15 minutes | STANDING TIME: 1 hour | GRILLING TIME: about 2 hours
SPECIAL EQUIPMENT: large disposable foil roasting tray, instant-read meat thermometer

2.75 kg/5½ lb boneless fore rib, trimmed of excess fat
125 ml/4 fl oz Dijon mustard
2 shallots, finely chopped
6 garlic cloves, finely chopped or crushed
2 teaspoons finely chopped fresh thyme
1 kg/2 lb meaty beef bones
350 ml/12 fl oz beef stock
Sea salt
Freshly ground black pepper

1 Season the roast evenly with 2 teaspoons salt and 1 teaspoon pepper. Combine the mustard, shallots, garlic and thyme. Set aside 4 tablespoons of the mustard mixture for the sauce. Spread the remaining mustard mixture all over the top and sides of the meat. Allow the joint to stand at room temperature for 1 hour before grilling.

2 Prepare the grill for roasting/indirect and grilling/direct cooking over medium heat (180–230°C/350–450°F).

3 Put the bones in a large disposable foil roasting tray and set the roast on top of the bones, fat side facing up. Position the tray on the cooking grate with the thicker end of the joint facing the hottest area of the grill. Grill over *roasting/indirect medium heat* for about 2 hours, with the lid closed, until an instant-read thermometer inserted into the thickest part of the joint registers 49–52°C/120–125°F for medium rare, rotating the meat once after 1 hour. Start checking the temperature of the meat after 1¼ hours. Keep the grill's temperature between 180 and 190°C/ 350 and 375°F.

4 Remove the roasting tray and the meat from the grill, loosely cover with aluminium foil, and let rest for 20–30 minutes (the internal temperature will rise 5–10 degrees during this time).

5 Transfer the joint to a carving board. Remove the bones from the roasting tray and discard. Pour off and discard the clear fat, leaving the browned bits in the tray. Return the tray to the grill over *grilling/direct medium heat*. Cook until the contents sizzle. Add the stock and the reserved mustard mixture. Holding the tray with insulated barbecue mitts or oven gloves and using a wooden spoon, scrape up any browned bits from the bottom. Continue cooking until the mixture is hot. Remove from the grill and season with salt and pepper.

6 Carve the joint into 1-cm/½-inch slices. Serve warm with the sauce.

TIP The appeal of a roast like this, for entertaining or otherwise, is that it is a showstopper that demands relatively little sweat. Just make sure your grill temperature is nice and even throughout the cooking time and use a reliable meat thermometer.

SLOW-COOKED COUNTRY RIBS

SERVES: 2–4 | PREP TIME: 15 minutes, plus about 20 minutes for the sauce | GRILLING TIME: about 2¼ hours
SPECIAL EQUIPMENT: large disposable foil tray fitted with a flat baking rack

RUB

2 tablespoons light brown sugar
1½ tablespoons smoked paprika
1½ teaspoons garlic granules
1½ teaspoons mustard powder
½ teaspoon ground cayenne pepper

SAUCE

150 ml/¼ pint tomato ketchup
25 g/1 oz unsalted butter
2 tablespoons cider vinegar
1 tablespoon light brown sugar
2 teaspoons prepared chilli seasoning
1 teaspoon Worcestershire sauce
1 large garlic clove, finely chopped or crushed
¼ teaspoon ground cayenne pepper

2.5 kg/5 lb rack meaty beef ribs (7 ribs), membrane
    removed, rack cut into individual ribs
125 ml/4 fl oz beef stock *or* water
Freshly ground black pepper
Sea salt
Corn cobs and watermelon wedges, to serve (optional)

1 Prepare the grill for grilling/direct and roasting/indirect
cooking over low heat (180–230°C/350–450°F).

2 Combine the rub ingredients, including 1 tablespoon
black pepper and 2½ teaspoons salt. Season the ribs
evenly with the rub. Grill the ribs over *grilling/direct low
heat* for 10–12 minutes, with the lid closed, until nicely
marked, turning once. Remove the ribs from the grill and
arrange them side by side in a large disposable foil tray
fitted with a flat baking rack. Add the stock and cover the
tray with aluminium foil. Place the pan over *roasting/
indirect low heat*, close the lid, and cook for 1 hour. Remove
the foil and turn the ribs over. Replace the foil and continue
cooking for about 1 hour, until the ribs are tender and the
meat has shrunk from the bones.

3 In a saucepan over a medium-low heat, combine the
sauce ingredients, including ¼ teaspoon salt and
¼ teaspoon pepper. Stir until the butter melts, cover, and
adjust the heat to maintain a gentle simmer. Cook for 15–20
minutes until the sauce is thickened, stirring occasionally.

4 Carefully remove the tray from the grill and lift the ribs
out. Serve immediately or, if you want the ribs a little
more charred, put them on the cooking grate over *grilling/
direct low heat*, leave the lid open and cook for an extra
5–10 minutes, turning once or twice. Serve warm with
the sauce and corn cobs and watermelon on the side,
if desired. (See page 260 for corn on the cob recipe).

BRAISED AND GLAZED SHORT RIBS

SERVES: 6 | PREP TIME: 25 minutes | GRILLING TIME: 2–2¾ hours | SPECIAL EQUIPMENT: large disposable roasting tray

BRAISING LIQUID

1 tablespoon extra-virgin olive oil
1 large onion, chopped
4 garlic cloves, chopped
450 g/14½ oz diced fire-roasted tomatoes in juice
250 ml/8 fl oz Merlot
250 ml/8 fl oz beef stock
1 tablespoon Italian herb seasoning
1 teaspoon sea salt
½ teaspoon freshly ground black pepper

12 meaty bone-in beef short ribs, about 3.75 kg/7½ lb total, each 7–10 cm/3–4 inches long

GLAZE

75 ml/3 fl oz balsamic vinegar
50 g/2 oz light brown sugar
3 tablespoons tomato purée

1 Prepare the grill for grilling/direct and roasting/indirect cooking over medium-low heat (about 180°C/350°F).

2 Warm the oil in a saucepan over a medium-high heat. Add the onion and cook for about 3 minutes until softened, stirring occasionally. Stir in the garlic and cook for about 1 minute until fragrant. Add the remaining braising liquid ingredients and bring to the boil. Arrange the ribs, bone side down, in a single layer in a large disposable foil roasting tray. Pour the braising liquid over the ribs and cover the tray tightly with aluminium foil. Place the pan over *roasting/indirect medium-low heat*, close the lid and cook for 1½–2 hours until the ribs are very tender when pierced with the tip of a knife. Transfer the ribs to a serving plate and tent loosely with foil.

3 Allow the braising liquid in the tray to stand for 5 minutes, then skim the fat from the surface. Pour half of the liquid into a blender, add the glaze ingredients and purée until smooth. Transfer to a bowl. Pour the remaining liquid into the blender, purée and add to the bowl. Pour the glaze back into the foil tray and cook over *grilling/direct medium-low heat* for about 25 minutes, with the lid closed, until thickened and reduced, stirring frequently.

4 Return the ribs over *grilling/direct medium-low heat*, close the lid, brush with some of the glaze and cook for 10–15 minutes until warmed through and nicely marked, turning often and brushing with more glaze at each turn. Serve the ribs warm with any remaining glaze.

LEG OF LAMB
WITH APRICOT AND CHICKPEA COUSCOUS

SERVES: 8–10 | PREP TIME: 15 minutes | MARINATING TIME: 4 hours | GRILLING TIME: 35–45 minutes
SPECIAL EQUIPMENT: large disposable foil pan

6 small fresh thyme sprigs
2–2.5 kg/4–5 lb boneless leg of lamb, butterflied and
    well trimmed
175 ml/6 fl oz Zinfandel
Extra-virgin olive oil
Sea salt
Freshly ground black pepper

COUSCOUS
500 ml/17 fl oz chicken stock
300 g/10 oz couscous
480-g/15½-oz can chickpeas, rinsed and drained
150 g/5 oz dried apricots, chopped into 5-mm/¼-inch dice
2 spring onions, finely chopped (white and light green
    parts only)
4 tablespoons almonds, toasted
3 tablespoons sherry vinegar
5 tablespoons roughly chopped fresh flat-leaf parsley

1 Tuck the thyme sprigs securely in the lamb. In a large
baking dish whisk the Zinfandel and 175 ml/6 fl oz oil.
Place the lamb in the baking dish. Cover and refrigerate
for 4 hours, turning once. Allow the lamb to stand at room
temperature for 30–40 minutes before grilling.

2 Place a large disposable foil tray underneath the cooking
grates (over an unlit burner) to catch the drippings.
Prepare the grill for grilling/direct and roasting/indirect
cooking over medium heat (180–230°C/350–450°F).

3 Remove the lamb from the dish and pat dry with kitchen
paper. Season with salt and pepper. Grill the lamb,
fat side up, over *grilling/direct medium heat* for about
15 minutes, with the lid closed, until nicely marked, turning
once after 10 minutes. Move the lamb, fat side up, over
roasting/indirect medium heat centred over the foil tray,
and continue cooking to your desired doneness, 20–30
minutes more for medium rare. Remove from the grill and
let rest for 5–10 minutes.

4 In a saucepan over a high heat, bring the stock to
the boil and add ½ teaspoon salt. In a heatproof bowl
combine the couscous, chickpeas, apricots and spring
onions. Stir in the stock. Cover and let stand for 5 minutes.
To the bowl add the almonds, 175 ml/6 fl oz oil, the vinegar,
half the parsley and ½ teaspoon pepper. Fluff with a fork.
Cut the lamb across the grain into thin slices and serve with
the couscous. Top with the remaining parsley.

RACKS OF LAMB
WITH WHOLEGRAIN MUSTARD AND APRICOT GLAZE

SERVES: 4 | PREP TIME: 15 minutes | MARINATING TIME: 20–30 minutes | GRILLING TIME: about 20 minutes

GLAZE
200 g/7 oz apricot jam
125 ml/4 fl oz wholegrain mustard
4 tablespoons extra-virgin olive oil
3 tablespoons finely chopped fresh thyme
6 garlic cloves, finely chopped or crushed

2 racks of lamb, each about 1 kg/2 lb, French trimmed
2 teaspoons sea salt
1½ teaspoons freshly ground black pepper

1 Whisk the glaze ingredients together. Transfer 5 tablespoons of the glaze to another bowl and set aside to brush on the racks of lamb when they come off the grill. Rub the remaining glaze all over the lamb, spreading more on the meaty side than the bone side. Marinate the lamb at room temperature for 20–30 minutes. Season evenly with the salt and the pepper.

2 Prepare the grill for grilling/direct cooking over medium heat (180–230°C/350–450°F).

3 Grill the lamb, bone side down first, over *grilling/direct medium heat*, with the lid closed, until cooked to your desired doneness, about 20 minutes for medium rare, turning occasionally and watching closely to avoid flare-ups. Remove from the grill and brush with the reserved glaze. Let rest for about 5 minutes.

4 Cut the lamb between the bones into individual chops. Serve warm.

BRISKET OF YOUR DREAMS

SERVES: 12–15 | PREP TIME: 30 minutes | MARINATING TIME: 1 hour | GRILLING TIME: 6–9 hours | RESTING TIME: 45 minutes
SPECIAL EQUIPMENT: 6 large handfuls mesquite wood chips, instant-read meat thermometer, extra-large disposable foil tray, large gravy separator, bamboo skewer

5–6 kg/10–12 lb untrimmed beef brisket

PASTE
4 tablespoons English mustard
2 tablespoons black treacle
2 tablespoons paprika
2 tablespoons light brown sugar
4 teaspoons sea salt
1 tablespoon Worcestershire sauce
2 teaspoons ground cumin
2 teaspoons prepared chilli seasoning
2 teaspoons garlic granules
1 teaspoon onion flakes
1 teaspoon freshly ground black pepper
¾ teaspoon celery salt
¾ teaspoon ground allspice

50 g/2 oz unsalted butter
350 ml/12 fl oz beef stock
2 teaspoons Worcestershire sauce
Shop-bought barbecue sauce
Hamburger buns, split
Dill pickles
Tomato slices
Mashed potatos, to serve (optional)

1 Using a very sharp knife, trim the fat on the fatty side of the brisket so that it is about 8 mm/⅓ inch thick, but no less. On the meatier side, remove the web-like membrane so that the coarsely grained meat underneath is visible. Remove any hard clumps of fat on either side of the brisket.

2 Combine the paste ingredients. Massage the paste all over the brisket and allow the brisket to stand at room temperature for 1 hour before cooking.

3 Soak the wood chips in water for at least 30 minutes.

4 Prepare the grill for roasting/indirect cooking over very low heat (110–130°C/225–250°F).

5 Drain and add two handfuls of the wood chips to the smoker box of a gas grill, following manufacturer's instructions, and close the lid. When the wood begins to smoke, cook the brisket, fat side up, over *roasting/indirect very low heat* for 4–5 hours, with the lid closed, until the internal temperature of the meat reaches 65°C/150°F. Drain and add a handful of the wood chips every 15–20 minutes (before the old chips burn out), until all of the wood chips are gone.

6 When the internal temperature of the brisket reaches 65°C/150°F, melt the butter in a saucepan over a medium heat and then add the beef stock and the Worcestershire sauce. Cook for 1–2 minutes until warmed through, stirring often. Pour the liquid into an extra-large disposable foil tray. Carefully transfer the meat, fat side up, from the grill to the tray. Close the grill lid to maintain the heat. Cover the tray with a double layer of aluminium foil and crimp the edges around the tray to seal it tightly.

7 Place the foil tray with the brisket on the cooking grates over *roasting/indirect very low heat,* close the lid and continue cooking for 2–4 hours more, until the meat is so tender that an instant-read thermometer easily tears the meat when it is pushed back and forth. The internal temperature should be 90.5–93°C/195–200°F, although tenderness is a more important indicator of doneness than temperature. Remove from the grill and let the brisket rest, still covered with foil in the tray, for 45 minutes.

8 Remove the meat from the tray and place on a carving board. Strain the pan juices into a large gravy separator. Allow the juices to stand for 3 minutes to let the fat rise to the top. Pour the pan juices into a saucepan and discard the fat. Bring to the boil over a high heat and cook for 8–10 minutes until the liquid is reduced by about a quarter and is starting to look slightly glossy, stirring frequently. Remove from the heat. Carve the 'flat' section of the brisket across the grain into thin slices. Dip each slice into the reduced pan juices. Roughly chop the fattier 'point' section. Serve the brisket warm, in hamburger buns, and side dishes of your choice, with any additional reduced pan juices, dill pickles, tomato slices and mashed potatoes, if liked.

For the sake of tenderness, brisket should be cut across the grain of the meat, but it is nearly impossible to see the grain when the meat is cooked. So, when the meat is raw, put a bamboo skewer through it (across the grain) to indicate where your knife should make parallel cuts later.

PORK

GRILLING PORK

CUT	THICKNESS/WEIGHT	APPROXIMATE GRILLING TIME
Bratwurst sausages, fresh	75-g/3-oz link	**20–25 minutes** grilling/direct medium heat
Bratwurst sausages, pre-cooked	75-g/3-oz link	**10–12 minutes** grilling/direct medium heat
Chop, boneless or bone-in	1.5 cm/¾ inch thick	**6–8 minutes** grilling/direct medium heat
	2.5 cm/1 inch thick	**8–10 minutes** grilling/direct medium heat
	3–3.5 cm/1¼–1½ inches thick	**10–12 minutes**: sear 6 minutes grilling/direct medium heat, grill 4–6 minutes roasting/indirect medium heat
Pork loin, boneless	1.75 kg/3½ lb	**28–40 minutes**: sear 8–10 minutes grilling/direct high heat, grill 20–30 minutes roasting/indirect high heat
Pork loin, bone-in	1.5–2.5 kg/3–5 lb	**1¼–1¾ hours** roasting/indirect low heat
Pork shoulder, boneless	2.5–3 kg/5–6 lb	**5–7 hours** roasting/indirect low heat
Pork, finely chopped	1 cm/½ inch thick	**8–10 minutes** grilling/direct medium heat
Ribs, baby back	750 g–1 kg/1½–2 lb	3–4 hours **roasting/**indirect low heat
Ribs, spareribs	1.25–1.75 kg/2½–3½ lb	3–4 hours **roasting/**indirect low heat
Ribs, boneless spareribs	2.5 cm/1 inch thick	**12–15 minutes** grilling/direct medium heat
Ribs, bone-in spareribs	2.5 cm/1 inch thick	**45–50 minutes** roasting/indirect medium heat
Fillet	500 g/1 lb	**15–20 minutes** grilling/direct medium heat

Official guidelines recommend that pork is cooked to 70°C/160°F, but most chefs today cook it to 63°C/145°F or 65°C/150°F, when it still has some pink in the centre and all the juices haven't been driven out. Of course, the doneness you choose is entirely up to you. Let roasts, larger cuts of meat and thick chops rest for 5–10 minutes before carving. The internal temperature of the meat will rise 5–10 degrees during this time.

TYPES OF PORK FOR THE GRILL

TENDER CUTS FOR GRILLING
▸ Centre-cut chop
▸ Fillet
▸ Loin or rib chop

MODERATELY TENDER CUTS FOR GRILLING
▸ Ham steak
▸ Shoulder steak
▸ Sirloin chop

BIGGER CUTS FOR GRILL-ROASTING
▸ Centre loin roast
▸ Boneless spareribs
▸ Cured ham
▸ Rack of pork

TOUGHER CUTS FOR BARBECUING
▸ Baby back ribs
▸ Shoulder
▸ Spareribs

GRILL SKILLS
PERFECT PORK CHOPS

CHOOSE WISELY

A lot of chops fall under the category of pork chops, but they are not all the same. They are all cut from a pig's loin, which extends from the shoulder blade to the hip, but along that loin you will find significant differences. The chops from the shoulder area (blade chops and boneless spareribs) have quite a bit of fat and chewy sinew, which makes them less than ideal for grilling. The chops cut from the hip area (sirloin chops) are often too lean and dry for this kind of cooking. The chops you should be grilling are from middle of the loin, aka the 'centre-cut rib chops' and 'centre-cut loin chops'. They are very similar to one another in taste and texture. Each loin chop features a T-shaped bone that separates the loin meat from some fillet meat on the other side. Each rib chop has a large bone (from a rack of baby back ribs) running down one side of some sumptuous loin meat. With either of these chops, try to find a thickness of at least 1.5 cm/¾ inch. Thinner chops tend to dry out too quickly.

MAKING MOCK CHOPS

Pork fillets are not chops, but if you cut them crossways into thick discs and flatten them with your hand, you've got little medallions that cook and taste very much like chops.

1 For brag-worthy results, brine your chops in a salt-and-sugar solution before grilling. This is how master grillers achieve especially juicy results. It only takes 30 minutes or so for pork chops to absorb some of that flavourful brine.

2 Once you have removed the chops from the brine, pat them dry with kitchen paper and then coat them with oil and a spice rub. Because of the salt in the brine, you will not need as much salt in the spice rub.

3 As with any piece of meat destined for the grill, it's smart to let it sit at room temperature for 15– 30 minutes before grilling. After that, the chops will cook faster and stay juicier.

GRILLING PERFECT PORK CHOPS

1 High heat tends to char the outside of pork chops too quickly and leave the centres rare or medium rare, like a steak, so go with medium heat instead for an even doneness. For chops that are less than 3.5 cm/1½ inches thick, direct medium heat is all you really need.

2 For chops that are thicker than 3.5 cm/1½ inches, grill them over grilling/direct medium heat until you have the colour of grill marks you like, and then move the chops to roasting/indirect heat for the final few minutes of cooking.

3 If any of your chops have a layer of undercooked fat around the perimeter, you might want to stand it on its edge over direct heat for up to 1 minute. Be mindful here because the fat can burn quickly, but if you work carefully, you will give your pork chop a crispy, sizzling edge.

WHEN IS IT DONE?

Chances are good that you learnt somewhere that 74°C/165°F is the safe internal temperature for pork. It's still true that ground pork must be cooked to 74°C/165°F, but chops are safe to eat when they reach 63°C/145°F. This is hot enough to eliminate the risk of trichinosis, a parasitic disease contracted from undercooked pork, but not so hot that you run every last drop of moisture out of the meat.

Remove the chops from the grill and give them a few minutes to rest at room temperature so that the juices settle throughout the meat. When you cut a perfect pork chop open, you should see a very light pink colour and a glistening sheen of moisture. The pork chop on the left, with raw meat in the centre, is clearly undercooked. The chop on the right, with a dry, grey appearance,

PORK CHOPS
WITH ROASTED PLUMS IN RED WINE REDUCTION

SERVES: 4 | PREP TIME: 30 minutes | MARINATING TIME: 2–4 hours | GRILLING TIME: 12–18 minutes

MARINADE
4 tablespoons soy sauce
2 tablespoons red wine vinegar
1 tablespoon dark brown sugar
1 tablespoon grated fresh ginger
1 garlic clove, finely chopped or crushed

Vegetable oil
4 bone-in pork loin chops, each about 250 g/8 oz and
   2.5 cm/1 inch thick, trimmed of excess fat
4 firm but ripe plums, about 500 g/1 lb total, each cut
   in half
2 garlic cloves, finely chopped or crushed
250 ml/8 fl oz fruity, full-bodied red wine
175 ml/6 fl oz beef stock
100 g/3½ oz plum jam or conserve
2 teaspoons red wine vinegar
1 sprig fresh rosemary, about 15 cm/6 inches long
15 g/½ oz cold unsalted butter
Sea salt
Freshly ground black pepper

REDUCTION SAUCES: WHEN LESS REALLY IS MORE

One way to add flavour to a dish is to keep adding ingredients, but of course that approach comes with limits and dangers, as the flavours can get muddled and confused. When you are making a sauce, there is an entirely different approach that does more with less. Borrowed from classical European cuisine, reduction sauces get more and more flavourful by concentrating whatever liquids you already have.

Take, for example, this red wine reduction sauce. You begin the process by sautéing some garlic. Then you add rich red wine and boil it until only a quarter of its original volume is left. All of the wine's richness, fruitiness and acidity have been packed into a much smaller volume now. Then you add beef stock to the wine and boil it, too. As the water evaporates, the remaining meaty flavours get stronger. Now you just need to thicken this liquid reduction with some syrupy jam, which is actually its own kind of reduction, but that's another story. The sweetness of the jam is a bit much, so add a little vinegar for balance. To smooth out the whole thing, swirl a little butter into the reduction sauce before combining it with roasted plums.

1 Whisk the marinade ingredients together, including 3 tablespoons oil. Place the pork chops in a large, resealable plastic bag and pour in the marinade. Press the air out of the bag and seal tightly. Turn the bag to distribute the marinade, place in a bowl and refrigerate for 2–4 hours, turning occasionally.

2 Prepare the grill for grilling/direct cooking over medium heat (180–230°C/350–450°F).

3 Lightly brush the plums on both sides with oil. Grill them over *grilling/direct medium heat* for 4–8 minutes, with the lid closed, until they begin to soften, turning once (the cooking time will vary depending on the ripeness of the plums). Remove from the grill and cut them into 5-mm/¼-inch slices.

4 Remove the chops from the bag and allow them to stand at room temperature for 15–30 minutes before grilling. Discard the marinade.

5 In a saucepan over a medium-high heat, warm 2 teaspoons oil. Add the garlic and sauté for about 1 minute until fragrant. Add the wine and bring to the boil. Boil rapidly for 7–8 minutes until it is reduced to 4 tablespoons. Add the stock, return to the boil and cook for 8–9 minutes until the mixture is again reduced to 4 tablespoons. Stir in the jam, vinegar and rosemary sprig, reduce the heat to medium-low and simmer for about 3 minutes until slightly thickened, stirring occasionally. Remove from the heat and discard the rosemary. Add the butter and swirl until melted. Season with ¼ teaspoon salt and ⅛ teaspoon pepper, add the plums and set aside.

6 Lightly season the chops on both sides with salt and pepper. Grill them over *grilling/direct medium heat* for 8–10 minutes, with the lid closed, until they are still slightly pink in the centre, turning once or twice. Remove from the grill and let rest for 3–5 minutes. Serve warm with the roasted plums.

BISTRO-STYLE PORK CHOPS
WITH CREAMY SHALLOT SAUCE

SERVES: 4 | PREP TIME: 35 minutes | GRILLING TIME: 8–10 minutes

4 bone-in pork loin chops, each about 250 g/8 oz and
   2.5 cm/1 inch thick, trimmed of excess fat
2 tablespoons extra-virgin olive oil
2 tablespoons finely chopped fresh tarragon
40 g/1½ oz unsalted butter
175 g/6 oz shallots, thinly sliced
100 g/3½ oz gherkins, thinly sliced
1½ tablespoons wholegrain mustard
175 ml/6 fl oz chicken stock
3 tablespoons concentrated apple juice
75 ml/3 fl oz whipping cream
Sea salt
Freshly ground black pepper

1 Lightly brush the pork chops on both sides with the oil
and season evenly with 1½ tablespoons of the tarragon,
1 teaspoon salt and ¾ teaspoon pepper. Allow the chops to
stand at room temperature for 15–30 minutes before grilling.

2 Prepare the grill for grilling/direct cooking over medium
heat (180–230°C/350–450°F).

3 Grill the chops over *grilling/direct medium heat* for
8–10 minutes, with the lid closed, until they are still
slightly pink in the centre, turning once or twice.

4 Meanwhile, in a large frying pan over a medium heat,
melt 25 g/1 oz butter. Add the shallots and sauté for
6–7 minutes until they are tender and deep golden brown.
Stir in the gherkins, mustard, stock and apple juice. Bring
to the boil and cook for 1–2 minutes until the mixture is
slightly thickened and the liquid is reduced. Add the cream,
return to a gentle boil, and cook for 2–3 minutes until
the mixture is thickened to a cream sauce consistency.
Season with the remaining tarragon, ¼ teaspoon salt and
¼ teaspoon pepper. Whisk in the butter. Remove from
the heat and cover to keep warm.

5 Remove the chops from the grill and let rest for 3–5
minutes to allow the juices to accumulate. Pour the juices
into the sauce and stir to blend. Serve the chops warm with
the sauce.

BACON-WRAPPED PORK CHOPS
WITH BOURBON SAUCE

SERVES: 4 | PREP TIME: 20 minutes | GRILLING TIME: 8–10 minutes

SAUCE
15 g/½ oz unsalted butter
1 onion, finely chopped
1 garlic clove, finely chopped or crushed
5 tablespoons tomato ketchup
5 tablespoons black treacle
4 tablespoons bourbon
1 tablespoon Worcestershire sauce
1 tablespoon balsamic vinegar
½ teaspoon hot pepper sauce

RUB
1 teaspoon prepared chilli seasoning
½ teaspoon sea salt
½ teaspoon freshly ground black pepper

4 boneless pork loin chops, each about 250 g/8 oz and
    2.5 cm/1 inch thick, trimmed of excess fat
Vegetable oil
4 rashers bacon

1 Melt the butter in a saucepan over a medium heat. Add the onion and cook for about 5 minutes until golden brown, stirring often. Stir in the garlic and cook for about 1 minute until fragrant. Add the remaining sauce ingredients and bring to a simmer for 10–15 minutes. Reduce the heat to low and simmer until the sauce is lightly thickened, stirring often. Reserve 4 tablespoons of the sauce for brushing on the pork chops while on the grill and the remaining sauce to serve with the chops.

2 Combine the rub ingredients. Brush the chops on both sides with oil and season with the rub. Allow the chops to stand at room temperature for 15–30 minutes before grilling.

3 Prepare the grill for grilling/direct cooking over medium heat (180–230°C/350–450°F).

4 In a frying pan over a medium heat or in a microwave oven on high, cook the bacon until the fat is slightly rendered, about 2 minutes. Wrap a slice of bacon around the edge of each chop and secure with a cocktail stick.

5 Grill the chops over *grilling/direct medium heat* for 8–10 minutes, with the lid closed, until they are still slightly pink in the centre and the bacon is crisp, turning once or twice and brushing with some of the sauce during the last 4–5 minutes of grilling time. Remove from the grill and let rest for 3–5 minutes. Serve warm with the remaining sauce.

HERB-CRUSTED PORK CHOPS
STUFFED WITH PROVOLONE AND PARMA HAM

SERVES: 4 | PREP TIME: 20 minutes | MARINATING TIME: 20–30 minutes | GRILLING TIME: 16–18 minutes

PASTE
4 tablespoons extra-virgin olive oil
2 tablespoons roughly chopped fresh rosemary
2 tablespoons fresh oregano
1 tablespoon fresh thyme
1 tablespoon finely grated lemon zest
2 large garlic cloves, peeled
1 teaspoon sea salt
½ teaspoon crushed red chilli flakes

4 double bone-in pork loin chops, each 375–425 g/12–14 oz
    and about 5 cm/2 inches thick, trimmed of excess fat
4 thin slices gruyere cheese
4 thin slices Parma ham
Grilled asparagus spears, to serve (optional)

1 In a food processor or a blender combine the paste ingredients and purée until the mixture forms a thick paste.

2 Place the pork chops on a work surface. Using a small, sharp knife, make a slit in the side of the meat opposite the bone. Enlarge this slit into a pocket by cutting to the left and right, slowly creating an opening that extends throughout the chop to within 1 cm/½ inch of the bone. Stuff each chop with one slice of the cheese and one slice of the Parma ham, folding them in half, if necessary, so that they will fit. Spread the paste all over the chops and marinate at room temperature for 20–30 minutes.

3 Prepare the grill for grilling/direct cooking over medium heat (180-230°C/350-450°F).

4 Grill the chops over *grilling/direct medium heat* for 16–18 minutes, with the lid closed, until they are still slightly pink in the centre, turning occasionally. Remove from the grill and let rest for 3–5 minutes. Serve warm with asparagus spears, if desired (see page 220 for recipe).

PORK TACOS
WITH GRILLED PINEAPPLE-ONION SALSA

SERVES: 6 | PREP TIME: **15 minutes** | MARINATING TIME: **30 minutes–1 hour** | GRILLING TIME: **19–21 minutes**

MARINADE
½ pineapple, coarsely chopped
1 onion, coarsely chopped
4 tablespoons tequila
2 tablespoons distilled white or cider vinegar
1 canned chipotle chilli in adobo sauce, or 1 large dried chilli
   marinated in passata
2 large garlic cloves
1 teaspoon dried oregano, preferably Mexican
1 teaspoon ground cumin
1 teaspoon sea salt
¼ teaspoon ground cinnamon

1 kg/2 lb boneless ribs or boneless blade pork chops,
   about 2.5 cm/1 inch thick, trimmed of excess fat

SALSA
½ pineapple, cut crossways into 1-cm/½-inch slices, cored
½ onion, cut crossways into 5-mm/¼-inch slices
5 tablespoons roughly chopped fresh coriander
1 jalapeño chilli, deseeded and finely chopped

12 corn or flour tortillas (15 cm/6 inches)
Sea salt
2 limes, cut into wedges

1 In a food processor purée the marinade ingredients until smooth. Place the pork chops in a large resealable plastic bag and pour in the marinade. Press the air out of the bag and seal tightly. Turn the bag to distribute the marinade, place in a bowl and refrigerate for 30 minutes–1 hour.

2 Prepare the grill for grilling/direct cooking over medium heat (180–230°C/350–450°F).

3 Grill the pineapple and onion slices over *grilling/direct medium heat* for about 8 minutes, with the lid closed, until grill marks appear, turning once or twice. Remove from the grill and cut into small dice. Combine all the salsa ingredients. Set aside.

4 Remove the chops from the bag, allowing some of the marinade to cling to the meat. Discard the remaining marinade. Season the chops with salt. Grill the chops over *grilling/direct medium heat* for 10–12 minutes, with the lid closed, until the meat is still slightly pink in the centre, turning once. (The grill may might be dark because of the natural sugar in the marinade.) Remove from the grill and let rest for 3–5 minutes. Warm the tortillas over *grilling/ direct medium heat* for about 1 minute, turning once. Cut the meat across the grain into 1-cm/½-inch slices. Fill each tortilla with pork and salsa. Serve with the lime wedges.

ROASTED PORK LOIN
WITH MAPLE-MUSTARD CREAM SAUCE

SERVES: 8–10 | PREP TIME: 20 minutes, plus about 40 minutes to make the sauce | GRILLING TIME: 28–40 minutes
SPECIAL EQUIPMENT: instant-read meat thermometer

SAUCE
40 g/1½ oz unsalted butter
75 g/3 oz shallots, finely chopped
3 tablespoons cider vinegar
575 ml/18 fl oz beef stock
250 ml/8 fl oz whipping cream
4 tablespoons maple syrup
3 tablespoons Dijon mustard
½ teaspoon sea salt

RUB
2 teaspoons smoked paprika
1 teaspoon garlic powder
1½ teaspoons sea salt
¾ teaspoon freshly ground black pepper

1.75 g/3½ lb boneless centre-cut pork loin joint
1 tablespoon extra-virgin olive oil
2 tablespoons finely chopped fresh flat-leaf parsley

1 In a saucepan over a medium heat, melt the butter. Add the shallots and cook for 5–6 minutes until slightly softened, stirring often. Add the vinegar and cook for 1–2 minutes until evaporated. Pour in the stock and the cream, increase the heat to high and bring to the boil. Reduce the heat to medium and gently simmer for 20–30 minutes until the mixture is reduced to 400 ml/14 fl oz and is thick enough to coat the back of a spoon, stirring occasionally. Stir in the syrup and simmer for 3 minutes. Remove from the heat and stir in the mustard and the salt. Set aside while you prepare the meat; or let cool, cover and refrigerate for up to 3 hours.

2 Combine the rub ingredients. Brush the joint all over with the oil and season evenly with the rub. Allow the meat to stand at room temperature for 30 minutes before grilling.

3 Prepare the grill for grilling/direct and roasting/indirect cooking over high heat (230–290°C/450–550°F).

4 Sear the pork over *grilling/direct high heat* for 8–10 minutes, with the lid closed, until the surface is well marked, turning occasionally (watch for flare-ups, especially when searing the fatty side). Move the pork over *roasting/indirect high heat* and grill, fat side up, for 20–30 minutes more, with the lid closed, until an instant-read thermometer inserted into the centre of the roast registers 60–63°C/140–145°F. Transfer to a carving board, tent loosely with foil, and let rest for about 15 minutes (the internal temperature will rise 5–10 degrees during this time).

5 Reheat the sauce gently over a medium-low heat and add the parsley. Carve the meat crossways into slices and serve warm with the sauce.

SEAR AND SLIDE

We roast pork for at least two reasons: the outside and the inside. We like the outside of the loin to have a glistening golden sheen with lightly charred edges of lip-smacking fat. We like the inside of the loin to have a succulent, delicate texture that gives easily to even an ordinary dinner knife. The trouble is, one heat alone will not get us to both outcomes.

That's why we sear the meat first over grilling/direct heat and then slide it over roasting/indirect heat to finish. While searing the meat right over the hot flames for 8–10 minutes, we dry the surface and develop the foundation of a sizzling, flavourful crust. If we continued to sear the meat over direct heat like that, the surface would get darker and darker and eventually burn; yet the inside would still be undercooked. So we slide the meat instead over indirect heat. With almost all the heat now circulating more gently around the roast, the inside of the meat cooks gradually, with only a little more browning of the crust. In a sense, the inside has an opportunity to catch up with the outside.

CITRUS-MARINATED PORK FILLET

MARINADE

175 ml/6 fl oz coca-cola (not diet)
4 tablespoons fresh orange juice
2 tablespoons fresh lime juice
1½ tablespoons peeled, grated fresh ginger
1 tablespoon dark brown sugar
2 teaspoons mustard powder
3 garlic cloves, finely chopped or crushed
1 teaspoon ground cumin
½ teaspoon ground cardamom
2 teaspoons sea salt
1 teaspoon freshly ground black pepper

2 pork fillets, each about 500 g/1 lb, trimmed of skin and any
   excess fat
1 tablespoon extra-virgin olive oil

1 Whisk the marinade ingredients together. Place the pork in a large, resealable plastic bag and pour in the marinade. Press the air out of the bag and seal tightly. Turn the bag to distribute the marinade, place in a bowl and refrigerate for 4 hours. Remove the pork from the bag and reserve the marinade. Allow the pork to stand at room temperature for 15–30 minutes before grilling.

2 Prepare the grill for grilling/direct cooking over medium heat (180–230°C/350–450°F).

3 Pour the marinade into a small saucepan. Bring to the boil over a medium-high heat and simmer for about 4 minutes until slightly reduced and thickened. Set aside.

4 Brush the pork all over with the oil. Grill over *grilling/ direct medium heat* for about 5 minutes, with the lid closed, until well marked on two sides, turning once. Lightly baste with the reduced marinade and continue to grill for 10–15 minutes more, until the outsides are evenly browned and the centres are barely pink, turning and basting every 5 minutes (if the fillets stick, move them to a clean part of the cooking grate when you turn them). Remove from the grill and let rest for 3–5 minutes. Cut into slices and serve warm. Serving suggestion: Summer Corn, Tomato and Avocado Salad (for the recipe, see page 263).

APPLE-GLAZED PORK FILLET
WITH SPRING GREENS

SERVES: 4 | PREP TIME: **30 minutes** | GRILLING TIME: **15–20 minutes**

GLAZE
375 g/12 oz apple jelly
3 tablespoons cider vinegar
25 g/1 oz unsalted butter
4 teaspoons Dijon mustard

4 teaspoons finely chopped fresh thyme
2 pork fillets, each about 500 g/1 lb, trimmed of skin and
    any excess fat
Extra-virgin olive oil
4 large garlic cloves, thinly sliced
⅛ teaspoon crushed red chilli flakes
500 g/1 lb spring greens, stems trimmed and leaves
    roughly chopped
50 g/2 oz sultanas
125 ml/4 fl oz chicken stock
2 teaspoons cider vinegar
4 rashers cooked bacon, finely chopped
Sea salt
Freshly ground black pepper

1 In a saucepan over a medium heat, cook the jelly for 1–2 minutes until it melts, stirring constantly. Add the remaining glaze ingredients, including ½ teaspoon salt and ¼ teaspoon pepper, and whisk until the mixture is smooth.

Remove from the heat and reserve 125 ml/4 fl oz of the glaze for brushing on the pork during grilling. Leave the remaining glaze in the saucepan.

2 Prepare the grill for grilling/direct cooking over medium heat (180–230°C/350–450°F).

3 Combine the thyme, 1½ teaspoons salt and 1 teaspoon pepper. Lightly brush the pork all over with oil and season with the thyme/seasoning. Grill over *grilling/direct medium heat* for 15–20 minutes, with the lid closed, until the outsides are evenly seared and the centres are barely pink, turning three times. During the last 3 minutes of grilling time, brush the pork with the reserved glaze. Remove from the grill and let rest for 3–5 minutes.

4 In a large, deep frying pan over medium-high heat, warm 2 tablespoons oil. Add the garlic and the chilli flakes and cook for about 1 minute until the garlic is fragrant, stirring constantly. Add the greens and toss for about 2 minutes until lightly wilted. Stir in the sultanas and stock and bring to the boil. Cook for 2–4 minutes until the stock is absorbed and the greens are tender. Stir in the vinegar and season with salt and pepper. Reheat the glaze in the saucepan. Cut the pork into slices. Divide the greens, pork and bacon among four plates. Spoon the glaze over and serve.

VIETNAMESE PORK SANDWICHES
WITH LEMON MAYONNAISE AND PICKLED VEGETABLES

SERVES: 6 | PREP TIME: 30 minutes | GRILLING TIME: 5–6 minutes

½ cucumber, about 175 g/6 oz, thinly sliced
1 red onion, about 125 g/4 oz, cut in half vertically,
    thinly sliced
1 carrot, peeled and grated using the large holes of
    a box grater
1 tablespoon granulated sugar
3 teaspoons sea salt
¾ teaspoon crushed red chilli flakes
4 tablespoons white wine vinegar
4 tablespoons extra-virgin olive oil
2 pork fillets, each about 500 g/1 lb, trimmed of skin and
    any excess fat
Vegetable oil
1 teaspoon freshly ground black pepper
175 ml/6 fl oz mayonnaise
1 tablespoon finely grated lemon zest
1 ciabatta loaf, about 500 g/1 lb, cut into 6 equal pieces,
    each piece halved horizontally
25 g/1 oz fresh coriander, coarsely chopped
25 g/1 oz fresh mint, coarsely chopped

1 Combine the vegetables with the sugar, 1 teaspoon of the
salt, the chilli flakes, vinegar and olive oil. Set aside.

2 Cut off the thin, tapered ends from each pork fillet and
reserve for another use. Cut each fillet crossways into
three equal pieces. Place the pieces of pork, cut side up, on a
work surface and, using your hand, pound each piece until it
is an even 1 cm/½ inch thick. Lightly brush the pork pieces
on both sides with vegetable oil and season them evenly
with the remaining 2 teaspoons salt and ½ teaspoon of
the pepper.

3 Combine the mayonnaise and the lemon zest.

4 Prepare the grill for grilling/direct cooking over high
heat (230–290°C/450–550°F).

5 Grill the pork over *grilling/direct high heat* for 5–6
minutes, with the lid closed, until barely pink in the
centre, turning once or twice. During the last minute of
grilling time, toast the ciabatta, cut side down, over *grilling/
direct heat*. Remove the pork and the ciabatta from the grill.
Let the pork rest for 3–5 minutes.

6 Thoroughly drain the vegetables and discard the liquid.
Build the sandwiches with lemon mayo, pork, pickled
vegetables, coriander and mint. Serve immediately.

SPANISH-STYLE PORK KEBABS

SERVES: 6–8 | PREP TIME: 15 minutes | MARINATING TIME: 4–8 hours | GRILLING TIME: 8–10 minutes
SPECIAL EQUIPMENT: metal or bamboo skewers

MARINADE

5 tablespoons finely chopped fresh flat-leaf parsley
  leaves and tender stems
4 tablespoons extra-virgin olive oil
2 tablespoons finely chopped red onion
1 tablespoon sherry vinegar
1 tablespoon smoked paprika
2 teaspoons ground cumin
2 teaspoons finely chopped garlic
¼ teaspoon ground cayenne pepper

2 pork fillets, each about 500 g/1 lb, trimmed
  of skin and any excess fat, cut into 3-cm/1¼-inch cubes
2 large peppers, 1 red and 1 green, cut into 3-cm/
  1¼-inch squares
Sea salt

1 Whisk the marinade ingredients together, including ½ teaspoon salt. Put the pork cubes in a large, resealable plastic bag and pour in the marinade. Press the air out of the bag and seal tightly. Turn the bag to distribute the marinade, place in a bowl, and refrigerate for 4–8 hours, turning occasionally.

2 If using bamboo skewers, soak in water for at least 30 minutes.

3 Prepare the grill for grilling/direct cooking over high heat (230–290°C/450–550°F).

4 Remove the pork from the bag and discard the marinade. Thread the pork and pepper squares alternately on to skewers.

5 Grill the kebabs over *grilling/direct high heat* for 8–10 minutes, with the lid closed, until the pork is barely pink in the centre, turning once or twice. Remove from the grill and season with salt. Serve warm.

PORK AND CHORIZO BURGERS
WITH LIME-JALAPEÑO SLAW

SERVES: 4 | PREP TIME: 30 minutes | CHILLING TIME: 30 minutes–6 hours | GRILLING TIME: 12–13 minutes
SPECIAL EQUIPMENT: instant-read meat thermometer

BURGERS

425 g/14 oz lean minced pork
300 g/10 oz fresh chorizo
300 g/10 oz panko breadcrumbs
3 tablespoons finely chopped shallots
2 tablespoons finely chopped fresh flat-leaf parsley
4 garlic cloves, finely chopped or crushed
1 teaspoon ground cumin
½ teaspoon smoked paprika
½ teaspoon dried thyme
½ teaspoon sea salt
¼ teaspoon freshly ground black pepper

SLAW

25 g/1 oz fresh coriander, finely chopped
½ jalapeño chilli, deseeded and finely chopped
2 tablespoons fresh lime juice
2 tablespoons soured cream
2 tablespoons mayonnaise
½ teaspoon sea salt
¼ teaspoon prepared chilli seasoning
375 g/12 oz green cabbage, cored and thinly sliced
1 carrot, peeled and coarsely grated

4 hamburger buns, split
Extra-virgin olive oil
Mayonnaise
8 thin slices tomato
4 lettuce leaves

1 In a large bowl gently combine the burger ingredients until thoroughly blended. With wet hands, form four loosely packed burgers, each about 10 cm/4 inches in diameter and 2.5 cm/1 inch thick. Don't compact the meat too much or the burgers will be tough. Using your thumb or the back of a spoon, make a shallow indentation about 2.5 cm/1 inch wide in the centre of each burger. This will help the burgers cook evenly and prevent them from puffing on the grill. Refrigerate in a single layer for at least 30 minutes or up to 6 hours (cover with clingfilm if chilling for more than 1 hour).

2 In a large bowl whisk the coriander, jalapeño, lime juice, soured cream, mayonnaise, salt and chilli seasoning. Add the cabbage and the carrot and toss to mix. If time allows, cover and refrigerate for 1 hour to allow the flavours to develop. Remove from the refrigerator about 20 minutes before serving (the slaw tastes better when it is not too cold).

3 Prepare the grill for grilling/direct cooking over medium heat (180–230°C/350–450°F).

4 Lightly brush the cut side of each bun with oil. Grill the burgers over *grilling/direct medium heat* for 12–13 minutes, with the lid closed, until an instant-read thermometer inserted into the centre of the burgers registers 63°C/145°F, turning once when the burgers release easily from the grate without sticking (if flare-ups occur, move temporarily over roasting/indirect heat). Looking at the burgers will not be an accurate measure of whether they are done since chorizo stays slightly pink when cooked. During the last minute of grilling time, toast the buns, cut side down, over *grilling/direct heat*. Remove the burgers and the buns from the grill.

5 Spread the cut sides of each bun with mayonnaise. Build each burger with lettuce, the meat and two tomato slices. Toss the slaw to redistribute the dressing and serve alongside the burgers.

TEXAS PORK SLIDERS
WITH BLACK BEAN SALSA

SERVES: 6 | PREP TIME: 20 minutes | GRILLING TIME: 6–8 minutes

SALSA
475-g/15-oz can black beans, rinsed and drained
2 small green peppers, finely chopped
½ red onion, coarsely grated
2 tablespoons extra-virgin olive oil
2 tablespoons finely chopped fresh coriander
1 tablespoon red wine vinegar
½ teaspoon dried oregano
¼ teaspoon hot pepper sauce, or to taste
¼ teaspoon smoked paprika
¼ teaspoon sea salt

BURGERS
750 g/1½ lb lean minced pork
½ red onion, coarsely grated
1 teaspoon mustard powder
1 teaspoon dried oregano
1 teaspoon sea salt
½ teaspoon smoked paprika
½ teaspoon freshly ground black pepper

12 small rolls, split
Crisps
Lime wedges

1 Combine the salsa ingredients. Set aside.

2 Prepare the grill for grilling/direct cooking over medium heat (180–230°C/350–450°F).

3 Gently combine the burger ingredients. With wet hands form 12 loosely packed burgers of equal size, each about 7 cm/3 inches in diameter. Don't compact the meat too much or the burgers will be tough. Using your thumb or the back of a spoon, make a shallow indentation about 1 cm/½ inch wide in the centre of each burger. This will help the burgers cook evenly and prevent them from puffing on the grill.

4 Grill the burgers over *grilling/direct medium heat* for 6–8 minutes, with the lid closed, until fully cooked, turning once or twice. During the last minute of grilling time, toast the rolls, cut side down, over grilling/direct heat. Remove from the grill and assemble the burgers in the rolls with the salsa on top (you may have leftover salsa). Serve immediately with crisps and lime wedges.

HUEVOS RANCHEROS
WITH CHORIZO

SERVES: 4 | PREP TIME: **30 minutes** | GRILLING TIME: **37–48 minutes** | SPECIAL EQUIPMENT: **25-cm/10-inch cast-iron frying pan**

3 poblano chillies, or green chilli, about 350 g/12 oz total
1½ teaspoons oil
375 g/12 oz fresh chorizo sausages, skins removed
3 large garlic cloves, finely chopped or crushed
250 g/8 oz spring onions (white and light green parts only)
2 teaspoons ground cumin
875 g/1¾ lb canned diced plum tomatoes in juice
475-g/15-oz can black beans, rinsed and drained
Sea salt
Freshly ground black pepper
100 g/3½ oz pepper jack Cheddar cheese, coarsely grated
4 large eggs
8 corn tortillas (15 cm/6 inches)
2 avocados, cut into 1-cm/½-inch dice
Soured cream
3 limes, cut into wedges

1 Prepare the grill for grilling/direct cooking over high heat (230–290°C/450–550°F). Chop the spring onions.

2 Grill the poblanos over *grilling/direct high heat* for 10–12 minutes, with the lid closed, until blackened and blistered all over, turning occasionally. Put the poblanos in a bowl and cover with clingfilm to trap the steam. Let stand for about 10 minutes. Peel off and discard the skin. Cut off and discard the stems and seeds and roughly chop the poblanos.

3 Place a 25-cm/10-inch cast-iron frying pan over *grilling/ direct high heat*, add the oil and warm for 1 minute. Add the chorizo and break into small pieces using a wooden spoon. Cook for 5–6 minutes until the chorizo is lightly browned, stirring occasionally. Stir in the garlic, spring onions and poblanos and cook for 2–3 minutes. Stir in the cumin, the tomatoes in juice, the beans, ½ teaspoon salt and ½ teaspoon pepper. Bring to the boil and cook for 12–16 minutes until the flavours are blended, the liquid is reduced by two-thirds and only a small amount of liquid remains in the bottom of the pan, stirring occasionally. Top evenly with the cheese and cook for 3–4 minutes until most of the cheese is melted. Keep the lid closed during grilling.

4 Make four shallow indentations in the chilli-bean mixture. Crack one egg into each indentation. Continue cooking over *grilling/direct high heat* for 3–5 minutes, with the lid closed, until the egg whites are set but the yolks are still soft and runny. Season the eggs with salt and pepper. Carefully remove the pan from the grill. Serve with the tortillas, soured cream, avocado and lime wedges.

5 Put four tortillas in each of two foil packets. Warm the packets over *grilling/direct high heat* for about 1 minute, turning once. Serve the huevos rancheros with the tortillas.

GRILLED PIZZAS
WITH SAUSAGE, PEPPERS AND HERBS

SERVES: 6–8 | PREP TIME: 30 minutes | GRILLING TIME: 18–22 minutes
SPECIAL EQUIPMENT: pizza stone at least 35 cm/14 inches in diameter, pizza peel (optional)

2 balls (each about 500 g/1 lb) prepared pizza dough
Extra-virgin olive oil
1 red or green pepper, cut into 5-mm/¼-inch strips
½ small onion, thinly sliced
250 g/8 oz mild or spicy Italian sausage
Plain flour
250-g/8-oz can tomato sauce
4 tablespoons thinly sliced black olives
2 tablespoons finely chopped fresh flat-leaf parsley
1 tablespoon finely chopped fresh thyme
2 teaspoons finely chopped fresh rosemary
150 g/5 oz mozzarella cheese, grated

1 Remove the balls of dough from the refrigerator, if necessary, about 1 hour before grilling so that the dough is easier to roll.

2 In a large frying pan over a medium-high heat, warm 1 tablespoon oil. Add the pepper and the onion and cook for about 3 minutes until softened but not browned, stirring occasionally. Remove the vegetables from the pan and set aside.

3 Add the sausage to the frying pan, breaking it into medium-sized pieces. Cook over a medium-high heat for about 3 minutes until lightly browned and fully cooked, stirring occasionally and breaking the sausage into smaller pieces. Remove the frying pan from the heat, and let the sausage cool in the pan.

4 Prepare the grill for grilling/direct cooking over medium heat (180–230°C/350–450°F) and preheat a pizza stone for at least 15 minutes, following manufacturer's instructions. Meanwhile, prepare your first pizza.

5 Using a rolling pin on a lightly floured work surface, roll out the dough, one ball at a time, into rounds about 30 cm/12 inches wide and 8 mm/⅓ inch thick. (If the dough retracts, cover it with kitchen paper, let it rest for 5 minutes and then continue.) Set the first round aside while you roll out the second.

6 Carefully transfer your first round of pizza dough on to a pizza peel (or a rimless baking sheet) lightly coated with flour. Spread the tomato sauce over the dough. Scatter half the sausage, half the pepper-and-onion mixture, half the olives and half the parsley, thyme and rosemary on top. Finish by scattering half the cheese on top of everything.

7 Slide your first pizza on to the preheated pizza stone and cook over *grilling/direct medium heat* for 9–11 minutes, with the lid closed, until the crust is golden brown and the cheese is melted. Using a pizza peel or a large spatula, remove the pizza from the pizza stone and let rest for a few minutes. Cut into wedges and serve warm.

8 Repeat steps 6 and 7 with the remaining dough, sauce and toppings.

1 Cold pizza dough is difficult to stretch, so take it out of the refrigerator about 1 hour before grilling, and then roll it to a thickness of about 8 mm/⅓ inch.

2 Move the dough on to a pizza peel or a rimless baking sheet lightly coated with flour so that it slides easily.

3 Use whatever toppings you like, but be sure all of them will be fully cooked after just 10 minutes on the grill.

4 Slide your pizza on to a preheated pizza stone so that the front edge of the dough grips the stone. Then slowly pull the peel or baking sheet back towards you.

STUFFED PIZZA WITH THE WORKS

SERVES: 6–8 | PREP TIME: 30 minutes | GRILLING TIME: 40–50 minutes | SPECIAL EQUIPMENT: 25-cm/10-inch cast-iron frying pan

FILLING

1 tablespoon extra-virgin olive oil
625 g/1¼ lb onions, finely chopped
3 green peppers, diced
500 g/1 lb button mushrooms, sliced
4 large garlic cloves, finely chopped or crushed
1 teaspoon sea salt
½ teaspoon freshly ground black pepper

SAUCE

250-g/8-oz can tomato sauce
4 tablespoons freshly grated Parmesan cheese
2 tablespoons tomato purée
1 tablespoon extra-virgin olive oil
½ teaspoon dried oregano
½ teaspoon dried basil
1 garlic clove, finely chopped or crushed
¼ teaspoon dried thyme

Extra-virgin olive oil
750 g/1½ lb prepared pizza dough (if you'd rather make
    your own dough, see page 282)
Plain flour
200 g/7 oz mozzarella cheese, grated
150 g/5 oz sliced pepperoni

1 Prepare the grill for grilling/direct and roasting/indirect cooking over medium heat (180–230°C/350–450°F).

2 Warm the oil in a large frying pan over a medium heat. Add the onions and green peppers and cook for about 3 minutes until slightly softened, stirring occasionally. Add the mushrooms and cook for about 12 minutes until tender and lightly browned and any liquid they have released is evaporated. During the last minute, stir in the garlic, salt and pepper. Remove the filling from the heat and set aside to cool.

3 Combine the sauce ingredients. Remove the dough from the refrigerator, if necessary, about 1 hour before grilling so that the dough is easier to roll.

4 Lightly coat a 25-cm/10-inch cast-iron frying pan with oil. Divide the dough into two balls, one with two-thirds of the dough and the other with the remaining third. On a lightly floured work surface, roll, pat and stretch the larger ball into a 35-cm/14-inch round. (If the dough retracts, cover it with kitchen paper, let it rest for 5 minutes, and then continue rolling.) Transfer the dough to the pan, letting the excess hang over the sides to keep the dough from sliding into the pan. Gently stretch the dough to fit the pan, pressing it into the corners but being careful not to tear the dough. Spread half the mozzarella on top of the dough. Spread half the filling on top of the cheese and then place half the pepperoni in a single layer on top of the filling. Repeat with another layer using the remaining filling and the remaining pepperoni. Top evenly with half of the remaining mozzarella. Roll, pat and stretch the remaining piece of dough into a 25-cm/10-inch round. Place the round on top of the filling and press down to remove any visible air pockets. Brush some water on the edges of the top and bottom pieces of dough where they come together, and then roll and pinch the edges to seal them. Prick the dough in several places to release any new air pockets that may have formed. Spread the sauce over the top crust, leaving the edges where the dough is sealed uncovered. Top the sauce with the remaining mozzarella.

5 Place the pan over *grilling/direct medium heat*, close the lid, and cook for about 5 minutes until the edges of the dough look set and somewhat dry. Move the frying pan over *roasting/indirect medium heat* and continue cooking for 35–45 minutes, with the lid closed, until the crust is golden. Remove the frying pan from the grill and let the pizza rest for 10 minutes. Using a wide spatula, slide the pizza on to a serving plate. Cut into wedges and serve.

1 Line the frying pan with two-thirds of the dough, gently pressing it into the corners.

2 Layer the mozzarella, the vegetable filling and the pepperoni inside the dough.

3 Place a round of the remaining dough on top, and press out any air pockets.

4 Moisten the top and bottom crusts, seal them snugly and prick the top crust in places.

POLISH SAUSAGE SANDWICHES
WITH BEER-BRAISED ONIONS

SERVES: 4 | PREP TIME: 15 minutes | GRILLING TIME: 31–36 minutes | SPECIAL EQUIPMENT: 25-cm/10-inch cast-iron frying pan

175 g/6 oz sauerkraut, rinsed and drained
2 red onions, 300–375 g/10–12 oz total, halved and
  very thinly sliced
2 bottles (each 350 ml/12 fl oz) beer
1 teaspoon granulated sugar
⅛ teaspoon caraway seeds
⅛ teaspoon celery seeds
500 g/1 lb Polish sausages, halved lengthways, each half cut
  crossways into 2 pieces
4 submarine rolls, each about 15 cm/6 inches long, split
English or German mustard, to serve

1 Prepare the grill for grilling/direct cooking over medium
heat (180–230°C/350–450°F).

2 In a 25-cm/10-inch cast-iron frying pan combine the
sauerkraut, onions, beer and sugar. Place the pan over
grilling/direct medium heat, close the lid and bring the
mixture to a simmer. Simmer for 25–30 minutes, stirring
occasionally. After 20 minutes, add the caraway seeds and
the celery seeds. At the same time, grill the sausages,
cut side down first, over *grilling/direct medium heat* for
7–8 minutes until nicely browned, turning once. Remove
the sausages from the grill and cut into 2.5-cm/1-inch
pieces. After the sauerkraut mixture has simmered for
25–30 minutes, add the sausages to the frying pan and
continue to cook for 5 minutes more, stirring occasionally.

3 Toast the rolls, cut side down, over *grilling/direct
medium heat* until warmed through and lightly browned
for about 1 minute.

4 Fill the rolls with the onion and sausage mixture. Serve
with mustard.

Everyone in the pool! After
these Polish sausages get a
good sear on the grill, they
join onions, sauerkraut and
beer in a simmering pool of
tasty flavours.

ROASTED PORK TORTAS
WITH GUACAMOLE

SERVES: 6–8 | PREP TIME: 25 minutes | GRILLING TIME: 2½–3 hours
SPECIAL EQUIPMENT: 2 large handfuls mesquite wood chips, large disposable foil roasting tray, instant-read meat thermometer

1 tablespoon prepared chilli seasoning
¾ teaspoon garlic granules
1.75 kg/3½ lb bone-in pork shoulder, trimmed of excess fat
Extra-virgin olive oil
8 crusty rolls, each about 15 cm/6 inches long, split
Sea salt

GUACAMOLE

2 avocados, cut into 1-cm/½-inch dice
2 plum tomatoes, deseeded and cut into 1-cm/½-inch dice
3 tablespoons finely chopped red onion
1 tablespoon finely chopped fresh coriander
1 tablespoon fresh lime juice
1 garlic clove, finely chopped or crushed
½ teaspoon prepared chilli seasoning

8 red lettuce leaves
8 slices tomato
1 red onion, thinly sliced and separated into rings
Pickled jalapeño chilli slices, drained

1 Soak the wood chips in water for at least 30 minutes. Prepare the grill for roasting/indirect cooking over medium-low heat (about 170°C/325°F).

2 Combine the chilli seasoning, garlic granules and 2 teaspoons salt. Lightly brush the meat all over with oil and season evenly with the spices. Place the joint in a large disposable foil roasting tray. Drain and add half the wood chips to the charcoal or to the smoker box of a gas grill, following manufacturer's instructions, and close the lid. When smoke appears, place the tray over *roasting/ indirect medium-low heat*, close the lid and cook for 1½ hours, draining and adding the remaining wood chips after 45 minutes. If you're using a charcoal grill, replenish the charcoal as needed to maintain a steady temperature. After 1½ hours, cover the tray tightly with aluminium foil and continue cooking for 1–1½ hours more, until an instant-read thermometer inserted into the thickest part of the joint (not touching the bone) registers 88°C/190°F. Remove from the grill, cover and let rest for 15–30 minutes. Save the pan juices. Toast the rolls, cut side down, over grilling/direct heat for about 1 minute.

3 Combine the guacamole ingredients and roughly mash with a fork. Season with salt. Carve the meat across the grain into thin slices. Skim the fat from the pan juices. Build the tortas on the rolls with lettuce, tomato, onion, jalapeño slices, pork, pan juices and guacamole. Serve warm.

APPLE-SMOKED PULLED PORK SANDWICHES

SERVES: 10–12 | PREP TIME: 30 minutes | GRILLING TIME: 6–7 hours | SPECIAL EQUIPMENT: 6 large handfuls apple wood chips, 1 large disposable foil roasting tray (2 if you're using a charcoal grill), instant-read meat thermometer

RUB

1 tablespoon dark brown sugar
1 tablespoon sea salt
2 teaspoons paprika
1 teaspoon garlic granules
1 teaspoon prepared chilli seasoning
1 teaspoon chipotle chilli powder

2.75 kg/5½ lb bone-in pork shoulder, trimmed of excess fat

SAUCE

15 g/½ oz unsalted butter
1 onion, finely chopped
250 ml/8 fl oz tomato ketchup
250 ml/8 fl oz unsweetened apple juice
125 ml/4 fl oz cider vinegar
2 tablespoons dark brown sugar
1 tablespoon black treacle
1 tablespoon soy sauce
½ teaspoon hot pepper sauce, or to taste

COLESLAW

75 ml/3 fl oz mayonnaise
3 tablespoons soured cream
2 tablespoons cider vinegar
1 tablespoon granulated sugar
¾ teaspoon sea salt
¼ teaspoon freshly ground black pepper
½ head green cabbage, thinly sliced
2 carrots, peeled and coarsely grated

12 hamburger buns, split

1 Soak the wood chips in water for at least 30 minutes.

2 Combine the rub ingredients. Coat the surface of the meat evenly with the rub. Allow the joint to stand at room temperature for 30 minutes before grilling.

3 Prepare the grill for roasting/indirect cooking over very low heat (130–150°C/250–300°F). If you're using a charcoal grill, make sure the charcoal covers no more than one-third of the charcoal grate. Place a large disposable foil tray on the empty side of the charcoal grate. Fill the tray about halfway with warm water.

4 Drain and add two handfuls of the wood chips to the charcoal or to the smoker box of a gas grill, following manufacturer's instructions, and close the lid. When the wood begins to smoke, cook the meat, fat side up, over *roasting/indirect very low heat* for 4 hours, with the lid closed. Drain and add one handful of the wood chips to the charcoal or to the smoker box every 45 minutes– 1 hour until they are gone. If you're using a charcoal grill, replenish the charcoal as needed to maintain a steady temperature, adding about eight unlit briquettes every 45 minutes–1 hour. Leave the lid off the grill for about 5 minutes to help the new briquettes light.

5 After 4 hours, use an instant-read thermometer to check the internal temperature of the roast. If it has not reached 70°C/160°F, continue cooking until it does. If it has reached 70°C/160°F, place the meat in a large disposable foil roasting tray and cover tightly with aluminium foil. Return the tray to the grill and cook over *roasting/indirect very low heat* for 2–3 hours more, with the lid closed, until the internal temperature in the thickest part of the roast (not touching the bone) registers 88°C/190°F. Remove from the grill and let rest, in the covered foil tray, for 1 hour. While the meat rests, make the sauce.

6 Melt the butter in a large saucepan over a medium heat. Add the onion and cook for 5–6 minutes until softened, stirring occasionally. Whisk in the remaining sauce ingredients, bring to a simmer, reduce the heat to medium-low, and cook for 10–15 minutes until slightly thickened, stirring occasionally. Remove from the heat.

7 In a large bowl whisk the mayonnaise, soured cream, vinegar, sugar, salt and pepper until smooth. Add the cabbage and the carrots. Mix until the vegetables are evenly coated.

8 When the joint is cool enough to handle, pull the meat apart into shreds. Discard any large pieces of fat and sinew. In a large saucepan over a low heat, moisten the pork with as much of the sauce as you like, and cook until warmed through, stirring occasionally. Pile the pork on the buns and top with coleslaw. Serve with any additional sauce.

SLOW-COOKED PERUVIAN PORK SHOULDER

SERVES: 8 | **PREP TIME:** 20 minutes | **MARINATING TIME:** 12–24 hours | **GRILLING TIME:** 4–5 hours
SPECIAL EQUIPMENT: large disposable foil roasting tray, instant-read meat thermometer

MARINADE

2 cans (each 350 ml/12 fl oz) cola (not diet)
1 onion, thinly sliced
2 lemons, peel and pith removed, cut crossways
    into 5-mm/¼-inch slices
125 ml/4 fl oz soy sauce
75 g/3 oz light brown sugar
3 garlic cloves, coarsely chopped
3 cinnamon sticks, each about 5 cm/2 inches long
1 canned chipotle chilli in adobo sauce, or 1 large dried chilli
    marinated in passata, coarsely chopped
1 tablespoon dried oregano

2.5–3 kg/5–6 lb bone-in pork shoulder roast, trimmed of
    excess fat
Cooked potato wedges, to serve (optional)

1 In a large bowl combine the marinade ingredients and stir until the sugar is dissolved. Score the fat on the meat in a cross-hatch pattern, cutting slashes through the fat just to the flesh about 5 cm/2 inches apart. Place the meat in the bowl with the marinade and turn to coat. Cover and refrigerate for 12–24 hours, turning occasionally. Allow the roast to stand at room temperature for 1 hour before grilling.

2 Prepare the grill for roasting/indirect cooking over low heat (130–180°C/250–350°F).

3 Place the joint, fat side down, in a large disposable foil roasting tray. Pour the marinade and the solids over the meat. Grill over *roasting/indirect low heat* for 4–5 hours, with the lid closed, until an instant-read thermometer inserted into the thickest part of the joint (not touching the bone) registers 88°C/190°F, turning once after 1½ hours. Remove the meat and the tray from the grill.

4 Transfer the meat to a serving plate, cover loosely with aluminium foil and let rest for 20 minutes. Discard the marinade. Cut the meat into 1-cm/½-inch slices. Serve warm with potato wedges, if desired.

HOISIN-GINGER PULLED PORK

SERVES: 6–8 | PREP TIME: 25 minutes | GRILLING TIME: 5–6 hours
SPECIAL EQUIPMENT: 4 large handfuls hickory wood chips, instant-read meat thermometer

2–2.5 kg/4–5 lb bone-in pork shoulder roast
1 tablespoon sea salt
1 teaspoon freshly ground black pepper

SAUCE
1 tablespoon vegetable oil
1 teaspoon toasted sesame oil
1 tablespoon peeled, grated fresh ginger
3 garlic cloves, finely chopped or crushed
125 ml/4 fl oz hoisin sauce
1 tablespoon soy sauce
2 tablespoons dry sherry
2 teaspoons hot chilli-garlic sauce
3 spring onions, ends trimmed, thinly sliced
½ teaspoon finely grated orange zest

500g/1 lb white rice, cooked
3 tablespoons roughly chopped fresh coriander

1 Soak the wood chips in water for at least 30 minutes. Trim the meat of excess fat and season with the salt and pepper. Cover and allow the meat to stand at room temperature for 30 minutes.

2 Prepare the grill for roasting/indirect cooking over low heat (130–180°C/250–350°F). Keep the grill's temperature as close to 150°C/300°F as possible.

3 Drain and add half the wood chips to the charcoal or to the smoker box of a gas grill, and close the lid. When the wood begins to smoke, cook the meat, fat side up, over *roasting/indirect low heat*, with the lid closed, for 1 hour. Drain and add the remaining wood chips after 30 minutes of cooking time. Continue cooking for 4–5 hours more, until an instant-read thermometer inserted into the thickest part of the joint (not touching the bone) registers 88°C/190°F. If you're using a charcoal grill, replenish the charcoal as needed to maintain a steady temperature. Transfer the meat to a carving board, cover loosely with foil, and let rest for about 20 minutes.

4 Warm the oils in a saucepan over a medium heat. Add the ginger and the garlic and cook for about 1 minute until fragrant and just starting to brown. Stir in the hoisin, soy sauce, sherry and chilli-garlic sauce, reduce the heat to medium, and cook for 2–3 minutes until warm, stirring occasionally. Remove from the heat and stir in half the spring onions and the orange zest. Pull the pork apart into shreds, discarding any large pieces of fat. Combine the pork and the sauce and toss to moisten. Serve warm, spooned over the rice and topped with the remaining spring onions and the coriander.

BLACK FOREST HAM, BRIE AND PEAR PANINI

SERVES: 4 | PREP TIME: 10 minutes | GRILLING TIME: 3–5 minutes
SPECIAL EQUIPMENT: grill-proof griddle, cast-iron grill press (optional)

4 soft rolls, each about 15 cm/6 inches long, split
4 tablespoons Dijon mustard
8 slices Black Forest ham, each about 2.5 mm/⅛ inch thick
125 g/4 oz Brie cheese, cut into 8 pieces, each about 5 mm/
  ¼ inch thick
1 large ripe pear or apple, cored and cut lengthways into
  8 slices
4 crisp romaine lettuce leaves
50 g/2 oz unsalted butter, melted

1 Prepare the grill for grilling/direct cooking over medium heat (180–230°C/350–450°F) and preheat a grill-proof griddle for about 10 minutes.

2 Spread the cut side of the rolls with the mustard. Top the bottom half of each roll with two ham slices, two cheese slices, two pear slices, a lettuce leaf and the top half of the roll. Press down on each sandwich so it is compacted. Brush the sandwiches on both sides with the melted butter.

3 Place the sandwiches on the griddle over *grilling/direct medium heat* and press them down, one at a time, with a grill press or a wide, sturdy spatula. Grill for 3–5 minutes until the rolls are toasted and golden and the cheese is melted, turning once and pressing them flat after turning. Remove from the grill and serve right away.

TIP You will need something to flatten these sandwiches as they grill. A cast-iron frying pan is too big and might slide off. You are better off using a small cast-iron grill press or a sturdy spatula to press straight down on each sandwich one at a time.

SMOKY MARMALADE-GLAZED GAMMON
WITH ORANGE-DILL SAUCE

SERVES: 8–10 | PREP TIME: 20 minutes | GRILLING TIME: 1¾–2½ hours
SPECIAL EQUIPMENT: large disposable foil roasting tray, instant-read meat thermometer

3–3.5 kg/6–7 lb bone-in gammon joint

GLAZE
5 tablespoons wholegrain mustard
100 g/3½ oz orange marmalade
2 tablespoons fresh lime juice
½ teaspoon freshly ground black pepper

SAUCE
150 ml/¼ pint mayonnaise
150 ml/¼ pint soured cream
4 tablespoons prepared horseradish
Finely grated zest and 4 tablespoons juice of 2 oranges
2 tablespoons finely chopped fresh dill
1 teaspoon white wine vinegar
½ teaspoon sea salt
¼ teaspoon freshly ground black pepper

1 Allow the gammon to stand at room temperature for 30–40 minutes before grilling.

2 Prepare the grill for roasting/indirect cooking over medium heat (180–230°C/350–450°F).

3 Combine the glaze ingredients. Score the gammon in a large criss-cross pattern about 1 cm/½ inch deep on all sides, except the cut side, and place it cut side down in a large disposable foil roasting tray. Brush half the glaze on the top and sides of the ham. Grill over *roasting/indirect medium heat* for 1 hour, with the lid closed. Baste with the remaining glaze and continue grilling for 45 minutes–1½ hours more, until an instant-read thermometer inserted into the thickest part of the ham (not touching the bone) registers 70°F/160°F. If the glaze gets too dark, cover the gammon loosely with aluminium foil for the remainder of the grilling time. Remove from the grill, tent loosely with foil and let rest for 15–45 minutes.

4 Whisk the sauce ingredients in a non-reactive bowl. Carve the gammon and serve warm with the sauce.

GRILL SKILLS
PERFECT RIBS

CRACKING THE CODE

If you ask ten barbecue fanatics about the features that add up to perfect ribs, you will get about ten different (and probably legitimate) answers. Ribs are that personal. Having said that, most of us agree on some basic elements. The meat itself should be so tender and moist that when you take a bite it pulls clean off the bone. The seasonings should be a complementary mélange of hot, sweet, savoury and salty, and no flavour should stick out from the crowd. The smoke from whatever kind of wood you like should blend into the meat as an ethereal background flavour. The sauce can vary from the sweet, smoky, tomato-based style of Missouri to the tangy, mustardy style of South Carolina to the spicy, chilli-laced style of New Mexico – but no sauce should ever smother the nuances of the meat underneath it. In the end, if you can get the meat, spices, smoke and sauce to play together nicely, you are well on your way to

REMOVING THE MEMBRANE

For the meat to be tender, you need to remove the tough membrane first. Slide a round-bladed knife under the membrane and along a bone far enough that you can prise an edge of the membrane

Then grab the loose edge and peel off the membrane in one big sheet or a few smaller pieces. You can use a kitchen paper if the membrane is hard to grip.

SEASON, SMOKE, MOP AND SAUCE

1 Season the racks generously, especially on the meaty side. Then let the racks stand at room temperature for 45 minutes so that they are not too cold going on to the grill.

2 If you stand them upright in a rib rack, you can cook twice as many racks in the same amount of space.

3 Create a small pile of charcoal to one side of the grill and feed it with more charcoal about once an hour (more often during cold or windy weather). A foil tray filled with water will help to maintain a steady temperature.

4 Once an hour, add a couple of dry wood chunks or a couple of handfuls of soaked and drained wood chips to the coals to maintain a steady stream of smoke during the first half of the cooking time.

5 Occasionally baste the ribs with a seasoned liquid called a 'mop'. Something as simple as apple juice with a little cider vinegar will moisten any areas that are drying out.

6 Barbecue sauce should not go on until the final 20–30 minutes of cooking; otherwise, the sugar in the sauce is likely to burn. Brush it on lightly – it should glaze the meat, not drown it.

7 For really tender ribs, glaze each rack with some sauce or mop, and wrap it in heavy-duty aluminium foil. Return each rack over roasting/indirect heat for the final 30 minutes– 1 hour of the cooking time.

WHEN IS IT DONE?

You will know you have reached perfect tenderness when each rack passes the bend test.

When you lift a rack at one end, bone side up, and the rack bends so easily in the middle that the meat tears open, the ribs are done.

KANSAS CITY PIT MASTER BABY BACK RIBS

SERVES: 6–8 | PREP TIME: 30 minutes | GRILLING TIME: 2¾–3 hours | SPECIAL EQUIPMENT: rib rack, 4 large handfuls hickory wood chips, large disposable foil tray (if you're using a charcoal grill), basting mop or brush

RUB

2 tablespoons paprika
1½ tablespoons dark brown sugar
1 tablespoon prepared chilli seasoning
1 tablespoon garlic granules
½ teaspoon dried thyme
½ teaspoon ground cayenne pepper
1½ teaspoons onion powder
1 tablespoon sea salt
1½ teaspoons freshly ground black pepper

4 racks baby back ribs, each 1.25–1.5 kg/2½–3 lb

SAUCE

250 ml/8 fl oz tomato ketchup
150 ml/¼ pint unsweetened apple juice
75 ml/3 fl oz cider vinegar
2 tablespoons dark brown sugar
2 tablespoons black treacle
1 tablespoon Worcestershire sauce
1 teaspoon prepared chilli seasoning
1 teaspoon smoked paprika
½ teaspoon ground cumin
¼ teaspoon freshly ground black pepper

250 ml/8 fl oz unsweetened apple juice
6 tablespoons sauce (from above)
4 tablespoons cider vinegar
Coleslaw
Corn bread

1 Mix the rub ingredients. Using a round-ended knife, slide the tip under the membrane covering the back of each rack of ribs. Lift and loosen the membrane until you can prise it up, then grab a corner of it with kitchen paper and pull it off. Season the racks evenly with the rub. Arrange the racks in a rib rack, standing each rack to face in the same direction. Allow the racks to stand at room temperature for 45 minutes before grilling. Soak the wood chips in water for at least 30 minutes.

2 Prepare the grill for roasting/indirect cooking over low heat (150–180°C/300–350°F). If you're using a charcoal grill, make sure the charcoal covers no more than a third of the charcoal grate. Place a large disposable foil tray on the empty side of the charcoal grate. Fill the tray about halfway with warm water.

3 Drain and add half the wood chips to the charcoal or to the smoker box of a gas grill, following manufacturer's instructions, and close the lid. When smoke appears, place the racks over *roasting/indirect low heat*, close the lid and cook for 1 hour. Maintain the temperature of the grill between 150 and 180°C/300 and 350°F. If you're using a charcoal grill, place the racks in the rib rack over the foil tray as far from the charcoal as possible, with the bone side towards the charcoal. Close the vent in the top lid halfway.

4 In a saucepan combine the sauce ingredients. Bring to a simmer over medium heat and cook for about 15 minutes until thickened, stirring occasionally. Remove from the heat.

5 Whisk the mop ingredients together. After the first hour of cooking, drain and add the remaining wood chips to the charcoal or to the smoker box. If you're using a charcoal grill, replenish the charcoal as needed to maintain a steady temperature, adding about eight unlit briquettes every 45 minutes–1 hour. Leave the lid off the grill for about 5 minutes to help the new briquettes light. Brush the racks with the mop, particularly the areas looking dry. Close the lid and cook for a second hour. Maintain the temperature of the grill between 150 and 180°C/300 and 350°F.

6 After the second hour of cooking, remove the racks from the rib rack, close the grill lid and brush the racks thoroughly with the remaining mop. Put the racks back in the rib rack, again all facing the same direction, but this time turned over so that the ends that were facing down earlier now face up. Also position any racks that appear to be cooking faster than the others towards the back of the rib rack, farthest from the heat. Cook for another 30 minutes. After 2½ hours, the meat will shrink back from most of the bones by 5 mm/¼ inch or more. Continue to cook until it does. Then remove the rib rack from the grill. Close the lid to maintain the heat. Remove the racks from the rib rack and brush each on both sides with some sauce.

7 Return the racks to the grill over *roasting/indirect low heat*. At this point you can pile the racks on top of one another. Continue to cook over *roasting/indirect low heat* for 15–30 minutes, with the lid closed, until tender and succulent. They are done when you lift a rack at one end with tongs, bone side up, and the rack bends so much that the meat tears. Continue to cook until it does. Remove from the grill and let rest for 5–10 minutes. Brush the racks with sauce and cut into ribs. Serve warm with extra sauce and coleslaw, and corn bread (for recipe see page 284).

1 The first step towards tender ribs is peeling off the tough membrane on the back of each rack.

2 Another step towards serious flavour is a spice rub that strikes a balance with salt, sugar, chilli powder and herbs.

3 Your next priority should be maintaining a steady, low temperature between 150 and 180°C/300° and 350°F, the lower the better.

4 Brushing the ribs with a tangy mop is a brilliant way of keeping them moist as well as adding another layer of flavour.

HONEY- AND LIME-GLAZED BABY BACK RIBS

SERVES: 4 | **PREP TIME:** 15 minutes | **MARINATING TIME:** 4–6 hours | **GRILLING TIME:** 2¼–2½ hours
SPECIAL EQUIPMENT: 45 cm/18-inch-wide heavy-duty aluminium foil

MARINADE

150 ml/¼ pint groundnut or vegetable oil
100 ml/3½ fl oz soy sauce
4 tablespoons fresh lime juice
2 tablespoons grated lemon zest
2 tablespoons finely chopped garlic
2 tablespoons Vietnamese or Thai fish sauce
2 tablespoons honey
2 teaspoons freshly ground black pepper

2 racks baby back ribs, each 750 g–1 kg/1½–2 lb, membrane
 removed (see page 156)
2 limes, cut into wedges
2 tablespoons chopped fresh basil leaves

1 Whisk the marinade ingredients together. Place the racks on a rimmed roasting tray and pour the marinade over the racks. Turn to coat both sides. Cover and refrigerate for 4–6 hours, turning occasionally. Allow the racks to stand at room temperature for 45 minutes.

2 Prepare the grill for roasting/indirect cooking over low heat (130–180°C/250–350°F).

3 Remove the racks from the roasting tray and pour the marinade into a small saucepan. Bring to the boil and then reduce the heat to maintain a simmer. Cook for 2 minutes, stirring occasionally. Remove from the heat.

4 Wrap each rack in a sheet of heavy-duty aluminium foil, crimping the seams well. Grill the foil-wrapped racks, bone side down, over *roasting/indirect low heat* for 1¼ hours, with the lid closed. Remove from the grill and let rest for about 10 minutes. When the packets are cool enough to handle, open them and pour any accumulated juices into the reduced marinade. Skim off the excess fat from the marinade. Return the ribs to the grill, meaty side down, and baste with the marinade. Cook over *roasting/indirect low heat*, with the lid closed, for 15 minutes. Turn the ribs over and cook for 45 minutes–1 hour until the meat has shrunk back from the ends of most of the bones by 5 mm/¼ inch or more, basting occasionally. The ribs are done when you lift a rack at one end with tongs, bone side up, and the rack bends so much in the middle that the meat tears easily. Remove from the grill and let rest for 5–10 minutes. Serve with lime wedges and top with the basil.

JERK-SPICED BABY BACK RIBS
WITH DARK RUM–PINEAPPLE SALSA

SERVES: 4 | PREP TIME: 20 minutes | MARINATING TIME: 3–4 hours | GRILLING TIME: 2½–3 hours

PASTE
1 onion, roughly chopped
1–2 serrano chillies, deseeded
3 spring onions, ends trimmed, roughly chopped
2 tablespoons extra-virgin olive oil
2 tablespoons fresh lime juice
2 tablespoons granulated sugar
6 garlic cloves, chopped
1 tablespoon ground allspice
1 teaspoon dried thyme
¾ teaspoon freshly ground black pepper

2 racks baby back ribs, each 875 g–1 kg/1¾–2 lb, membrane removed (see page 156)
Sea salt
Lime wedges, to serve

SALSA
375 g/12 oz finely diced fresh pineapple
½ red pepper, finely diced
¼ onion, finely diced
2 tablespoons roughly chopped fresh coriander
½ teaspoon hot pepper sauce, or to taste
1 tablespoon fresh lime juice
1 tablespoon dark or spiced rum

1 In a food processor combine the paste ingredients, including 1½ teaspoons salt, and process until fairly smooth. Spread the paste all over the racks. Cover and refrigerate for 3–4 hours, turning occasionally. Allow the ribs to stand at room temperature for 45 minutes.

2 Prepare the grill for roasting/indirect cooking over low heat (130–180°C/250–350°F). In a non-reactive bowl combine the salsa ingredients, including 1 teaspoon salt. Cover and refrigerate until just before serving.

3 Season the racks evenly with salt. Grill, bone side down first, over *roasting/indirect low heat* for 2½–3 hours, with the lid closed, turning the racks over, rotating them, and switching their positions about every 40 minutes so that both sides of each rack spend the same amount of time closest to the heat. Also, baste them occasionally with water to keep the surface moist. The ribs are done when the meat has shrunk back from the ends of most of the bones by 5 mm/¼ inch or more. Lift a rack by picking up one end with tongs. It should bend in the middle and the meat should tear easily. If it does not, continue to cook for up to 1 hour more. Transfer to a serving plate and let rest for 5–10 minutes. Stir the lime juice and rum into the salsa. Cut each rack into ribs and serve with the salsa and lime wedges.

BABY BACK RIBS
WITH SPICY RUB AND BLACK BARBECUE SAUCE

SERVES: 4 | PREP TIME: **20 minutes** | GRILLING TIME: **3¼–4¼ hours**

RUB
2 tablespoons light brown sugar
2 teaspoons chipotle chilli powder
2 teaspoons garlic powder
1 teaspoon prepared chilli seasoning
1 teaspoon ground cayenne pepper
1 tablespoon sea salt
1 teaspoon freshly ground black pepper

2 racks baby back ribs, each 1–1.25 kg/2–2½ lb

SAUCE
25 g/1 oz unsalted butter
1 large onion, finely chopped
250 ml/8 fl oz tomato ketchup
175 ml/6 fl oz black treacle
125 ml/4 fl oz beer, preferably lager
4 tablespoons cider vinegar
3 tablespoons tomato purée
1½ teaspoons mustard powder
1 teaspoon garlic powder

250 ml/8 fl oz beer, preferably lager

1 Combine the rub ingredients. Using a round-bladed knife, slide the tip under the membrane covering the back of each rack of ribs. Lift and loosen the membrane until you can prise it up, then grab a corner of it with kitchen paper and pull it off. Season the racks all over with the rub, and allow them to stand at room temperature for 45 minutes before grilling.

2 Prepare the grill for roasting/indirect cooking over low heat (130–180°C/250–350°F).

3 Meanwhile, melt the butter in a saucepan over a medium-high heat. Add the onion and cook for 3–4 minutes until slightly softened, stirring occasionally. Stir in the remaining sauce ingredients and bring to the boil. Reduce the heat to medium-low and simmer for 18–20 minutes, uncovered, until thickened. Remove from the heat.

4 Place the racks, bone side down, over *roasting/indirect low heat*, as far from the heat as possible, close the lid, and cook for 3 hours. After the first hour, baste the racks with beer, particularly any areas that are looking a little dry. Continue to baste with beer every hour or so. After 3 hours, check to see if one or both racks are ready to come off the grill. They are done when the meat has shrunk back from the ends of most of the bones by 5 mm/¼ inch or more. Lift a rack by picking up one end with tongs. It should bend in the middle and the meat should tear easily. If the meat does not tear easily, return the racks to the grill, close the lid and continue cooking for up to 1 hour more.

5 Remove the racks from the grill and lightly brush them on both sides with some of the sauce. Return the racks to the grill and cook over *roasting/indirect low heat* for 10–20 minutes, with the lid closed, until the surface is slightly crispy, turning occasionally. Remove from the grill and let rest for 5–10 minutes. Cut the racks between the bones into individual ribs and serve warm with the remaining sauce.

SPARERIBS
WITH HONEY-ORANGE GLAZE

SERVES: 4 | PREP TIME: **15** minutes | GRILLING TIME: about 1½ hours
SPECIAL EQUIPMENT: 1 large handful hickory wood chips, 45-cm/18-inch-wide heavy-duty aluminium foil

GLAZE
175 g/6 oz honey
2 tablespoons orange juice
1 tablespoon balsamic vinegar

RUB
2 teaspoons ancho chilli powder
2 teaspoons ground cumin
2 teaspoons dried oregano
1 tablespoon sea salt
1 teaspoon freshly ground black pepper

2 racks trimmed spareribs, each 1.5–1.75 kg/3–3½ lb,
   membrane removed (see page 156)

1 Soak the wood chips in water for at least 30 minutes.

2 Prepare the grill for grilling/direct cooking over medium heat (180–230°C/350–450°F).

3 Whisk the glaze ingredients together.

4 Combine the rub ingredients. Cut each rack in half to create two smaller racks. Season the racks evenly with the rub. Using eight 45-by-60-cm/18-by-24-inch sheets of heavy-duty aluminium foil, double wrap each half rack in its own packet and seal tightly. Place the foil-wrapped racks on the grill over *grilling/direct medium heat*, close the lid, and cook for 1¼ hours, turning the packets over once or twice for even cooking, making sure not to pierce the foil. If you're using a charcoal grill, replenish the charcoal as needed to maintain a steady temperature. Remove the packets from the grill and let rest for about 10 minutes. Carefully open the packets, remove the racks and discard the rendered fat and foil.

5 Drain and add the wood chips to the charcoal or to the smoker box of a gas grill, following manufacturer's instructions, and close the lid. When the wood begins to smoke, return the racks to the grill. Cook over *grilling/ direct medium heat* for about 5 minutes, with the lid closed, until the racks are sizzling, turning once or twice. Brush both sides with the glaze and cook until the racks are shiny and slightly crispy, about 5 minutes more, turning once or twice and applying more glaze after each turn. Remove from the grill and let rest for 5–10 minutes. Serve warm.

GINGER-RUBBED SPARERIBS
WITH APRICOT GLAZE

SERVES: 4 | PREP TIME: 20 minutes | GRILLING TIME: about 3½ hours
SPECIAL EQUIPMENT: 45-cm/18-inch-wide heavy-duty aluminium foil

RUB
3 tablespoons light brown sugar
1 teaspoon ground ginger
½ teaspoon mustard powder
½ teaspoon Chinese five spice powder
2 teaspoons freshly ground black pepper

2 racks trimmed spareribs, each 1.5–1.75 kg/3–3½ lb,
    membrane removed (see page 156)
2 teaspoons toasted sesame oil
1 tablespoon peeled, grated fresh ginger
3 garlic cloves, finely chopped or crushed
150 g/5 oz apricot jam
3 tablespoons soy sauce
Sea salt
Grilled pineapple chunks, to serve (optional)

1 Prepare the grill for roasting/indirect and grilling/direct cooking over low heat (130–180°C/250–350°F).

2 Combine the rub ingredients and ¾ teaspoon salt. Season the racks with the rub, putting most on the meaty side. Let the racks stand at room temperature for 45 minutes.

3 Grill the racks, bone side down, over *roasting/indirect low heat* for 2 hours, with the lid closed. Meanwhile, in a saucepan over a medium-high heat, warm the oil. Add the ginger and the garlic and cook for about 1 minute until fragrant and just starting to brown, stirring often. Stir in ¾ teaspoon salt, the jam and the soy sauce. Bring to the boil and cook for 2–3 minutes until thickened, stirring occasionally. Remove from the heat.

4 Remove the racks from the grill and brush both sides with three-quarters of the apricot-soy glaze. Wrap each rack in heavy-duty aluminium foil. Return the foil-wrapped racks to the grill and continue cooking over *roasting/ indirect low heat* for 1½ hours more, with the lid closed, until the meat has shrunk back from the ends of most of the bones at least 5 mm/¼ inch or more and the meat tears easily when you lift each rack. Remove from the grill and let rest until cool enough to handle. Remove the racks from the foil and discard the rendered fat and foil. Brush the racks with the remaining glaze, return to the grill over *grilling/ direct low heat* for about 5 minutes, close the lid and cook until charred, turning occasionally. Remove from the grill and let rest for 5–10 minutes. Serve warm with the grilled pineapple chunks, if desired.

POULTRY

GRILLING POULTRY

CUT	THICKNESS/WEIGHT	APPROXIMATE GRILLING TIME
Chicken breast, bone-in	300–375 g/10–12 oz	**23–35 minutes:** 3–5 minutes grilling/direct medium heat, 20–30 minutes roasting/indirect medium heat
Chicken breast, boneless, skinless	175–250 g/6–8 oz	**8–12 minutes** grilling/direct medium heat
Chicken drumstick	75–125 g/3–4 oz	**26–40 minutes:** 6–10 minutes grilling/direct medium heat, 20–30 minutes roasting/indirect medium heat
Chicken thigh, bone-in	150–175 g/5–6 oz	**36–40 minutes:** 6–10 minutes grilling/direct medium heat, 30 minutes roasting/indirect medium heat
Chicken thigh, boneless, skinless	125 g/4 oz	**8–10 minutes** grilling/direct medium heat
Chicken thigh, minced	1.5 cm/¾ inch thick	**12–14 minutes** grilling/direct medium heat
Chicken, whole	2–2.5 kg/4–5 lb	**1¼–1½ hours** roasting/indirect medium heat
Chicken, whole leg	300–375 g/10–12 oz	**48 minutes–1 hour:** 40–50 minutes roasting/indirect medium heat, 8–10 minutes grilling/direct medium heat
Chicken wing	50–75 g/2–3 oz	**35–43 minutes:** 30–35 minutes roasting/indirect medium heat, 5–8 minutes grilling/direct medium heat
Cornish game hen	750–1 kg/1½–2 lb	**50 minutes–1 hour** roasting/indirect high heat
Duck breast, boneless	300–375 g/10–12 oz	**9–12 minutes:** 3–4 minutes grilling/direct low heat, 6–8 minutes roasting/indirect high heat
Duck, whole	2.75–3 kg/5½–6 lb	**40 minutes** roasting/indirect high heat
Turkey breast, boneless	1.25 kg/2½ lb	**1–1¼ hours** roasting/indirect medium heat
Turkey, whole, not stuffed	5–6 kg/10–12 lb	**2½–3½ hours** roasting/indirect medium-low heat

The cuts, thicknesses, weights and grilling times are meant to be guidelines rather than hard and fast rules. Cooking times are affected by such factors as altitude, wind and outside temperature. Cooking times are for the official guideline recommendation of 74°C/165°F. Let whole poultry rest for 10–15 minutes before carving. The internal temperature of the meat will rise 5–10 degrees during this time.

GRILL SKILLS
PERFECT CHICKEN PARTS

CHOOSE WISELY

Most chicken parts these days are mass-produced for the lowest cost possible. With the help of a lively mix of spices or an interesting marinade, along with some solid grilling technique, these conventional parts can be good. If, however, you are willing to spend more for organic, free-range chicken parts, you will appreciate an obvious difference. When chickens are fed a diet free of artificial ingredients and growth-promoting antibiotics, and when they are able to run and forage in the great outdoors, they have a cleaner, more pronounced chicken flavour and their texture is firm without being tough.

EVERY MINUTE COUNTS

When you take the bones away from a chicken, especially the breasts, and expose that lean meat to the grill, there is a matter of only a couple of minutes between underdone and overcooked. The precise timing depends on the heat of the grill and the thickness of each breast, so you must pay close attention to those details. With grilling/direct medium heat (about 200°C/400°F), the thin breast on the left will be fully cooked in about 8 minutes, but the thicker breast on the right will require at least 10 minutes, and maybe 12, to cook all the way to the centre.

The darker meat on the far left comes from an organic, free-range chicken with pure, natural flavours. Whenever you see chicken like the paler breast, left, with thin white lines, you are looking at a conventional chicken that will be relatively bland and a little chewier.

CUTTING UP A WHOLE CHICKEN

1 Using a sharp knife, cut off each wing at the second joint.

Leave the rest of each wing attached to the breast.

5 Run your knife down the middle of the breast to divide it.

This technique will give you six meaty pieces.

2 Cut through the skin between each leg and the rest of the body.

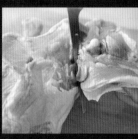

Bend each leg to expose the thigh joint, and cut through it.

3 Cut off the part of the rib cage below the breast on each side.

Finish each cut just below the remaining part of each wing.

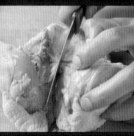

4 Make a shallow cut at the top of the rib cage.

Bend the chicken with both hands to crack the rib cage.

THE BONES MATTER

Boneless chicken pieces are thin enough that you can grill them entirely over direct heat, but when bones are involved the parts take longer to cook, so it is important to use both grilling/direct and roasting/indirect heat. Otherwise the surface will burn to a crisp before the meat at the bones has lost its pink colour.

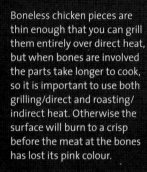

You can start grilling bone-in parts over direct heat to brown the outer surfaces and then finish the parts over roasting/indirect heat, or you can start the parts slowly over roasting/indirect heat and finish them over grilling/direct heat for a final crisping of the skin. Either way works, though it is usually safest to begin the cooking over roasting/indirect heat. That way you are less likely to experience flare-ups, because some fat will render out of the skin before you set the parts right over the flames.

WHEN IS IT DONE?

Check the thigh meat by inserting the probe of an instant-read meat thermometer into the thickest part (but not touching the bone). If you don't have a thermometer, cut into the centre of the meat. The juices should run clear and the meat should no longer be pink at the bone.

CHICKEN BREASTS ON SWISS CHARD
WITH WARM BACON DRESSING

SERVES: 4 | PREP TIME: 45 minutes | GRILLING TIME: 8–12 minutes

500 g/1 lb red Swiss chard
4 boneless, skinless chicken breasts, each about
   175 g/6 oz
Extra-virgin olive oil
2½ tablespoons finely chopped fresh thyme
4 rashers apple-wood smoked bacon, cut crossways into
   8-mm/⅓-inch strips
3 tablespoons sherry vinegar
125 ml/4 fl oz chicken stock
1 tablespoon Dijon mustard
3 large shallots, thinly sliced
3 large garlic cloves, thinly sliced
Sea salt
Freshly ground black pepper

1 Cut the thick centre stalks from the chard and finely chop them. Roughly chop the leaves and set them aside separately.

2 Prepare the grill for grilling/direct cooking over medium heat (180–230°C/350–450°F).

3 Lightly brush the chicken breasts on both sides with 1 tablespoon oil and season evenly with 1½ tablespoons of the thyme, 1 teaspoon salt and ¾ teaspoon pepper.

4 To make the dressing: in a frying pan over a medium-high heat, cook the bacon for 8–10 minutes until crisp, stirring occasionally. Using a slotted spoon, transfer the bacon to kitchen paper to drain. Add 1 tablespoon oil to the pan with the bacon drippings and warm over a medium heat. Carefully add 2 tablespoons of the vinegar, the remaining 1 tablespoon thyme, ¼ teaspoon salt and ¼ teaspoon pepper (it will bubble vigorously) and cook for 30 seconds, stirring constantly. Remove the pan from the heat.

5 Grill the chicken, smooth (skin) side down first, over *grilling/direct medium heat* for 8–12 minutes, with the lid closed, until the meat is firm to the touch and opaque all the way to the centre, turning once or twice.

6 Meanwhile, in a small bowl whisk the chicken stock, the remaining 1 tablespoon vinegar and the mustard. In a large deep frying pan over a medium-high heat, warm 2 tablespoons oil. Add the shallots and sauté for 3–4 minutes until tender and golden. Add the garlic and the chard stalks and cook for 2 minutes, stirring occasionally. Increase the heat to high, add the chard leaves and toss with tongs for about 2 minutes until just wilted. Stir in the stock-mustard mixture and toss for 2–4 minutes longer, until the liquid is almost evaporated but the chard is still bright green. Season with salt and pepper.

7 Remove the chicken from the grill and let rest for 3–5 minutes. Divide the chard among four plates and top each with a chicken breast. Return the pan with the dressing to a medium heat. Add the bacon and warm through for about 1 minute. Spoon the dressing over the chicken and serve warm.

MARINATED CHICKEN
WITH GREEN OLIVE AND CAPER VINAIGRETTE

SERVES: **4** | PREP TIME: **15 minutes** | MARINATING TIME: **1–2 hours** | GRILLING TIME: **8–12 minutes**

VINAIGRETTE
3 tablespoons red wine vinegar
1 tablespoon finely chopped shallot
2 teaspoons finely chopped fresh rosemary
1 garlic clove, finely chopped
¼ teaspoon crushed red chilli flakes
1 teaspoon sea salt
150 ml/¼ pint extra-virgin olive oil

4 boneless, skinless chicken breasts, each about 175 g/6 oz
75 g/3 oz green olives, chopped
2 tablespoons capers, rinsed and drained

1 Whisk together all the vinaigrette ingredients except the oil. Add the oil in a steady stream, whisking constantly to emulsify. Pour half of the vinaigrette into a 33-by-23-cm/13-by-9-inch glass or ceramic baking dish and reserve the remaining vinaigrette at room temperature for serving. Add the chicken breasts to the baking dish and turn to coat. Cover and refrigerate for at least 1 hour or up to 2 hours.

2 Prepare the grill for grilling/direct cooking over medium heat (180–230°C/350–450°F).

3 Remove the chicken from the dish, letting any excess vinaigrette drip back into the dish, and discard the vinaigrette. Grill the chicken, smooth (skin) side down first, over *grilling/direct medium heat* for 8–12 minutes, with the lid closed, until the meat is firm to the touch and opaque all the way to the centre, turning once or twice. Remove from the grill and let rest for 3–5 minutes.

4 Stir the olives and the capers into the reserved vinaigrette. Serve each chicken breast with a spoonful of the vinaigrette on top.

CHICKEN BREAST SKEWERS
WITH CHIPOTLE MAYO AND AVOCADO SALSA

SERVES: **4** | PREP TIME: **30 minutes** | GRILLING TIME: **9–10 minutes** | SPECIAL EQUIPMENT: **8 metal or bamboo skewers**

½ teaspoon grated lime zest
½ teaspoon ground cumin
4 boneless, skinless chicken breasts, each about
    175 g/6 oz, cut into 2.5-cm/1-inch cubes
½ onion, separated into layers, cut into 2.5-cm/1-inch pieces
125 ml/4 fl oz mayonnaise
2 teaspoons fresh lime juice
2 teaspoons chopped canned chipotle chilli in adobo sauce,
    or chilli marinated in passata
Sea salt
Freshly ground black pepper

SALSA

2 large or 3 small avocados, diced
2 plum tomatoes, deseeded and finely diced
3 spring onions, finely chopped (white and light green
    parts only)
2 tablespoons fresh lime juice
1 tablespoon finely chopped fresh coriander
¼ teaspoon hot pepper sauce

Extra-virgin olive oil
8 flour tortillas (20 cm/8 inches)

1 If using bamboo skewers, soak in water for at least
30 minutes.

2 In a large bowl mix the lime zest, ¼ teaspoon of the
cumin, ½ teaspoon salt and ¼ teaspoon pepper. Place
the chicken cubes and the onion pieces in the bowl with the
seasonings and toss to combine; thread the chicken and the
onion alternately on to skewers.

3 Prepare the grill for grilling/direct cooking over medium
heat (180–230°C/350–450°F).

4 Whisk together the mayonnaise, lime juice, chipotle
chilli and the remaining ¼ teaspoon cumin. Stir in
water, 1 teaspoon at a time, until the mixture reaches a
thick drizzling consistency.

5 Combine all of the salsa ingredients, including
½ teaspoon salt.

6 Brush the skewers all over with oil and season with salt
and pepper. Grill over *grilling/direct medium heat* for
about 8 minutes, with the lid closed, until the meat is firm to
the touch and opaque all the way to the centre, turning once
or twice. Remove from the grill and let rest for 2–3 minutes.
Meanwhile, warm the tortillas over *grilling/direct medium
heat* for 1–2 minutes, with the lid open, turning once. Push
the chicken and onion off the skewers on to the tortillas and
serve with the chipotle mayo and salsa.

MOROCCAN-SPICED CHICKEN KEBABS
WITH LEMON YOGURT SAUCE

SERVES: 4 | PREP TIME: **30 minutes** | MARINATING TIME: **4 hours** | GRILLING TIME: **8–10 minutes**
SPECIAL EQUIPMENT: **metal or bamboo skewers**

MARINADE

4 tablespoons extra-virgin olive oil
4 tablespoons chopped fresh coriander
4 tablespoons chopped fresh mint
2 tablespoons fresh lemon juice
2 teaspoons honey
1 teaspoon paprika
1 teaspoon ground cumin
2 garlic cloves, finely chopped or crushed
½ teaspoon ground coriander
½ teaspoon ground cinnamon
¼ teaspoon ground cayenne pepper
1½ teaspoons sea salt

4 boneless, skinless chicken breasts, each about
    175 g/6 oz, cut into 3.5-cm/1½-inch pieces

SAUCE

475 g/15 oz full-fat Greek yogurt
1 teaspoon finely grated lemon zest
125 ml/4 fl oz fresh lemon juice
4 tablespoons finely chopped fresh mint
2 medium garlic cloves, finely chopped or crushed
1 teaspoon sea salt

2 large peppers, 1 green and 1 red, each cut into
    3.5-cm/1½-inch squares
1 small red onion, cut into 8 wedges and separated
    into layers

1 Whisk the marinade ingredients together. Pour 4 tablespoons of the marinade into a non-reactive bowl and reserve for the vegetables. Place the chicken pieces in a large, resealable plastic bag and pour in the marinade. Press the air out of the bag and seal tightly. Turn the bag to distribute the marinade, place in a bowl and refrigerate for 4 hours, turning occasionally.

2 If using bamboo skewers, soak in water for at least 30 minutes.

3 Whisk the sauce ingredients together. Cover and refrigerate until ready to serve.

4 Prepare the grill for grilling/direct cooking over medium heat (180–230°C/350–450°F).

5 Put the vegetables in the bowl with the reserved marinade, and turn to coat. Remove the chicken from the bag and discard the marinade. Remove the vegetables from the bowl. Thread the chicken, peppers and onion alternately on to skewers.

6 Grill the kebabs over *grilling/direct medium heat* for 8–10 minutes, with the lid closed, until the meat is firm to the touch and opaque all the way to the centre, turning once or twice. Remove from the grill and let rest for 2–3 minutes. Serve warm with the sauce.

To avoid soaking bamboo skewers each time you need them, soak a big batch once for an hour or so, drain them, and then freeze them in a plastic bag. When it's time to grill, pull out as many skewers as you need.

CHICKEN BREAST AND PECAN SALAD
WITH WHEATBERRIES

SERVES: 4 | PREP TIME: 20 minutes, plus 1 hour for the wheatberries | MARINATING TIME: 2 hours | GRILLING TIME: 8–12 minutes

2 boneless, skinless chicken breasts, each about
    175 g/6 oz
250 ml/8 fl oz sweet pickle brine (from the jar of gherkins)
125 g/4 oz wheatberries
3 celery stalks, finely chopped
175 g/6 oz gherkins, chopped
75 g/3 oz chopped pecans
125 ml/4 fl oz mayonnaise
4 tablespoons cider vinegar
1 tablespoon chopped fresh dill or 1 teaspoon dried dill
¼ teaspoon celery seeds
½ teaspoon sea salt
1 teaspoon freshly ground black pepper
2 large tomatoes, cut crossways into thick slices

1 Place the chicken breasts in a small baking dish and pour the pickle brine on top. Cover and refrigerate for 2 hours, turning once or twice.

2 Meanwhile, place the wheatberries in a small saucepan and fill about two-thirds full of water. Bring to the boil over a high heat. Reduce the heat to low, partially cover and cook for about 1 hour until tender. Drain and then rinse with cool water to bring the wheatberries to room temperature. Drain again.

3 Prepare the grill for grilling/direct cooking over medium heat (180–230°C/350–450°F).

4 Remove the chicken from the dish and discard the brine. Grill the chicken, smooth (skin) side down first, over *grilling/direct medium heat* for 8–12 minutes, with the lid closed, until the meat is firm to the touch and opaque all the way to the centre, turning once or twice. Remove from the grill and let rest for 3–5 minutes. Cut the chicken into 1-cm/½-inch pieces.

5 Place the chicken and the wheatberries in a large serving bowl and add all the remaining ingredients except the tomatoes. Stir until well combined. Serve warm or at room temperature over the sliced tomatoes.

CHOPPED CHICKEN SHEPHERD'S SALAD

SERVES: 4 | PREP TIME: 45 minutes | MARINATING TIME: 1–1½ hours | GRILLING TIME: 8–12 minutes

MARINADE

2 tablespoons extra-virgin olive oil
2 tablespoons fresh lemon juice
2 teaspoons paprika
3 garlic cloves, finely chopped or crushed
1 teaspoon sea salt
½ teaspoon freshly ground black pepper

4 boneless, skinless chicken breasts, each about 175 g/6 oz

SALAD

3 tomatoes, about 500 g/1 lb total, deseeded and diced
1 cucumber, about 375 g/12 oz, diced
1 green pepper, diced
4 spring onions, chopped (white and light green
    parts only)
4 tablespoons fresh lemon juice
4 tablespoons extra-virgin olive oil
4 tablespoons roughly chopped fresh flat-leaf parsley
2 tablespoons roughly chopped fresh mint
1 teaspoon sea salt
½ teaspoon freshly ground black pepper

125 g/4 oz feta cheese, crumbled

1 In a non-reactive bowl whisk the marinade ingredients together. Add the chicken, turn to coat, cover and refrigerate for 1–1½ hours.

2 Prepare the grill for grilling/direct cooking over medium heat (180–230°C/350–450°F).

3 Combine the salad ingredients in a large serving bowl.

4 Remove the chicken from the bowl and discard the marinade. Grill the chicken, smooth (skin) side down first, over *grilling/direct medium heat* for 8–12 minutes, with the lid closed, until the meat is firm to the touch and opaque all the way to the centre, turning once or twice. Remove from the grill and let rest for 3–5 minutes. Cut the chicken into 5-mm/¼-inch cubes, add to the salad and toss well to combine. Top with the feta and serve immediately.

CHICKEN AND ROMAINE SALAD
WITH HOMEMADE RANCH DRESSING

SERVES: 4 | PREP TIME: **20 minutes** | MARINATING TIME: **4–6 hours** | GRILLING TIME: **10–14 minutes**

DRESSING
250 ml/8 fl oz mayonnaise
150 ml/¼ pint buttermilk
½ onion, coarsely grated
1 tablespoon cider vinegar
½ teaspoon celery seeds
½ teaspoon celery salt
1 garlic clove, finely chopped or crushed
¼ teaspoon freshly ground black pepper

4 boneless, skinless chicken breasts, each about 175 g/6 oz
2 hearts of romaine, about 375 g/12 oz total, each cut
    lengthways in half, trimmed
Extra-virgin olive oil
500 g/1 lb small cherry tomatoes, each cut in half
2 tablespoons finely chopped fresh flat-leaf parsley
Sea salt
Freshly ground black pepper

1 Whisk the dressing ingredients together. Place the chicken in a large, resealable plastic bag and pour in 250 ml/8 fl oz of the dressing. Press the air out of the bag and seal tightly. Turn the bag to distribute the dressing, place in a bowl and refrigerate for 4–6 hours, turning occasionally. Cover and refrigerate the remaining dressing.

2 Prepare the grill for grilling/direct cooking over medium heat (180–230°C/350–450°F).

3 Remove the chicken from the bag, shaking off and discarding the excess dressing. Grill the chicken, smooth (skin) side down first, over *grilling/direct medium heat* for 8–12 minutes, with the lid closed, until the meat is firm to the touch and opaque all the way to the centre, turning once or twice. Remove from the grill and let rest for 3–5 minutes. Cut the chicken into chunks.

4 Lightly brush the romaine halves on both sides with oil and grill over *grilling/direct medium heat* for about 2 minutes, with the lid closed, until slightly wilted, turning once. Remove from the grill.

5 Serve the lettuce warm with the chicken, dressing, tomatoes and parsley. Season with salt and pepper.

180 POULTRY

CALIFORNIA CHICKEN BREAST SALAD
WITH TANGERINE VINAIGRETTE

SERVES: 4 | PREP TIME: 25 minutes | SOAKING TIME: 30–45 minutes | GRILLING TIME: 8–12 minutes

1 red onion, thinly sliced
3 large tangerines
3 boneless, skinless chicken breasts, each about 175 g/6 oz
2 tablespoons extra-virgin olive oil
3 small bunches watercress, thick stems trimmed
3 avocados, cut into thick slices
½ teaspoon sea salt
¼ teaspoon freshly ground black pepper

VINAIGRETTE
100 ml/3½ fl oz extra-virgin olive oil
2 tablespoons sherry vinegar
1 tablespoon Dijon mustard
¼ teaspoon sea salt
1 teaspoon coarsely ground black pepper

1 Soak the onion for 30–45 minutes in a medium bowl filled with iced water, until it is crisp.

2 Finely grate enough zest from the tangerines to make 1 teaspoon. Remove the peel and white pith from the tangerines. Cut between the flesh and the white membranes separating the individual segments, working over a sieve set over a bowl so you can catch the tangerine juice for the dressing. Set aside the tangerine zest, segments and juice.

3 Prepare the grill for grilling/direct cooking over medium heat (180–230°C/350–450°F). Brush the chicken breasts with the oil and season with the salt and pepper.

4 Whisk the vinaigrette ingredients, including the reserved 1 teaspoon tangerine zest and 2 tablespoons of the reserved tangerine juice, until smooth and emulsified.

5 Grill the chicken, smooth (skin) side down first, over *grilling/direct medium heat* for 8–12 minutes, with the lid closed, until the meat is firm to the touch and opaque all the way to the centre, turning once or twice. Remove from the grill and let rest for 3–5 minutes.

6 Meanwhile, drain the onions and pat dry with kitchen paper. Combine the onions, tangerine segments and watercress. Drizzle with enough vinaigrette to coat the ingredients and toss gently. Cut the chicken breasts crossways into slices. Divide the salad, chicken and avocado among four plates and serve with the remaining vinaigrette.

PULLED CHICKEN SLIDERS
WITH ROOT BEER BARBECUE SAUCE

SERVES: 4 | PREP TIME: 15 minutes, plus about 20 minutes for the sauce | GRILLING TIME: 8–10 minutes

SAUCE
1 tablespoon extra-virgin olive oil
1 onion, finely chopped
150 ml/¼ pint tomato ketchup
125 ml/4 fl oz root beer
2 tablespoons black treacle
2 tablespoons fresh lemon juice
1 teaspoon prepared chilli seasoning
½ teaspoon garlic powder
⅛ teaspoon ground cayenne pepper

RUB
2 teaspoons smoked paprika
1 teaspoon ground cumin
1 teaspoon garlic powder
1 teaspoon sea salt

750 g/1½ lb boneless, skinless chicken thighs
Extra-virgin olive oil
8 small, soft hamburger buns or rolls, split
Mixed salad (optional)

1 Warm the oil in a medium saucepan over a medium heat. Add the onion and cook for 3–5 minutes until softened, stirring occasionally. Stir in all the remaining sauce ingredients. Increase the heat to medium-high, bring to the boil, reduce the heat to medium, and simmer for 10–15 minutes until slightly thickened, stirring occasionally.

2 Prepare the grill for grilling/direct cooking over medium heat (180–230°C/350–450°F).

3 Combine the rub ingredients. Lightly brush the chicken thighs on both sides with oil and season evenly with the rub.

4 Grill the chicken over *grilling/direct medium heat* for 8–10 minutes, with the lid closed, until the meat is firm to the touch and the juices run clear, turning once or twice. Remove from the grill and let rest for 3–5 minutes until just cool enough to handle. Shred the chicken, add to the sauce and heat through over a medium heat, stirring occasionally.

5 Fill the buns with the chicken mixture. Serve with salad, if liked.

> **TIP** The sauce can be made several days ahead of time and kept refrigerated until ready to use. Try it brushed on grilled pork, or slather it on top of your favourite burger.

CHICKEN AND BROCCOLI STIR-FRY
WITH PEANUTS AND SPRING ONIONS

SERVES: **4** | PREP TIME: **15 minutes** | GRILLING TIME: **7–9 minutes**
SPECIAL EQUIPMENT: grill-proof wok or 30-cm/12-inch cast-iron frying pan

SAUCE
75 ml/3 fl oz hoisin sauce
4 tablespoons chicken stock
1 tablespoon low-sodium soy sauce
1 teaspoon hot chilli-garlic sauce or ½–1 teaspoon crushed
    red chilli flakes

2 tablespoons vegetable oil
1 tablespoon peeled, finely chopped fresh ginger
2 teaspoons finely chopped garlic
500 g/1 lb boneless, skinless chicken thighs, cut into
    1.5-cm/¾-inch pieces
375 g/12 oz broccoli florets
1 red pepper, cut into 1.5-cm/¾-inch pieces
75 g/3 oz lightly salted peanuts
3 spring onions, thinly sliced on the diagonal (white and
    light green parts only)
250 g/8 oz rice, cooked

TIP Cut all the vegetables and meat into similar-sized
pieces so that they all finish cooking at the same time.

1 Whisk the sauce ingredients together.

2 In a large bowl whisk the oil, ginger and garlic. Add the chicken pieces and turn to coat.

3 Prepare the grill for grilling/direct cooking over high heat (230–290°C/450–550°F).

4 Place a grill-proof wok on the cooking grate over *grilling/direct high heat*, close the lid and preheat it for about 10 minutes. Bring the sauce, chicken mixture, broccoli, red pepper, peanuts and spring onions out to-hand.

5 When the wok is smoking hot, add the chicken mixture and stir-fry over *grilling/direct high heat*, with the grill lid open, for 3 minutes, using wok spatulas or wooden spoons to toss the chicken frequently. Add the broccoli and red pepper and continue to stir-fry for 2–3 minutes until the broccoli is bright green, stirring frequently. Add the sauce and stir well. Close the grill lid and cook for about 1 minute until the sauce is bubbling. Add the peanuts and the spring onions. Cook for 1–2 minutes until the broccoli is crisp-tender and the chicken is cooked through. Remove from the grill and serve immediately over warm rice.

SOFT CHICKEN TACOS
WITH EASY TOMATILLO SALSA

SERVES: **6** | PREP TIME: **15 minutes** | GRILLING TIME: **14–18 minutes**

SALSA
¼ onion, cut through the root end and peeled
8 tomatillos, about 500 g/1 lb total, papery skins removed
    and tomatillos rinsed, or green tomatoes
Extra-virgin olive oil
5 tablespoons fresh coriander
2 garlic cloves, roughly chopped
½ jalapeño chilli, deseeded and roughly chopped
Sea salt

RUB
2 teaspoons pure ancho chilli powder
½ teaspoon ground cumin
½ teaspoon garlic powder
1 teaspoon sea salt

750 g/1½ lb boneless, skinless chicken thighs
2 tablespoons extra-virgin olive oil
12 corn or flour tortillas (15 cm/6 inches)
175 g/6 oz shredded lettuce

1 Prepare the grill for grilling/direct cooking over medium heat (180–230°C/350–450°F).

2 Lightly coat the onion and the tomatillos with oil. Grill the onion, cut side down, and the tomatillos over *grilling/direct medium heat*, with the lid closed, until the onion is lightly charred and the tomatillos are softened and beginning to collapse, turning as needed. The onion will take 4–6 minutes and the tomatillos will take 6–8 minutes. Remove from the grill as they are done. Roughly chop the onion and the tomatillos, and place them in a food processor or a blender with the coriander, garlic and jalapeño. Purée until smooth. Season with salt.

3 Combine the rub ingredients. Lightly brush the chicken thighs on both sides with the oil and season evenly with the rub. Grill the chicken over *grilling/direct medium heat* for 8–10 minutes, with the lid closed, until the meat is firm to the touch and the juices run clear, turning once or twice. Remove from the grill and let rest for 3–5 minutes. Cut the chicken into slices.

4 Warm the tortillas over *grilling/direct medium heat* for about 30 seconds, with the lid open, turning once. Remove from the grill and gently fold in half. Fill each tortilla with some chicken, lettuce and salsa. Serve immediately.

SMOKED CHICKEN ENCHILADA PIE

SERVES: 6–8 | PREP TIME: 20 minutes | GRILLING TIME: about 50 minutes
SPECIAL EQUIPMENT: 2 large handfuls mesquite wood chips, 30-cm/12-inch cast-iron frying pan

750 g/1½ lb boneless, skinless chicken thighs
Extra-virgin olive oil
½ teaspoon sea salt
¼ teaspoon freshly ground black pepper
18 corn tortillas (15 cm/6 inches)
1 onion, chopped
2 large garlic cloves, finely chopped or crushed
875 g/1¾ lb canned enchilada sauce
275 g/9 oz fresh or frozen and thawed corn kernels
200-g/7-oz can chopped fire-roasted green
    chillies, drained
250 g/8 oz Cheddar cheese, grated
Soured cream
Chopped fresh coriander
Shop-bought guacamole

TIP As an alternative, substitute drained canned black or pinto beans for some or all of the corn. The enchilada sauce will determine the heat level of the overall dish, so choose carefully.

1 Soak the wood chips in water for at least 30 minutes.

2 Prepare the grill for grilling/direct and roasting/indirect cooking over medium heat (180–230°C/350–450°F).

3 Brush the chicken thighs on both sides with 1 tablespoon oil and season evenly with the salt and pepper.

4 Grill the tortillas over *grilling/direct medium heat* for about 1 minute, with the lid open, until lightly browned, turning once. Remove from the grill and place the tortillas in a single layer on baking sheets to cool. Once cooled, tear the tortillas into quarters.

5 Drain and add half the wood chips to the lit charcoal or to the smoker box of a gas grill, following manufacturer's instructions, and close the lid. When smoke appears, cook the chicken over *grilling/direct medium heat* for 8–10 minutes, with the lid closed, until the meat is firm to the touch and the juices run clear, turning once or twice. Remove from the grill and set aside. When the chicken is cool enough to handle, shred it into bite-sized pieces.

6 Meanwhile, in a frying pan over a medium heat, warm 1 tablespoon oil. Add the onion and the garlic and cook for about 3 minutes until softened, stirring occasionally. Remove from the heat.

7 Lightly oil a 30-cm/12-inch cast-iron frying pan. Spread 125 ml/4 fl oz of the enchilada sauce in the bottom of the pan. Top with a third of the tortilla pieces, and cover with 250 ml/8 fl oz of the enchilada sauce. Scatter with half the chicken, half the corn, half the onion-garlic mixture and half the chillies. Top with 75 g/3 oz of the cheese. Repeat these layers (chicken, corn, onion-garlic mixture, chillies), and then add the remaining tortilla pieces, sauce and cheese.

8 Drain and add the remaining wood chips to the charcoal or to the smoker box. If using a charcoal grill, replenish the charcoal as needed to maintain a steady temperature, adding 6–10 unlit briquettes after 45 minutes to help the new briquettes light. Cover the frying pan with aluminium foil and cook the enchilada pie over *roasting/indirect medium heat* for about 20 minutes, with the lid closed, until the sauce starts to bubble and the cheese is melted. Remove the foil and continue to cook for about 20 minutes more, until the centre of the pie is hot. Remove the frying pan from the grill, uncover and let rest for 5 minutes. Serve warm with soured cream, coriander and guacamole.

CREOLE CHICKEN BREASTS
WITH BLACK-EYED PEA AND TOMATO SALAD

SERVES: 4 | PREP TIME: **25 minutes** | GRILLING TIME: **30–45 minutes**

DRESSING
4½ tablespoons extra-virgin olive oil
3 tablespoons cider vinegar
1 tablespoon Creole, or wholegrain, mustard
1 tablespoon honey

SALAD
2 cans (each 475 g/15 oz) black-eyed peas, rinsed
    and drained
300 g/10 oz cherry tomatoes, each cut in half
125 g/4 oz smoked ham, cut into 8-mm/⅓-inch cubes
1 stalk celery, finely chopped

4 chicken breasts (with bone and skin),
    each 300–375 g/10–12 oz
1 tablespoon extra-virgin olive oil
2½ teaspoons Cajun seasoning
100 ml/3½ fl oz Creole, or wholegrain, mustard
1 tablespoon honey
2 teaspoons finely chopped fresh thyme
1 bunch watercress sprigs, thick stems trimmed
Sea salt
Freshly ground black pepper

1 Whisk the dressing ingredients together in a large bowl. Add the salad ingredients and toss to coat with the dressing. Season with salt and pepper. Cover and refrigerate until ready to serve.

2 Prepare the grill for roasting/indirect cooking over medium heat (180–230°C/350–450°F).

3 Brush the chicken breasts on both sides with the oil and season evenly with the Cajun seasoning, 1½ teaspoons salt and 1 teaspoon pepper.

4 Whisk the mustard and the honey together. Place close by the grill.

5 Grill the chicken, bone side down, over *roasting/indirect medium heat* for 25–35 minutes, with the lid closed, until the meat is almost firm to the touch. Brush the honey mustard evenly over the chicken. Continue to grill for 5–10 minutes more until the juices run clear and the meat is no longer pink at the bone, brushing occasionally with the remaining honey mustard. Remove from the grill and season the skin side of the chicken evenly with the thyme. Let the chicken rest for 3–5 minutes.

6 Add the watercress to the salad and toss gently to combine. Serve the chicken warm with the salad.

THE CAJUN-CREOLE CONNECTION

North of New Orleans, there's an assumption that 'Cajun' and 'Creole' are interchangeable. Don't ever tell a Louisianan that. Yes, the two styles of cooking have technique and ingredient overlap, but Cajun tends to be humbler, more casual, and reflective of its history as the rustic 'peasant' cooking of French Canadian immigrants who settled in the bayous. Creole is a little richer and fancier, with the European flair and Caribbean and African flavours of Louisiana's previous settlers. Our chicken owes its Creole connection to the use of its signature mustard, a zippier, concentrated version of the condiment often found in rémoulade sauce. And, as a nod to the Cajuns, we use their peppery, robust seasoning to add unmistakable spice (but not heat). The result is a simple, elegant dish that will make all Louisianans proud.

SPICY CRUSTED LEMONGRASS CHICKEN
WITH CORIANDER PESTO

SERVES: 4 | PREP TIME: **20 minutes** | MARINATING TIME: **1–6 hours** | GRILLING TIME: **8–12 minutes**

MARINADE

2 stalks lemongrass
4 tablespoons cider vinegar
4 tablespoons groundnut oil
2 spring onions, ends trimmed and roughly chopped
2 tablespoons finely chopped fresh coriander
1 tablespoon peeled, finely chopped fresh ginger
1 teaspoon finely chopped garlic

4 boneless chicken breasts (with or without skin),
    each 175 g/6 oz
Sea salt
Freshly ground black pepper

PESTO

125 g/4 oz fresh coriander, coarsely chopped
40 g/1½ oz fresh flat-leaf parsley
75 ml/3 fl oz extra-virgin olive oil
1 tablespoon peeled, coarsely chopped fresh ginger
1 garlic clove, coarsely chopped
⅛ teaspoon ground cayenne pepper

50 g/2 oz panko breadcrumbs
15 g/½ oz plain flour
1 teaspoon crushed red chilli flakes
Olive oil cooking spray

1 Peel away the dry outer layers of the lemongrass stalks, trim the ends and chop the tender parts. In a large non-reactive bowl whisk the lemongrass with the remaining marinade ingredients, including ¾ teaspoon salt and ½ teaspoon pepper. Place the chicken in the bowl with the marinade and turn to coat. Cover and refrigerate for 1–6 hours, turning occasionally.

2 In a food processor combine the pesto ingredients, including ½ teaspoon salt and ¼ teaspoon pepper. Purée until fairly smooth.

3 Prepare the grill for grilling/direct cooking over medium heat (180–230°C/350–450°F). Remove the chicken from the bowl and discard the marinade. Using kitchen paper, blot the chicken mostly dry, leaving some of the solid bits clinging to the chicken. In a shallow dish stir the panko with the flour, chilli flakes and ¼ teaspoon salt. Coat the chicken with the mixture, pressing so that the mixture adheres. Spray the chicken all over with oil.

4 Grill the chicken, smooth (skin) side down first, over *grilling/direct medium heat* for 8–12 minutes, with the lid closed, until the meat is firm to the touch and opaque all the way to the centre, turning once. Remove from the grill and let rest for 3–5 minutes. Serve warm with the pesto.

CHILLI- AND TEQUILA-MARINATED CHICKEN BREASTS
WITH CAJUN-SPICED RICE

SERVES: 4 | PREP TIME: **30 minutes, plus 25 minutes for the rice** | MARINATING TIME: **4–8 hours** | GRILLING TIME: **8–12 minutes**

MARINADE

4 tablespoons gold tequila
4 tablespoons fresh lime juice
1 tablespoon light brown sugar
2 teaspoons Dijon mustard
2 teaspoons ancho chilli powder
2 garlic cloves, smashed
1 teaspoon ground cumin
1 teaspoon freshly ground black pepper

Extra-virgin olive oil
4 boneless chicken breasts (with skin), each about 175 g/6 oz
Sea salt
Parsley sprigs

RICE

15 g/½ oz unsalted butter
½ onion, finely chopped
1 garlic clove, finely chopped or crushed
1 teaspoon paprika
1 teaspoon dried oregano
¼ teaspoon ground cayenne pepper
300 g/10 oz long-grain white rice
575 ml/18 fl oz chicken stock
50 g/2 oz spring onions, thinly sliced

1 Whisk the marinade ingredients together, including 1 tablespoon oil and 1 teaspoon salt. Place the chicken in a large resealable plastic bag and pour in the marinade. Press the air out of the bag and seal tightly. Turn the bag to distribute the marinade, place in a bowl and refrigerate for 4–8 hours.

2 Prepare the grill for grilling/direct cooking over medium heat (180–230°C/350–450°F). In a saucepan over a medium heat, warm the butter and 1 tablespoon oil. Add the onion and the garlic and sauté for about 3 minutes until the onion softens and begins to turn golden brown. Add the paprika, oregano, cayenne pepper and 1 teaspoon salt and sauté for about 30 seconds until fragrant. Add the rice and stir for about 1 minute until coated in the oil. Add the stock and bring to the boil. Cover the pan and reduce the heat to low. Simmer for 20–25 minutes until all of the liquid is absorbed. Remove from the heat, fluff the rice with a fork and stir in the spring onions. Cover and keep warm.

3 Remove the chicken from the bag and discard the marinade. Grill the chicken, skin side up first, over *grilling/direct medium heat* for 8–12 minutes, with the lid closed, until the meat is firm to the touch and no longer pink in the centre, turning once after 7–9 minutes. Remove from the grill and let rest for 3–5 minutes. Serve warm with the rice and parsley sprigs, to garnish.

HERBED CHICKEN THIGHS
WITH HONEY-LEMON GLAZE

SERVES: 4 | PREP TIME: **20 minutes** | GRILLING TIME: **36–40 minutes**

GLAZE

2 teaspoons extra-virgin olive oil
3 medium garlic cloves, finely chopped or crushed
1 tablespoon peeled, grated fresh ginger
175 g/6 oz honey
3 tablespoons fresh lemon juice
2 teaspoons cornflour dissolved in 2 teaspoons water
1 teaspoon finely grated lemon zest

RUB

1 teaspoon dried marjoram
1 teaspoon dried basil
1 teaspoon garlic powder
¼ teaspoon ground cinnamon
1 teaspoon sea salt
¾ teaspoon freshly ground black pepper

8 chicken thighs (with bone and skin), each
    150–175 g/5–6 oz, trimmed of excess fat and skin

1 Prepare the grill for grilling/direct cooking and roasting/indirect cooking over medium heat (180–230°C/350–450°F).

2 Warm the oil in a small saucepan over a medium-high heat. Stir in the garlic and the ginger and cook for 1–2 minutes until they just start to brown, stirring often. Add the honey, bring to the boil and cook for 2 minutes, watching carefully and reducing the heat if necessary so the mixture doesn't boil over. Add the lemon juice and cook for 1 minute. Stir in the cornflour mixture, return to the boil and cook for about 1 minute until slightly thickened. Remove from the heat and stir in the lemon zest. The glaze will continue to thicken as it cools.

3 Combine the rub ingredients. Season the chicken thighs evenly with the rub.

4 Grill the chicken, skin side down first, over *grilling/ direct medium heat* for 6-10 minutes, with the lid closed, until golden brown, turning occasionally. Move the chicken over *roasting/indirect medium heat*, brush with some of the glaze, and cook for about 30 minutes more, until the juices run clear and the meat is no longer pink at the bone, turning once or twice and occasionally brushing with the remaining glaze. Remove from the grill and let rest for 3–5 minutes. Serve warm.

> **TIP** Coat a measuring cup with oil before adding the honey to ensure the honey will come out easily with no mess.

CRISPY CHICKEN THIGHS
WITH BASIL AND PARMA HAM BUTTER

SERVES: **4** | PREP TIME: **15 minutes** | GRILLING TIME: **20–24 minutes**

BUTTER
50 g/2 oz unsalted butter, softened
25 g/1 oz Parma ham, finely chopped
1 shallot, finely chopped
1 tablespoon finely chopped fresh basil
1 tablespoon finely grated Parmesan cheese
¼ teaspoon sea salt
¼ teaspoon freshly ground black pepper

8 chicken thighs (with bone and skin), each
   150–175 g/5–6 oz, trimmed of excess fat and skin
½ teaspoon sea salt
¼ teaspoon freshly ground black pepper

Lift the skin and put the butter mixture on to the exposed meat.

1 Using a fork, combine the butter ingredients. Divide the seasoned butter into eight equal portions.

2 Prepare the grill for roasting/indirect and grilling/direct cooking over medium-high heat (200–260°C/400–500°F).

3 Pat the chicken thighs dry with kitchen paper. Using your fingertips, gently loosen the skin of the thighs, being careful not to completely separate the skin from the meat. Lift the skin up and place a portion of the butter underneath. Smooth the skin over the butter and massage it gently to spread it evenly over the top of the meat. Season the thighs on both sides with the salt and pepper.

4 Grill the thighs, skin side up first, over *roasting/indirect medium-high heat* for 18–20 minutes, with the lid closed, until sizzling, slightly firm and lightly marked on the bottom. Then turn the thighs over and cook over *grilling/ direct medium-high heat* for 2–4 minutes more, with the lid closed, until the juices run clear, the skin is blistered and crisp, and the meat is no longer pink at the bone (if flare-ups occur, move the thighs temporarily over indirect heat). Remove from the grill and let rest for 3–5 minutes. Serve warm.

SPICY DRUMSTICKS
WITH GRILLED PEACHES

SERVES: 4 | PREP TIME: 20 minutes | GRILLING TIME: 25–30 minutes

GLAZE
300 g/10 oz peach conserve
125 ml/4 fl oz peach nectar
4 teaspoons prepared chilli seasoning
1 teaspoon finely grated lime zest
2 tablespoons fresh lime juice
25 g/1 oz chopped fresh coriander

12 chicken drumsticks, 1.4–1.5 kg/2¾–3 lb total
4 firm but ripe peaches, each cut in half
2 teaspoons rapeseed oil
Sea salt
Freshly ground black pepper

1 In a small saucepan over a medium-high heat, combine the conserve, nectar and chilli seasoning. Bring to a simmer, whisking for about 1 minute until the mixture is well blended and almost smooth. Remove the saucepan from the heat and whisk in the lime zest and juice. Let cool to lukewarm, then whisk in the coriander, ⅛ teaspoon salt and ⅛ teaspoon pepper.

2 Divide the glaze equally between two small bowls: one for brushing on the chicken while grilling and the other for serving.

3 Prepare the grill for grilling/direct cooking over medium heat (180–230°C/350–450°F).

4 Pat the drumsticks dry with kitchen paper and season evenly with 1¼ teaspoons salt and 1 teaspoon pepper. Brush the cut side of the peach halves lightly with the oil.

5 Grill the drumsticks over *grilling/direct medium heat* for about 20 minutes, with the lid closed, until the skin is golden brown and the meat is almost firm to the touch, turning occasionally. Brush the peach glaze from the first bowl evenly over the drumsticks. Continue grilling for 5–10 minutes more, with the lid closed, until the juices run clear and the meat is no longer pink at the bone, turning once or twice and brushing occasionally with more of the glaze. During the last 5 minutes of grilling time, grill the peach halves, cut side down, over *grilling/direct medium heat* until lightly charred and beginning to soften (check after 3 minutes). Remove the drumsticks and the peaches from the grill and let the drumsticks rest for 3–5 minutes. Serve the drumsticks and the peaches warm with the reserved glaze.

SPICE-RUBBED CHICKEN
WITH ORANGE-CHIPOTLE BARBECUE SAUCE

SERVES: 4 | PREP TIME: **30 minutes** | GRILLING TIME: **40–50 minutes**

RUB

1 teaspoon garlic, granules
1 teaspoon dried thyme
¼ teaspoon ground allspice
1½ teaspoons sea salt
1 teaspoon freshly ground black pepper

4 whole chicken legs, each 300–375 g/10–12 oz,
    excess skin and fat removed
Extra-virgin olive oil

SAUCE

1 onion, finely chopped
2 garlic cloves, finely chopped or crushed
250 ml/8 fl oz fresh orange juice
250 ml/8 fl oz tomato ketchup
2 canned chipotle chillies in adobo sauce, finely chopped
1 tablespoon light brown sugar
1 tablespoon cider vinegar
1 teaspoon Worcestershire sauce
¼ teaspoon ground allspice

Corn cobs and tomato quarters, to serve (optional)

1 Prepare the grill for roasting/indirect and grilling/direct cooking over medium heat (180–230°C/350–450°F).

2 Combine the rub ingredients. Lightly brush the chicken on both sides with oil and season evenly with the rub.

3 In a small saucepan over a medium heat, warm 2 tablespoons oil. Add the onion and the garlic and cook for 3–5 minutes until the onion is tender but not browned, stirring occasionally. Add the remaining sauce ingredients and whisk until smooth. Simmer over a medium heat for 5–7 minutes, stirring occasionally. Remove from the heat.

4 Grill the chicken, skin side up, over *roasting/indirect medium heat* for 35–40 minutes, with the lid closed, until the juices run clear and the meat is no longer pink at the bone, brushing once with the sauce after 30 minutes. Brush with the sauce again and then move the chicken over *grilling/direct medium heat*. Continue cooking for 5–10 minutes, with the lid open, until the skin is well browned, turning once or twice. Remove from the grill and let rest for 3–5 minutes. Serve the chicken with the remaining sauce and corn cobs and tomato quarters if desired.

TIP Trimming the excess skin and fat from the chicken legs helps to minimise flare-ups on the grill. When you move the chicken over grilling/direct heat to finish cooking it, watch for excess smoke coming from the grill, which could be an indicator that you need to move the chicken temporarily over roasting/indirect heat.

GRILL SKILLS
PERFECT WHOLE CHICKEN

Done right, a roast chicken dinner from the grill is spectacular. When its golden skin turns crisp and warm juices run throughout the tender meat, it is worth every minute and every pound spent. The first step towards such a dinner happens at the shop, because nowadays there is a big difference between a factory-farmed, commodity chicken and an organic, free-range chicken. Commodity birds are often fed hormones and artificial ingredients to grow quickly with large breasts and yellowish skins. They may look good, but organic birds are definitely more flavourful and their texture has a tender, meaty integrity that is also quite moist if you cook it right.

CLASSIC ROAST CHICKEN

1 Prepare the grill for roasting/indirect medium heat (180–230°C/350–450°F). For a particularly crisp skin, get the temperature somewhere between 200 and 230°C/400 and 450°F.

2 Remove any excess fat from inside the cavity and any giblets. The wing tips tend to burn and they don't have much meat, so either cut them off or tuck the tips under the back of the chicken.

3 Lightly coat the surface of the chicken with good olive oil and season inside and outside with salt and pepper, especially the outside of the chicken. Salt is crucial for a deliciously crisp skin. If you like, stuff the cavity with some herb sprigs and a quartered lemon for added flavours.

4 Truss the chicken to make it evenly compacted and to protect the top of the breasts with the ends of the drumsticks.

5 Set the chicken over roasting/indirect heat and let it roast for an hour or so. Let it rest at room temperature for 10–15 minutes, cut it up, and serve warm.

1 Set the chicken, with the breast side facing down, on a work surface. Using sharp kitchen shears, make incisions on both sides of the backbone and cut from the tail end.

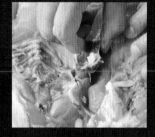

3 Run your fingertips alongside both sides of the breastbone to expose it. Dig your fingertips down along the breastbone until it comes loose from the meat. Then pull it out and discard it.

2 Cut along both sides of the backbone. Remove the backbone and discard it. Flatten the chicken with both hands to crack the rib cage. Use a sharp knife to cut a shallow slit at the top of the rib cage.

4 Cut a small hole in the loose skin on both sides at the leg end of the chicken. Pull the end of each drumstick through the hole on its side. This will hold the legs in place on the grill.

BEER CAN CHICKEN

This wacky-looking idea is actually brilliant. With the chicken standing upright on a can, you have a solution to an age-old problem of cooking whole birds, which is that the breast meat cooks faster than the leg meat and tends to turn dry by the time the leg meat is done. In this showstopping situation, the legs are closer to the heat source, so they get a little hotter and cook a little faster than the breasts. Now both areas are done at the same time. Genius! Also, the entire surface of the bird gets full exposure to the dry, caramelising heat of the grill, so you get a handsome, crisp skin all the way round. But wait, there's more. The beer left in the can steams the chicken from the inside, producing moist, succulent meat. The key for that is to have less than a third of the beer in the can; otherwise, the beer doesn't get hot enough to steam.

1 Pour out at least two-thirds of the beer, poke a couple of extra holes in the top of the can, season the chicken, and lower the hollow cavity of the chicken on to the can.

2 Tuck the wing tips behind the back of the chicken. Transfer the chicken on the beer can to the grill's cooking grate, balancing it on its two legs and the can, like a tripod.

3 Grill over roasting/indirect medium heat until done. For a smoked beer can chicken, add soaked and drained wood chips to the charcoal or to the smoker box of a gas grill once or twice during the first half of the cooking time. For a full recipe, see page 204.

WHEN IS IT DONE?

As a chicken overcooks, the meat loses its flavour and gradually shrivels to a chalky texture. To avoid that, take your chicken off the grill just in time.

As long as you have a reliable instant-read thermometer, the 'temperature test' works perfectly. Insert the sensor of the thermometer into the deepest part of the thigh, not touching the bone. The temperature there should be about 77°C/170°F. The meat is safe to eat above 70°C/160°F, but the dark meat is not really tender until it reaches 77°C/170°F. Ideally, the breast meat will be about 74°C/165°F.

If you don't have an instant-read thermometer, cut through the skin between a leg and the rest of the body. Bend that leg away from the body to expose the thigh joint. When the chicken is done, the meat at the joint should be opaque and the juices should run clear with no trace of pink.

CHICKEN UNDER BRICKS
WITH WHITE BARBECUE SAUCE

SERVES: 4 | PREP TIME: 20 minutes | GRILLING TIME: 40–50 minutes
SPECIAL EQUIPMENT: poultry shears, 2 foil-wrapped bricks or a cast-iron frying pan, instant-read meat thermometer

SAUCE

300 ml/½ pint mayonnaise
4 tablespoons cider vinegar
2 teaspoons prepared horseradish
2 teaspoons Dijon mustard
2 teaspoons granulated sugar
1 teaspoon fresh lemon juice
¼ teaspoon hot pepper sauce or ground cayenne pepper
¾ teaspoon sea salt
1 teaspoon freshly ground black pepper

RUB

1 teaspoon prepared chilli seasoning
1 teaspoon garlic powder
1 teaspoon ground cumin
1 teaspoon sea salt
¼ teaspoon ground cayenne pepper

2–2.5 kg/4–5 lb whole chicken, spatchcocked
   (see page 199)
2 tablespoons extra-virgin olive oil

1 Prepare the grill for roasting/indirect cooking over high heat (230–290°C/450–550°F).

2 Whisk the sauce ingredients together. Cover and refrigerate until ready to serve.

3 Combine the rub ingredients.

4 Brush the chicken on both sides with the oil and season evenly with the rub. Place the chicken, skin side down, over *roasting/indirect high heat*, and put two foil-wrapped bricks or a cast-iron frying pan on top of the chicken. Close the lid and grill for 20–25 minutes until golden around the edges. Remove the bricks or pan and, using a large spatula, carefully turn the chicken over, being careful not to tear the skin. Replace the bricks or frying pan and continue cooking for 20–25 minutes more, with the lid closed, until the juices run clear and an instant-read thermometer inserted into the thickest part of the thigh (not touching the bone) registers 70–74°C/160–165°F. Remove from the grill and let rest for 10–15 minutes (the internal temperature will rise 5–10 degrees during this time). Cut into serving pieces and serve warm with the sauce.

BUTTERMILK-BRINED CHICKEN

SERVES: 4 | PREP TIME: 20 minutes | BRINING TIME: 8–24 hours | GRILLING TIME: 1¾–2 hours
SPECIAL EQUIPMENT: kitchen string, large disposable foil roasting tray, instant-read meat thermometer

BRINE

1.5 litres/2½ pints buttermilk
1 onion, finely chopped
4 tablespoons granulated sugar
2 tablespoons hot pepper sauce
6 garlic cloves, finely chopped or crushed
1 tablespoon ground coriander
½ teaspoon ground cayenne pepper
4 tablespoons sea salt

2.75–3 kg/5½–6 lb whole chicken, neck, giblets,
   wing tips and excess fat removed
2 tablespoons extra-virgin olive oil

1 Whisk the brine ingredients in a non-reactive container just wide enough to hold the chicken.

2 Submerge the chicken in the brine, breast side down, and refrigerate for 8–24 hours.

3 Prepare the grill for roasting/indirect cooking over medium heat (180–230°C/350–450°F).

4 Remove the chicken from the container and discard the brine. Pat the chicken dry with kitchen paper and tie the drumsticks together with kitchen string (see page 202). Place the chicken in a large disposable foil tray and drizzle with the oil.

5 Grill the chicken in the tray over *roasting/indirect medium heat* for 1¾–2 hours, with the lid closed, until the juices run clear and an instant-read thermometer inserted into the thickest part of the thigh (not touching the bone), registers 70–74°C/160–165°F, basting the chicken with the pan juices and rotating the pan occasionally. Remove the pan and the chicken from the grill and let the chicken rest for 10–15 minutes (the internal temperature will rise 5–10 degrees during this time). Cut the chicken into serving pieces. Serve warm.

SUMMER HERB-ROASTED CHICKEN

SERVES: 4 | PREP TIME: **15 minutes** | GRILLING TIME: **1¼-1½ hours**
SPECIAL EQUIPMENT: **kitchen string, instant-read meat thermometer**

BUTTER

25 g/1 oz unsalted butter, softened
2 tablespoons fresh thyme
1 tablespoon finely chopped fresh chives
1 teaspoon finely grated lemon zest
1 garlic clove, finely chopped or crushed
⅛ teaspoon sea salt
⅛ teaspoon freshly ground black pepper

2-2.5 kg/4-5 lb chicken neck, giblets and any excess
    fat removed
1 lemon, cut into quarters
3 sprigs fresh thyme
2 garlic cloves, crushed

1 Prepare the grill for roasting/indirect cooking over medium heat (180-230°C/350-450°F).

2 Mix the butter ingredients. Gently lift the skin from the chicken breast meat and the thighs, taking care not to cause any tears. Distribute half the butter under the skin on the breast and thigh meat and the other half over the skin.

3 Insert the lemon quarters into the chicken's cavity, squeezing them gently as you do, along with the thyme and the garlic. Tie the drumsticks together with kitchen string (see below). Fold the wings tips behind the chicken's back.

4 Grill the chicken over *roasting/indirect medium heat* for 1¼-1½ hours, with the lid closed, until the juices run clear and an instant-read thermometer inserted into the thickest part of the thigh (not touching the bone) registers 70-74°C/160-165°F. Remove from the grill and let rest for 10-15 minutes (the internal temperature will rise 5-10 degrees during this time). Cut the chicken into serving pieces. Serve warm.

1 Wrap a piece of kitchen string under and around the drumsticks, cross it in the middle, and pull the ends to draw the drumsticks together.

2 Cross the twine above the drumsticks and tie a knot. This will hold the chicken in a compact shape and will help the meat cook more evenly.

HICKORY-SMOKED BEER CAN CHICKEN

SERVES: 4 | PREP TIME: **15 minutes** | DRY-BRINING TIME: **2 hours** | GRILLING TIME: **1¼–1½ hours**
SPECIAL EQUIPMENT: **4 large handfuls hickory or oak wood chips, instant-read meat thermometer**

2–2.5 kg/4–5 lb whole chicken, neck, giblets
and any excess fat removed
2 tablespoons sea salt

RUB
2 teaspoons onion flakes
2 teaspoons paprika
1 teaspoon light brown sugar
½ teaspoon freshly ground black pepper

1 tablespoon extra-virgin olive oil
1 can (350 ml/12 oz) beer, at room temperature

1 Sprinkle the salt evenly over the meaty parts of the chicken and inside the cavity (but not on the back). The chicken will be coated with a visible layer of salt. Cover with clingfilm and refrigerate for 2 hours.

2 Combine the rub ingredients.

3 Soak the wood chips in water for at least 30 minutes.

4 Prepare the grill for roasting/indirect cooking over medium heat (180–230°C/350–450°F). Keep the temperature as close to 200°C/400°F as possible throughout the cooking time.

5 Rinse the chicken with cold water, inside and outside, to remove the salt, and then pat dry with kitchen paper. Brush the chicken with the oil and season all over, including inside the cavity, with the rub. Fold the wing tips behind the chicken's back.

6 Open the can of beer and pour out about two-thirds. Using a can opener with a pointed end, make two more holes in the top of the can. Place the can on a solid surface and then lower the chicken cavity over the can.

7 Drain and add two handfuls of wood chips to the charcoal or to the smoker box of a gas grill, following manufacturer's instructions, and close the lid. When the wood begins to smoke, transfer the chicken-on-a-can to the grill, balancing it on its two legs and the can like a tripod. Cook the chicken over *roasting/indirect medium heat* for 1¼–1½ hours, with the lid closed, until the juices run clear and an instant-read thermometer inserted into the thickest part of the thigh (not touching the bone), registers 70–74°C/160–165°F. After the first 15 minutes of cooking time, drain and add the remaining wood chips to the charcoal or to the smoker box. If using a charcoal grill, replenish the charcoal as needed to maintain a steady temperature, adding 6–10 unlit briquettes after 45 minutes. Leave the lid off the grill for about 5 minutes to help the new briquettes light.

8 Carefully remove the chicken-on-a-can from the grill (do not spill the contents of the beer can, which will be very hot). Let the chicken rest for 10–15 minutes (the internal temperature will rise 5–10 degrees during this time) before lifting it from the beer can and carving it into serving pieces. Serve warm.

SMOKE SIGNALS

Near and dear to the griller's heart – right up there with a really great pair of tongs and bacon-wrapped anything – is smoke. Simple, hard-working and dependable, smoke is the work horse of grilling. Sure, smoke adds flavour, and sometimes a little flair, but did you know it can clue you in on what's going on under the lid?

The colour of the smoke can tell you a lot about how things are going. Seeing grey smoke shimmying from the fire is a good thing. It means juices from the meat are hitting the hot coals or the Flavourizer® bars, flashing and creating flavour. Everything is fine. Good, even. But seeing black, sooty smoke frantically waving its arms at you means trouble is at hand and it's time to spring into action.

Black smoke signals that you might have a grease fire. This happens when fatty meats are placed over coals or burners that are too hot, or when the grill needs cleaning. To extinguish the flames when cooking on a charcoal grill, carefully remove the lid, shielding your face from the fire. Remove the meat using long-handled tongs and insulated barbecue mitts or oven gloves. Replace the lid with the damper closed. On a gas grill, turn off the burners and slowly lift the lid. Remove the meat, assess the situation, let the fire burn out, pledge to clean your grill and offer smoke some thanks.

BEER-BRINED TURKEY

SERVES: 4 | PREP TIME: 25 minutes | BRINING TIME: 12–14 hours | GRILLING TIME: 2½–3 hours
SPECIAL EQUIPMENT: sturdy plastic bag; 10-litre/16-pint or larger stockpot; kitchen string; 2 large disposable foil roasting trays;
6 large handfuls hickory wood chips; instant-read meat thermometer; gravy separator

BRINE

4 bottles (each 350 ml/12 oz) lager
250 g/8 oz light brown sugar
3 tablespoons smoked paprika
1½ tablespoons dried thyme
1 tablespoon coarsely cracked black peppercorns
1 tablespoon garlic granules
1 tablespoon onion flakes
½ teaspoon ground cayenne pepper
100 g/3½ oz sea salt
3 litres/5 pints iced water

6–7 kg/12–14 lb turkey, thawed if frozen
875 g/1¾ lb onions, coarsely chopped
4 sprigs fresh thyme
40 g/1½ oz unsalted butter, melted
1 litre/1¾ pints chicken stock

1 About 14 hours before grilling, in a very large bowl combine all of the brine ingredients, except the iced water, and whisk until the salt and sugar are dissolved. Stir in the iced water. The brine should be very cold.

2 Remove the giblets, neck and lumps of fat from the turkey and reserve (discard the liver). Place in a bowl, cover and refrigerate until ready to grill. If the turkey has a plastic truss or a pop-up timer, remove and discard it. Place the turkey inside a sturdy plastic bag and put it in a 10-litre/16-pint or larger stockpot. Pour enough of the brine into the bag to cover the turkey as much as possible when the bag is closed and tightly tied. Discard any extra brine. Seal the bag. Refrigerate the turkey for at least 12 hours and no longer than 14 hours.

3 Remove the turkey from the bag and discard the brine. Rinse the turkey under cold water and pat it dry inside and outside with kitchen paper. Put a third of the chopped onions and all of the thyme sprigs into the body cavity. Tuck the wing tips behind the turkey's back and loosely tie the drumsticks together with kitchen string (see page 202). Brush the turkey all over with the melted butter. Place one large disposable roasting tray inside the other to create a single tray of double thickness. Put the remaining onions into the tray and place the turkey, breast side down, on top of the onions. Allow the turkey to stand at room temperature for 1 hour before grilling.

4 Soak the wood chips in water for at least 30 minutes. Prepare the grill for roasting/indirect cooking over medium-low heat (about 180°C/350°F).

5 Place the reserved giblets, neck and lumps of fat in the roasting tray and pour in the chicken stock. Drain and add two handfuls of the wood chips to the charcoal or to the smoker box of a gas grill, following manufacturer's instructions, and close the lid. When the wood begins to smoke, cook the turkey over *roasting/indirect medium-low heat*, with the lid closed, for 1 hour, keeping the grill's temperature as close to 180°C/350°F as possible. If using a charcoal grill, replenish the charcoal as needed to maintain a steady temperature, adding 8–10 unlit briquettes every 45 minutes–1 hour. Leave the lid off the grill for about 5 minutes to help the new briquettes light.

6 After 1 hour, turn the turkey over so that the breast faces up. Drain and add two handfuls of wood chips to the charcoal or to the smoker box. Cook the turkey for another 45 minutes, then drain and add the remaining two handfuls of wood chips to the charcoal or to the smoker box. Continue cooking the turkey for 45 minutes–1 hour more, with the lid closed, until an instant-read thermometer inserted into the thickest part of the thigh (not touching the bone), registers 77°C/170°F.

7 Remove the tray with the turkey from the grill. Tilt the turkey so the juices run out of the body cavity and into the tray. Transfer the turkey to a carving board and let rest for 20–30 minutes (the internal temperature will rise 5–10 degrees during this time). Save the pan juices to make the gravy (see recipe on the opposite page).

8 Carve the turkey and serve with the warm gravy.

1 Remove each half of the turkey breast by cutting lengthways along each side of the breastbone.

2 Pull the first half of the breast away from the breastbone, using a knife to carefully release the meat from the rib cage, and transfer to a carving board.

GRAVY

Chicken stock, as needed
Melted unsalted butter, as needed
50 g/2 oz plain flour
125 ml/4 fl oz lager
1 teaspoon chopped fresh thyme
Sea salt
Freshly ground black pepper

1 Strain the pan juices into a gravy separator. Let stand for about 3 minutes until the fat rises to the surface. Pour the pan juices into a measuring jug, reserving the fat. If necessary, add chicken stock to the jug so that you have 1 litre/1¾ pints of liquid.

2 Measure the reserved fat. If necessary, add melted butter to make 125 ml/4 fl oz. In a saucepan heat the fat (and butter) over a medium heat. Whisk in the flour and let it bubble for 1 minute, whisking constantly. Whisk in the pan juices and the lager. Bring the gravy to a simmer, whisking frequently. Reduce the heat to medium-low, stir in the thyme and simmer for 3–5 minutes until slightly thickened. Remove from the heat and season with salt and pepper, if liked (the salt and pepper in the brine may have provided enough seasoning already). Serve warm.

MARINATED TURKEY STEAKS
WITH DRIED CHERRY-CRANBERRY RELISH

SERVES: 4–6 | PREP TIME: **15 minutes** | MARINATING TIME: **1–4 hours** | GRILLING TIME: **5–7 minutes**

MARINADE
4 tablespoons extra-virgin olive oil
1 tablespoon Dijon mustard
1 tablespoon chopped fresh rosemary
3 large garlic cloves, finely chopped
1 teaspoon sea salt
¼ teaspoon freshly ground black pepper

8 turkey steaks, each about 125 g/4 oz and
   1.5 cm/¾ inch thick

RELISH
200 g/7 oz fresh or frozen cranberries
250 ml/8 fl oz 100% cranberry juice (no sugar added)
75 g/3 oz light brown sugar
40 g/1½ oz dried sour cherries, roughly chopped
¼ teaspoon sea salt

Summer vegetables, to serve (optional)

1 Whisk the marinade ingredients together in a large bowl. Place the turkey steaks in the bowl and turn to coat. Cover and refrigerate for 1–4 hours.

2 Prepare the grill for grilling/direct cooking over medium heat (180–230°C/350–450°F).

3 In a saucepan over a high heat, combine the relish ingredients and bring to the boil. Lower the heat to a simmer and cook for 4–6 minutes until the cranberries are soft, stirring and crushing the cranberries against the side of the saucepan often. Remove the saucepan from the heat, transfer the relish to a bowl and allow to cool to room temperature.

4 Grill the steaks over *grilling/direct medium heat* for 5–7 minutes, with the lid closed, until the meat is firm to the touch and no longer pink in the centre, turning once after 3–4 minutes. Remove from the grill and serve warm with the relish and green vegetables, if desired.

SUN-DRIED TOMATO TURKEY CHEESEBURGERS

SERVES: 4 | PREP TIME: **15 minutes** | GRILLING TIME: **8–10 minutes**

BURGERS

10 sun-dried tomato halves packed in oil, drained
10 large fresh basil leaves
750 g/1½ lb minced turkey thigh meat
¾ teaspoon sea salt
½ teaspoon dried oregano
¼ teaspoon freshly ground black pepper

4 tablespoons mayonnaise
2 teaspoons finely grated lemon zest
Extra-virgin olive oil
4 slices fresh mozzarella cheese, each about 5 mm/¼ inch
   thick (about 125 g/4 oz)
4 ciabatta rolls, split
40 g/1½ oz baby rocket

1 Prepare the grill for grilling/direct cooking over medium heat (180–230°C/350–450°F).

2 Chop the sun-dried tomatoes and together as finely as possible to make a paste. Gently mix the remaining burger ingredients with the paste. With wet hands, form four loosely packed burgers of equal size, each about 2.5 cm/¾ inch thick. Don't compact the meat too much or the burgers will be tough. With your thumb or the back of a spoon, make a shallow indentation about 2.5 cm/1 inch wide in the centre of each burger. This will help the burgers cook evenly and prevent them from puffing on the grill.

3 Combine the mayonnaise and the lemon zest and set aside.

4 Lightly brush the burgers on both sides with oil. Grill the burgers over *grilling/direct medium heat* for 8–10 minutes, with the lid closed, until fully cooked but still juicy, turning once when the burgers release easily from the grate without sticking. During the last 1–2 minutes of grilling time, top each burger with a slice of cheese to melt, and toast the rolls, cut side down, over grilling/direct heat. Remove from the grill and build the burgers with rocket and lemon mayonnaise. Serve warm.

SPICE-RUBBED DUCK BREASTS
WITH ORANGE-CUMIN SAUCE

SERVES: 4 | PREP TIME: **20 minutes** | GRILLING TIME: **about 8 minutes**

RUB
2 teaspoons ground cumin
1 teaspoon ground coriander
1 teaspoon ground cardamom
1 teaspoon sea salt
1 teaspoon freshly ground black pepper

4 boneless duck breasts, each about 175 g/6 oz,
    skin removed, patted dry
Extra-virgin olive oil

SAUCE
250 ml/8 fl oz fresh orange juice
4 tablespoons balsamic vinegar
1 tablespoon light brown sugar
1 teaspoon ground cumin
½ teaspoon ground cardamom
⅛ teaspoon freshly ground black pepper
2 teaspoons cornflour dissolved in 1 tablespoon fresh
    orange juice
1 teaspoon sea salt

250 g/8 oz rice, cooked
Vegetables, to serve (optional)

1 Combine the rub ingredients.

2 Lightly brush the duck breasts on both sides with oil and season evenly with the rub. Set aside at room temperature while you prepare the grill and make the sauce.

3 Prepare the grill for grilling/direct cooking over medium heat (180–230°C/350–450°F).

4 In a small saucepan whisk the orange juice, vinegar, brown sugar, cumin, salt, cardamom and pepper. Bring to the boil over a medium-high heat and cook for about 10 minutes until the liquid is reduced by a third, stirring often. Reduce the heat to medium and whisk in the cornflour mixture. Bring the sauce back to a simmer and simmer for about 1 minute until the sauce thickens slightly, stirring constantly. Remove from the heat.

5 Grill the duck breasts over *grilling/direct medium heat*, with the lid closed, until cooked to your desired doneness, about 8 minutes for medium rare, turning once. Remove from the grill and let rest for 3–5 minutes. Meanwhile, rewarm the sauce over a low heat. Cut the duck breasts crossways into 8-mm/⅓-inch slices. Serve the duck warm with the sauce, with the rice and vegetables, if liked.

DUCK BREAST SALAD
WITH HOISIN DRESSING

SERVES: 4 | PREP TIME: **15 minutes** | GRILLING TIME: **about 8 minutes**

4 boneless duck breasts (with skin), each about
    175 g/6 oz, patted dry
1 teaspoon Chinese five spice powder
1 teaspoon sea salt

DRESSING
150 ml/¼ pint vegetable oil
4 tablespoons rice vinegar
2 tablespoons toasted sesame oil
2 tablespoons water
4 teaspoons hoisin sauce
1 tablespoon peeled, finely chopped fresh ginger
1 tablespoon sesame seeds
1 garlic clove, roughly chopped

150 g/5 oz mixed baby salad leaves
3 spring onions, thinly sliced (white and light
    green parts only)
375 g/12 oz fresh raspberries
50 g/2 oz flaked almonds, preferably toasted

1 Prepare the grill for grilling/direct cooking over medium heat (180–230°C/350–450°F).

2 Score the skin of each duck breast on the diagonal in a criss-cross pattern (do not cut through the breast meat). Season evenly with the five spice powder and the salt.

3 In a blender combine the dressing ingredients and purée until smooth.

4 Grill the duck breasts, skin side down first, over *grilling/ direct medium heat*, with the lid closed, until the skin is browned and the meat is cooked to your desired doneness, about 8 minutes for medium rare, turning once (if flare-ups occur, move the breasts temporarily over roasting/indirect heat). Remove from the grill and let rest for 3–5 minutes. Cut the meat crossways into 8-mm/⅓-inch slices.

5 In a large bowl toss the mixed leaves, spring onions, raspberries and almonds with 125 ml/4 fl oz of the dressing. Divide the salad and duck evenly among four plates. Serve with the remaining dressing on the side.

SEAFOOD

GRILLING SEAFOOD

TYPE	THICKNESS / WEIGHT	APPROXIMATE GRILLING TIME
Fish, fillet or steak: halibut, salmon, sea bass, swordfish and tuna	1 cm/½ inch thick	**6–8 minutes** grilling/direct high heat
	2.5 cm/1 inch thick	**8–10 minutes** grilling/direct high heat
	2.5–3 cm/1–1¼ inches thick	**10–12 minutes** grilling/direct high heat
Fish, whole	500 g/1 lb	**15–20 minutes** roasting/indirect medium heat
	1–1.25 kg/2–2½ lb	**20–30 minutes** roasting/indirect medium heat
	1.5 kg/3 lb	**30–45 minutes** roasting/indirect medium heat
Clam (discard any that do not open)	50–75 g/2–3 oz	**6–8 minutes** grilling/direct high heat
Lobster tail	175 g/6 oz	**7–11 minutes** grilling/direct medium heat
Mussel (discard any that do not open)	25–50 g/1–2 oz	**5–6 minutes** grilling/direct high heat
Oyster	75–125 g/3–4 oz	**5–7 minutes** grilling/direct high heat
Scallop	40 g/1½ oz	**4–6 minutes** grilling/direct high heat
Prawn	40 g/1½ oz	**2–4 minutes** grilling/direct high heat

The types, thicknesses, weights and grilling times are meant to be guidelines rather than hard and fast rules. Cooking times are affected by such factors as altitude, wind, outside temperature and desired doneness. The general rule of thumb for grilling fish: 8–10 minutes per 2.5 cm/1 inch thickness.

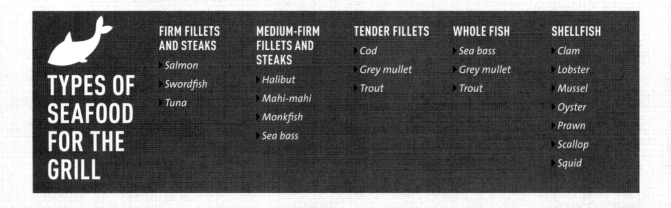

TYPES OF SEAFOOD FOR THE GRILL

FIRM FILLETS AND STEAKS
▸ *Salmon*
▸ *Swordfish*
▸ *Tuna*

MEDIUM-FIRM FILLETS AND STEAKS
▸ *Halibut*
▸ *Mahi-mahi*
▸ *Monkfish*
▸ *Sea bass*

TENDER FILLETS
▸ *Cod*
▸ *Grey mullet*
▸ *Trout*

WHOLE FISH
▸ *Sea bass*
▸ *Grey mullet*
▸ *Trout*

SHELLFISH
▸ *Clam*
▸ *Lobster*
▸ *Mussel*
▸ *Oyster*
▸ *Prawn*
▸ *Scallop*
▸ *Squid*

SEARED SCALLOPS AND GRITS

SERVES: 4 | PREP TIME: 30 minutes | GRILLING TIME: 4–6 minutes

100 g/3½ oz unsalted butte
40 g/1½ oz panko breadcrumbs
1 garlic clove, finely chopped or crushed
2 teaspoons finely chopped fresh thyme
Sea salt

GRITS

900 ml/1½ pints full-fat milk, plus more if needed
2 garlic cloves, finely chopped or crushed
125 g/4 oz quick-cooking grits, or polenta
125 g/4 oz extra-mature Cheddar cheese, grated
Freshly ground black pepper

16 large scallops, each about 50 g/2 oz
1¼ teaspoons Cajun seasoning
4 spring onions, ends trimmed
Hot pepper sauce
1 tablespoon finely chopped fresh flat-leaf parsley

1 Melt the butter in a frying pan over a medium heat. Pour 75 ml/3 fl oz of the melted butter into a bowl; set aside. Add the panko breadcrumbs and the garlic to the remaining butter in the frying pan and cook for 3–4 minutes until the breadcrumbs are crisp and golden, stirring often. Stir in the thyme and ⅛ teaspoon salt. Remove from the heat.

2 Prepare the grill for grilling/direct cooking over high heat (230–290°C/450–550°F).

3 In a saucepan combine the milk, the garlic, and ¾ teaspoon salt. Bring to a simmer over a medium-high heat. Gradually whisk in the grits or polenta. Reduce the heat to low and continue cooking for 6–9 minutes until the mixture thickens and the grits are very tender, whisking often and adding water several tablespoons at a time if the mixture seems too thick. Stir in the cheese and season with pepper. Remove from the heat and cover to keep warm.

4 Pat the scallops dry. Remove and discard the small tough side muscle that might be left on each one (see below left). In a bowl combine the scallops, Cajun seasoning, ½ teaspoon salt and ¼ teaspoon pepper. Turn the scallops in the seasonings and then add 2 tablespoons of the melted butter and toss to coat.

5 Grill the scallops over *grilling/direct high heat* for 4–6 minutes, with the lid closed, until they are lightly browned and just opaque in the centre, turning once or twice. During the last minute of grilling time, grill the spring onions over *grilling/direct high heat*, turning once. Transfer the scallops to a clean bowl. Add the remaining melted butter and 1 tablespoon hot pepper sauce, or to taste; toss to coat. Roughly chop the spring onions.

6 If the grits have solidified, loosen with a few tablespoons of water or milk and then warm through. Divide the grits among four plates. Top the grits with the spring onions, scallops and breadcrumbs. Garnish with parsley and serve right away with more hot pepper sauce, if liked.

1 Before grilling, remove any tough little side muscle that may still be attached to the scallop.

2 Pinch one end of the muscle between your thumb and your index finger, and peel it off gently.

CRUSTY PRAWN AND SCALLOP SKEWERS

SERVES: 4 | PREP TIME: **15 minutes** | GRILLING TIME: **about 6 minutes** | SPECIAL EQUIPMENT: metal or bamboo skewers

COATING
50 g/2 oz fresh breadcrumbs
1 tablespoon finely chopped fresh flat-leaf parsley
1 teaspoon dried oregano
½ teaspoon smoked paprika
½ teaspoon freshly ground black pepper
1 garlic clove, finely chopped or crushed
¼ teaspoon sea salt

Extra-virgin olive oil
12 sea scallops, each 25–40 g/1–1½ oz
12 large prawns, peeled and deveined, tails removed
1 lemon, cut into wedges
Roasted peppers

1 If using bamboo skewers, soak in water for at least 30 minutes.

2 Prepare the grill for grilling/direct cooking over high heat (230–290°C/450–550°F).

3 In a shallow dish combine the coating ingredients, including 1 tablespoon oil.

4 Pat the scallops dry. Remove and discard the small tough side muscle that might be left on each scallop (see page 216). Thread the prawns and scallops on their own skewers. Lightly brush the shellfish on both sides with oil and then press them into the coating mixture, patting the crumbs firmly to help them adhere. Let stand for 5 minutes to allow the coating to set.

5 Grill the skewers over *grilling/direct high heat*, with the lid closed, until the shellfish are just opaque in the centre and the crumbs are golden brown, turning once or twice (some of the crumbs may become slightly charred). The scallops will take about 6 minutes, and the prawns will take about 4 minutes. Remove from the grill and serve immediately with the lemon wedges and roasted peppers.

TIP Serve the skewers with a grilled pepper medley. Cut four peppers into thin slices. Coat them lightly with oil and season with salt. Spread them in a single layer on a preheated perforated grill pan and grill over grilling/direct medium heat for 4–6 minutes until crisp-tender, turning occasionally.

PRAWN KEBABS
WITH PISTACHIO-TARRAGON PESTO

SERVES: 4 | PREP TIME: 50 minutes | GRILLING TIME: 3–5 minutes | SPECIAL EQUIPMENT: metal or bamboo skewers

20 g/¾ oz fresh flat-leaf parsley, roughly chopped
4 tablespoons roughly chopped fresh tarragon
25 g/1 oz shelled unsalted pistachios
5 teaspoons fresh lemon juice
1 garlic clove, peeled and smashed
Extra-virgin olive oil
1 tablespoon water
32 large prawns, peeled and deveined, tails left on
24 cherry tomatoes
2 small courgettes, each halved lengthways and
    cut crossways into 24 half-moons
1 large yellow pepper, cut into 24 pieces
12 spring onions, cut into 24 pieces (white and light
    green parts only)
Lemon wedges, for squeezing
Sea salt
Freshly ground black pepper

1 If using bamboo skewers, soak in water for at least
30 minutes.

2 In a food processor combine the parsley, tarragon,
pistachios, lemon juice, garlic, ¼ teaspoon salt and
¼ teaspoon pepper. Process until the mixture is finely
ground, 30 seconds–1 minute. With the motor running,
slowly pour 125 ml/4 fl oz oil through the feed tube and
process until smooth, scraping down the sides of the bowl
once or twice. Transfer 5 tablespoons of the pesto to a bowl
for brushing on the kebabs. Transfer the remaining pesto
to another bowl and stir in the water to loosen the pesto
slightly. Set aside for serving.

3 Prepare the grill for grilling/direct cooking over high
heat (230–290°C/450–550°F).

4 Thread the prawns, tomatoes, courgettes, yellow pepper
and spring onions alternately on to skewers. Brush
the ingredients with oil, then brush them evenly with the
reserved pesto. Lightly season with salt and pepper. Grill
the kebabs over *grilling/direct high heat* for 3–5 minutes,
with the lid closed, until the prawns are just firm to the
touch and opaque in the centre, turning once or twice.
The vegetables will be crisp-tender. Remove from the grill.
Drizzle the remaining pesto over the kebabs and squeeze
the lemon on top.

LEMON RISOTTO
WITH GRILLED ASPARAGUS AND PRAWNS

SERVES: 6–8 | PREP TIME: about 20 minutes, plus 30–40 minutes for the risotto | GRILLING TIME: 6–8 minutes

500 g/1 lb asparagus
Extra-virgin olive oil
18 jumbo prawns, peeled and deveined, tails removed
1 tablespoon fresh lemon juice
Sea salt

RISOTTO

1.5 litres/2½ pints chicken stock
40 g/1½ oz unsalted butter
2 tablespoons extra-virgin olive oil
1 onion, finely chopped
1 teaspoon sea salt
400 g/13 oz arborio rice
125 ml/4 fl oz dry white wine
50 g/2 oz Parmesan cheese, finely grated
1 tablespoon finely grated lemon zest
4 tablespoons fresh lemon juice
2 tablespoons finely chopped fresh flat-leaf parsley
1 tablespoon finely chopped fresh mint
Freshly ground black pepper

1 Prepare the grill for grilling/direct cooking over medium heat (230–290°C/450–550°F).

2 Remove and discard the tough bottom of each asparagus spear by grasping each end and bending it gently until it snaps at its natural point of tenderness, usually about two-thirds of the way down the spear. Place the asparagus on a plate and drizzle with oil, turning to coat. Season with salt.

3 Brush the prawns with oil and lightly season with salt.

4 Grill the asparagus (at right angles to the bars on the cooking grate) over *grilling/direct medium heat* for 6–8 minutes, with the lid closed, until browned in spots and crisp-tender, turning occasionally. At the same time, grill the prawns over *grilling/direct medium heat* for 3–5 minutes until slightly firm on the surface and opaque in the centre, turning once. Remove from the grill as they are done. Toss the prawns with the lemon juice. When the asparagus and prawns are cool enough to handle, cut them into 2.5 cm/1-inch pieces. Set aside.

5 In a saucepan over a high heat, bring the stock to a simmer. Keep warm.

6 In a large saucepan over a medium heat, melt 25 g/1 oz of the butter with the oil. Add the onion and ½ teaspoon of the salt. Sauté for 3–4 minutes until the onion is softened but not browned. Add the rice and cook for about 2 minutes until the grains are coated with the butter mixture and turn opaque, stirring frequently. Add the wine and stir for about 1 minute until evaporated. Add 250 ml/8 fl oz of the warm stock. Simmer until the rice has absorbed nearly all of the liquid, stirring occasionally. Add the remaining 125 ml/ 4 fl oz of stock gradually, stirring until nearly all of the liquid is absorbed before adding more, 25–30 minutes in all. At this point the risotto should be creamy and the grains should be plump and tender, yet firm to the bite.

7 Remove the risotto from the heat and stir in the remaining butter, half the cheese, the lemon zest and juice and the remaining ½ teaspoon salt. Fold in the asparagus, prawns, parsley and mint and season with pepper. Divide the risotto among serving bowls, garnish with the remaining cheese and serve immediately.

PRAWN AND CHORIZO TACOS
WITH FIRE-ROASTED CORN SALSA

SERVES: 4 | PREP TIME: 25 minutes | GRILLING TIME: 20–27 minutes

3 fresh corn cobs, outer leaves and silk removed
Extra-virgin olive oil
2 jalapeño chillies
1 avocado, cut into 5-mm/¼-inch pieces
½ red onion, finely chopped
2 tablespoons chopped fresh coriander
5 teaspoons fresh lime juice
24 large prawns, peeled and deveined, tails removed
¾ teaspoon prepared chilli seasoning
3 fresh chorizo sausages, about 375 g/12 oz total *or*
    2 hot linguica sausages, about 400 g/13 oz total
8 corn or flour tortillas (15–20 cm/6–8 inches)
Sea salt
Freshly ground black pepper

1 Prepare the grill for grilling/direct cooking over medium heat (180–230°C/350–450°F).

2 Lightly brush the corn all over with oil. Grill the corn and the jalapeños over *grilling/direct medium heat,* with the lid closed, until the corn is browned in spots and tender and the jalapeños are blackened and blistered, turning as needed. The corn will take 10–15 minutes and the jalapeños will take 7–9 minutes. Remove from the grill as they are done; let cool. Cut the corn kernels off the cobs.

Scrape off and discard the loosened skin, and remove and discard the stems and seeds from the jalapeños; finely chop the jalapeños. Combine the corn kernels, jalapeños, avocado, onion, coriander, lime juice, ½ teaspoon salt and ⅛ teaspoon pepper.

3 Brush the prawns on both sides with 1 tablespoon oil and season with the chilli seasoning, ¼ teaspoon salt and ⅛ teaspoon pepper. Grill the chorizo over *grilling/direct medium heat* for 10–12 minutes, with the lid closed, until cooked through, turning occasionally. At the same time, grill the prawns over *grilling/direct medium heat* for 3–5 minutes until they are firm to the touch and opaque in the centre, turning once. During the last minute of grilling time, warm the tortillas over grilling/direct heat, turning once or twice. Remove everything from the grill and cut the chorizo into 5-mm/¼-inch slices. Serve the prawns, chorizo and salsa with the warm tortillas.

MARINATED PRAWN SALAD
WITH FETA CHEESE AND OLIVES

SERVES: 4 | PREP TIME: 25 minutes | MARINATING TIME: 1 hour | GRILLING TIME: 2–4 minutes

MARINADE
½ onion, finely chopped
4 tablespoons fresh lemon juice
2 tablespoons chopped fresh dill
1 tablespoon Dijon mustard

Extra-virgin olive oil
24 large prawns, peeled and deveined, tails removed
Sea salt
Freshly ground black pepper

DRESSING
2 tablespoons fresh lemon juice
1 tablespoon red wine vinegar
1 small garlic clove, finely chopped or crushed

SALAD
375 g/12 oz cherry tomatoes, each cut in half
175 g/6 oz pitted kalamata olives
125 g/4 oz feta cheese, crumbled
1 small red pepper, thinly sliced
1 red onion, thinly sliced
25 g/1 oz fresh flat-leaf parsley

1 Whisk the marinade ingredients, including 4 tablespoons oil, ½ teaspoon salt and ½ teaspoon pepper. Place the prawns in a large, resealable plastic bag and pour in the marinade. Press the air out of the bag and seal tightly. Turn the bag to distribute the marinade, place in a bowl and refrigerate for 1 hour.

2 Prepare the grill for grilling/direct cooking over high heat (230–290°C/450–550°F).

3 Whisk the dressing ingredients together, then add 4 tablespoons oil in a steady stream, whisking constantly to emulsify. Season with ½ teaspoon salt and ½ teaspoon pepper.

4 Remove the prawns from the bag and discard the marinade. Grill the prawns over *grilling/direct high heat* for 2–4 minutes, with the lid closed, until they are firm to the touch and just turning opaque in the centre, turning once. Remove from the grill.

5 Combine the salad ingredients in a large bowl. Drizzle half of the dressing over the salad and toss to coat. Divide the salad among four serving plates and top with the prawns. Drizzle with additional dressing and serve immediately.

PRAWN ROLLS
WITH LEMON-CHIVE MAYO

SERVES: 6 | PREP TIME: 25 minutes | GRILLING TIME: 3–5 minutes | SPECIAL EQUIPMENT: perforated grill pan

MAYO
125 ml/4 fl oz mayonnaise
2 tablespoons finely chopped fresh chives
1 tablespoon finely chopped fresh tarragon
1 tablespoon finely chopped fresh dill
½ teaspoon finely grated lemon zest
1 teaspoon fresh lemon juice

75 g/3 oz unsalted butter
2 garlic cloves, finely chopped or crushed
32 large prawns, peeled and deveined, tails removed
6 hot dog buns, cut vertically from the top, sides trimmed
65 g/2½ oz romaine lettuce, thinly sliced
1 large tomato, deseeded and diced
Sea salt
Freshly ground black pepper
Hot pepper sauce
Lemon wedges

1 Combine the mayo ingredients, including ¼ teaspoon salt and ¼ teaspoon pepper. Set aside.

2 Prepare the grill for grilling/direct cooking over high heat (230–290°C/450–550°F) and preheat a perforated grill pan.

3 In a saucepan over a medium-low heat, melt the butter with the garlic. Remove from the heat. Pat the prawns dry and put in a bowl. Add 2 tablespoons of the garlic butter, ¼ teaspoon salt and ½ teaspoon pepper. Turn to coat. Brush the remaining garlic butter on the cut sides (outside only) of the buns.

4 Spread the prawns in a single layer on the grill pan and grill over *grilling/direct high heat* for 2–4 minutes, with the lid closed, until they are firm to the touch and just turning opaque in the centre, turning once or twice. Remove from the grill to cool. Toast the buns, buttered sides only, over *grilling/direct high heat* for about 1 minute, rotating once.

5 Roughly chop the prawns, add to the mayo and stir to combine. Open the buns and add lettuce and the prawn mixture. Top with tomatoes and serve immediately with hot pepper sauce and lemon wedges.

OYSTER PO'BOYS
WITH LEMONY RÉMOULADE

SERVES: 4 | PREP TIME: **30 minutes** | GRILLING TIME: **6–8 minutes** | SPECIAL EQUIPMENT: oyster knife

RÉMOULADE
125 ml/4 fl oz mayonnaise
50 g/2 oz spring onions, finely chopped (white and light
    green parts only)
1½ teaspoons Dijon mustard
½ teaspoon finely grated lemon zest
1½ teaspoons fresh lemon juice
¼ teaspoon hot pepper sauce
¼ teaspoon paprika
¼ teaspoon garlic powder
¼ teaspoon sea salt

32 large fresh oysters in the shell, each about 7 cm/
    3 inches long
4 soft French rolls, each about 15 cm/6 inches long, split
3 tablespoons extra-virgin olive oil
75 g/3 oz romaine lettuce, shredded
3 tomatoes, sliced
16 dill pickle chips
250 g/8 oz French fried onions

1 Combine the rémoulade ingredients.

2 Prepare the grill for grilling/direct cooking over high heat (230–290°C/450–550°F).

3 Grill the oysters over *grilling/direct high heat* for 5–7 minutes, with the lid closed, until they open 5 mm– 1 cm/¼–½ inch. Using tongs, carefully remove the oysters from the grill, place on a roasting tray, and cover tightly with aluminium foil. Discard any oysters that are not open.

4 Use an oyster knife to open the shells. Carefully cut each oyster loose from the top shell and then from the bottom shell by running the oyster knife carefully under the body. Cover the shucked oysters with foil to keep them warm.

5 Brush the cut side of each roll with the oil. Grill the rolls, cut side down, over *grilling/direct high heat* for 30 seconds–1 minute until lightly toasted.

6 Spread the bottom half of each roll with rémoulade and fill the rolls with lettuce, tomatoes, pickles, oysters and French fried onions. Serve immediately.

LOBSTER TAILS
WITH BASIL-LEMON BUTTER

SERVES: 4 | PREP TIME: **10 minutes** | GRILLING TIME: **7–11 minutes** | SPECIAL EQUIPMENT: **kitchen shears**

BUTTER
300 g/10 oz unsalted butter
2 tablespoons finely chopped fresh basil
1 tablespoon finely grated lemon zest
1 tablespoon fresh lemon juice
½ teaspoon hot pepper sauce
½ teaspoon sea salt

4 fresh lobster tails, each 175–300 g/6–10 oz, thawed

1 Prepare the grill for grilling/direct cooking over medium heat (180–230°C/350–450°F).

2 In a small saucepan over a low heat, melt the butter, swirling the saucepan occasionally. When the butter is melted, skim off the foam and discard. Stir in the remaining butter ingredients and heat for 1 minute. Remove from the heat. Pour off 4 tablespoons of the butter to use for grilling the lobster. Cover the saucepan to keep the remaining butter warm for serving.

3 Using kitchen shears, cut along the centre of the top (rounded) side of one of the lobster shells, cutting from the wider end to the tail. Turn the lobster tail over and make the same cut, again starting at the wider end and cutting towards the tail. Using a knife, cut through the meat and the tail to divide the tail lengthways into two pieces. Repeat with the remaining lobster tails.

4 Brush the meat side of the lobster with some of the butter reserved for grilling. Grill the lobster tails, meat side down, over *grilling/direct medium heat* for 2–3 minutes, with the lid closed, depending on their size. Brush the tops of the shells with a little more of the butter, turn them over, and grill for 5–8 minutes more, just until the meat is white and firm but not dry. Remove from the grill and serve the lobster warm with the reserved butter.

1 Use kitchen shears to cut through the hard back shell all the way to the tail.

2 Turn the lobster tail over, and cut through the centre of the shell on the underside.

3 Use a sharp, heavy knife to cut each tail in half lengthways, passing through the openings that you've already made.

> **TIP** It is possible to buy the lobster tails frozen. If you do, allow them to thaw gently. Don't attempt to rush the process in a microwave oven, or the delicate meat will turn tough.

CIOPPINO WITH GRILLED SHELLFISH
AND GARLIC CROUTONS

SERVES: 4–6 | PREP TIME: 40 minutes | GRILLING TIME: 8–10 minutes

Extra-virgin olive oil
2 onions, finely chopped
1 fennel bulb, cored and thinly sliced
3 garlic cloves, crushed
1 small red pepper, cut into 5-mm/¼-inch dice
1 teaspoon dried oregano
¼ teaspoon crushed red chilli flakes
875 g/28 oz canned Italian plum tomatoes in juice
1 litre/1¾ pints chicken stock
1 tablespoon tomato purée
1 bay leaf
24 large prawns, peeled and deveined, tails left on
12 large scallops, each about 40 g/1½ oz
1 large garlic clove, finely grated, chopped or crushed
½ ciabatta loaf or other Italian bread, cut into
    3.5-cm/1½-inch cubes (12–16 pieces)
24 live mussels, about 500 g/1 lb total, scrubbed
    and debearded
Sea salt
Freshly ground black pepper
4 tablespoons finely chopped fresh flat-leaf parsley

1 Warm 2 tablespoons oil in a large saucepan over a medium heat. Add the onions and the fennel and sauté for about 5 minutes until the vegetables begin to soften. Add the crushed garlic, pepper, oregano and chilli flakes and sauté for 2 minutes. Add the tomatoes and their juice (crushing the tomatoes with your hands before adding them to the pan), the stock, tomato purée, bay leaf, 1 teaspoon salt and ¼ teaspoon pepper. Bring to the boil, reduce the heat to medium-low and simmer, partially covered, for 30 minutes, stirring occasionally.

2 While the stew is simmering, prepare the grill for grilling/direct cooking over high heat (230–290°C/450–550°F).

3 Rinse the prawns and the scallops under cold water and pat dry. Remove the small tough side muscle that might be left on each scallop (see page 216§). Brush the shellfish on all sides with oil and lightly season with salt and pepper.

4 Combine 2 tablespoons oil, the finely grated garlic and the bread cubes and toss to coat.

5 Grill the prawns and the scallops over *grilling/direct high heat*, with the lid closed, until they are just opaque in the centre, turning once. The prawns will take 2–4 minutes and the scallops will take 4–6 minutes. Remove from the grill as they are done.

6 Lower the temperature of the grill to medium heat (180–230°C/350–450°F). Grill the bread cubes over *grilling/direct medium heat* for about 4 minutes, with the lid closed, until lightly browned on all sides, turning several times.

7 Just before serving, return the stew to a vigorous simmer over a medium heat. Add the mussels, cover the pan and cook for 3–5 minutes until the mussels open (discard any unopened mussels). Stir in the scallops and prawns. Ladle the stew into wide soup bowls. Top with the parsley, garnish with the croutons and serve warm.

TIP Cioppino, a fisherman's stew originating in San Francisco, typically includes shellfish that are gently poached in a tomato-based stock. In this recipe, prawns and scallops are grilled separately and then added near the end, bringing charred, smoky flavours to the stew. The garlic croutons require some vigilance to avoid burning, but it's worth the trouble because the crunchy bread does a great job of soaking up the amazing stock.

GRILL SKILLS
PERFECT FISH

CHOOSE WISELY

1 Fresh fish have a firm, shiny flesh that bounces back a bit when you touch it. If the fish has started to separate, or if it's discoloured, don't buy it.

2 High-quality fish smells like the ocean, not like cooked fish.

3 For whole fish, look for clear, bright eyes. If a fish has eyes that have clouded over, it's way past its prime.

4 The scales of whole fish should be smooth. Breaks or cracks in the scaling pattern indicate poor handling or age.

FILLETING A WHOLE FISH

Begin by scaling and rinsing the fish in the sink. Then remove the head by making a diagonal cut just behind the small fin at the base of the head. Cut all the way through the bones.

1 Using a very sharp knife with a flexible blade, begin a cut about 1 cm/½ inch deep just above the backbone near the tail end. Continue the cut along the length of the back until you reach the other end of the fish.

2 Then go back and make the cut deeper and deeper with each gentle stroke, keeping the blade of the knife as close to the bones as possible. Gently lift the top fillet with one hand so you can see where your knife is cutting.

3 Lay the fillet back in place and cut through the tail end, always moving the blade of the knife away from you in case the knife slips. Turn the fish over and repeat the process on the other side.

FIRM FILLETS

Salmon and halibut are good choices for grilling because their flesh is firm. Look for fillets that are at least 2.5/1 inch thick from end to end. Thinner fillets cook too quickly and tend to break apart.

WHEN IS IT DONE?

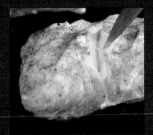

PEEK TEST
When the flesh turns from translucent to opaque all the way to the centre and just begins to flake around the edges, the fish is done. This typically happens when the internal temperature reaches 52–55°C/125–130°F.

SKEWER TEST
If you don't have an instant-read thermometer, insert a metal skewer into the thickest part of the fish for a few seconds and then touch the skewer on a sensitive part of your skin.

If the skewer feels cold to an area like the base of your thumb, the fish is underdone. If the skewer feels warm, the fish is cooked. If the skewer feels hot, the fish is overcooked.

PREVENTING STICKING

1 The first step is to get your cooking grate hot and clean enough that it will dry the watery surface of the fillets quickly so they can brown. Once they begin to brown on a clean grate, they start to release.

2 Oil is a natural lubricant that will prevent sticking, so brush it evenly and generously over the fillets. But don't overdo it. If the fish is dripping with oil, you will probably get flare-ups.

3 Don't touch any fillet until it is browned and ready to turn. It is often a good idea to grill the first side a little longer than the second side. An extra few minutes on the first side (with the lid closed) will help the fillet to release from the grate more easily.

USING A PERFORATED GRILL PAN

If you are concerned about turning your fillets on the grill, just set them on a preheated grill pan over roasting/indirect high heat. There is no need to turn them. They will roast fairly evenly on both sides, but the side touching the pan should develop a nice golden crust.

HALIBUT
WITH ROASTED VEGETABLES AND BASIL

SERVES: 4 | PREP TIME: 30 minutes | GRILLING TIME: 26–28 minutes | SPECIAL EQUIPMENT: perforated grill pan

175 g/6 oz fresh basil
2 tablespoons fresh lemon juice
¼ teaspoon crushed red chilli flakes
Extra-virgin olive oil
1 teaspoon dried thyme
½ teaspoon dried oregano
2 large red peppers, cut into 1-cm/½-inch strips
2 red onions, cut crossways into 1-cm/½-inch slices
    and separated into rings
3 garlic cloves, finely chopped
500 g/1 lb cherry tomatoes
18 oil-cured black olives, pitted and halved
4 halibut fillets (with skin), each 175–250 g/6–8 oz
    and about 2.5 cm/1 inch thick
Sea salt
Freshly ground black pepper

1 In a food processor combine the basil, 1 tablespoon of
the lemon juice, the chilli flakes and ½ teaspoon salt.
Pulse a few times to roughly chop the basil. With the motor
running, add 4 tablespoons oil in a steady stream and
process until the mixture forms a chunky sauce. Transfer
to a bowl and press a piece of clingfilm on to the surface to
prevent discolouring.

2 Prepare the grill for grilling/direct cooking over medium
heat (180–230°C/350–450°F) and preheat a perforated
grill pan.

3 In a large bowl whisk 4 tablespoons oil, the thyme,
oregano, 1 teaspoon salt and ½ teaspoon pepper. Add the
red peppers, onions, garlic and tomatoes and toss to coat.
Spread the vegetables in a single layer on the grill pan and
grill over *grilling/direct medium heat* for about 20 minutes,
with the lid closed, until the vegetables have softened
and the tomatoes have begun to break down, stirring
occasionally. Transfer the vegetables to a heatproof bowl.
Stir in the olives. Keep warm. Increase the temperature of
the grill to medium-high heat (200–260°C/400–500°F).

4 Brush the flesh side of the halibut fillets with oil and
season evenly with 1 teaspoon salt and ½ teaspoon
pepper. Grill the fillets over *grilling/direct medium-high
heat* for 6–8 minutes, with the lid closed, until the flesh just
begins to flake when poked with the tip of a knife, turning
once. Remove from the grill. Remove the skin from the
fillets. Divide the vegetables among four serving plates.
Nestle a fillet in the centre of the vegetables. Drizzle with
the remaining lemon juice, then spoon the sauce over the
fish. Serve right away.

SPICY HALIBUT
WITH RÉMOULADE COLESLAW

SERVES: 4 | PREP TIME: **30 minutes** | GRILLING TIME: **6–8 minutes**

RÉMOULADE
5 tablespoons mayonnaise
2 spring onions, ends trimmed, finely chopped
1 tablespoon finely chopped fresh chives
1 tablespoon capers, rinsed and chopped
1½ teaspoons finely chopped fresh flat-leaf parsley
1½ teaspoons fresh lemon juice
1 teaspoon finely chopped garlic
¼ teaspoon freshly ground black pepper

250 g/8 oz green cabbage, shredded
1 carrot, cut into small dice
1 spring onion, cut into thin strips about 5 cm/2 inches long
    (white and light green parts only)
Sea salt

MARINADE
4 tablespoons groundnut oil
3 tablespoons chopped fresh basil
2 tablespoons fresh lemon juice
2 teaspoons finely chopped fresh ginger
½ teaspoon crushed red chilli flakes
½ teaspoon ground cayenne pepper
¼ teaspoon ground turmeric

4 skinless halibut fillets, each about 175 g/6 oz
    and 2.5 cm/1 inch thick

1 Combine the rémoulade ingredients. Season with salt, if liked. In a large bowl combine the cabbage, carrot and spring onion. Add the rémoulade and toss until mixed.

2 Prepare the grill for grilling/direct cooking over high heat (230–290°C/450–550°F).

3 Whisk the marinade ingredients together, including ¾ teaspoon salt. Pat the halibut fillets dry with kitchen paper, place them in a shallow baking dish and brush them thoroughly with some of the marinade. Reserve the remaining marinade.

4 Grill the fillets over *grilling/direct high heat* for 4–5 minutes, with the lid closed, until they release from the cooking grate without sticking. Carefully turn the fillets over and brush with the reserved marinade. Discard any remaining marinade. Continue cooking for 2–3 minutes more, until the fish just begins to flake when poked with the tip of a knife. Remove from the grill and serve warm with the slaw.

HALIBUT AND PRAWN BURGERS
WITH GRILLED VEGETABLE SALAD

SERVES: 4 | PREP TIME: 20 minutes | CHILLING TIME: 30 minutes–1 hour | GRILLING TIME: 10–12 minutes
SPECIAL EQUIPMENT: perforated grill pan

BURGERS

500 g/1 lb skinless halibut fillets
250 g/8 oz prawns, peeled and deveined, tails removed
3 tablespoons finely chopped fresh chives
1½ tablespoons finely chopped fresh dill
1 tablespoon Dijon mustard
1 tablespoon fresh lemon juice

Sea salt
Freshly ground black pepper
Extra-virgin olive oil
2 courgettes, cut crossways into 1-cm/½-inch slices
2 thin aubergines, cut crossways into 1-cm/½-inch slices
2 red peppers, cut into bite-sized pieces
250 g/8 oz romaine lettuce, shredded
Homemade or shop-bought ranch dressing
   (see page 180)

1 In a food processor combine the burger ingredients, including ½ teaspoon salt and ½ teaspoon pepper, and pulse until the mixture forms a chunky paste, scraping down the sides of the bowl once or twice. With wet hands, gently form four loosely packed burgers of equal size, each about 10 cm/4 inches in diameter, and place them on a baking sheet. Refrigerate for 30 minutes–1 hour.

2 Prepare the grill for grilling/direct cooking over medium heat (180–230°C/350–450°F) and preheat a perforated grill pan.

3 Brush the burgers on both sides with oil. Brush the courgettes, aubergines and red peppers with oil and season evenly with salt and pepper.

4 Spread the vegetables in a single layer on the grill pan and grill over *grilling/direct medium heat* for 6–8 minutes, with the lid closed, until crisp-tender, turning once or twice. At the same time, grill the burgers on the cooking grates over *grilling/direct medium heat* for 10–12 minutes until fully cooked, turning once or twice. Remove from the grill when they are done.

5 Divide the lettuce among each of four serving plates. Top with grilled vegetables and a burger. Drizzle with the ranch dressing and serve immediately.

TIP Pureéd prawns take the place of the egg or breadcrumbs used in other recipes to bind all the ingredients together.

FRESH TUNA SANDWICHES
WITH RED PEPPER MAYO AND CUCUMBER SALAD

SERVES: 4 | PREP TIME: 15 minutes | GRILLING TIME: 3–4 minutes

SALAD
1 cucumber, about 375 g/12 oz, very thinly sliced
½ large sweet onion, thinly sliced
4 tablespoons seasoned rice vinegar
1 teaspoon ground coriander

½ roasted red pepper (from a jar), drained
125 ml/4 fl oz mayonnaise
4 tuna fillets, each about 175 g/6 oz and 2.5 cm/1 inch thick
1 tablespoon extra-virgin olive oil
½ teaspoon sea salt
¼ teaspoon paprika
⅛ teaspoon freshly ground black pepper
4 small ciabatta rolls, split
40 g/1½ oz baby rocket

1 Prepare the grill for grilling/direct cooking over high heat (230–290°C/450–550°F).

2 Combine the salad ingredients and toss thoroughly. Set aside at room temperature until ready to serve, stirring occasionally.

3 In a food processor or a blender combine the red pepper and the mayonnaise and purée until fairly smooth, scraping down the sides of the bowl as needed.

4 Lightly brush the tuna fillets on both sides with the oil and season evenly with the salt, paprika and pepper. Grill the fillets over *grilling/direct high heat*, with the lid open, until cooked to your desired doneness, 3–4 minutes for medium rare, turning once. During the last minute of grilling time, toast the rolls, cut side down, over grilling/direct heat. Remove the tuna and the rolls from the grill. Cut the tuna into thin slices.

5 Spread the cut side of the rolls generously with the red pepper mayo and top with tuna and rocket. Drain any excess liquid from the cucumber salad and serve with the warm sandwiches.

> **TIP** If you have a mandoline or a food processor equipped with a slicing blade, use it to slice the cucumber and the onion as thinly as possible.

TUNA STEAKS
WITH FIG AND BLACK OLIVE TAPENADE

SERVES: 6 | PREP TIME: 15 minutes | GRILLING TIME: 2–3 minutes

TAPENADE
40 g/1½ oz dried figs, finely chopped
125 ml/4 fl oz medium-dry sherry
250 ml/8 fl oz shop-bought black olive or mixed
   olive tapenade
4 tablespoons finely chopped fresh mint
Finely grated zest of 1 lemon
1 tablespoon fresh lemon juice
¼ teaspoon freshly ground black pepper

Extra-virgin olive oil

RUB
½ teaspoon paprika
½ teaspoon sea salt
¼ teaspoon freshly ground black pepper

6 tuna steaks, each about 250 g/8 oz and 2.5 cm/1 inch thick

1 In a small bowl stir the figs and sherry thoroughly and let stand for 10 minutes. Drain, discarding any remaining sherry. Combine the figs with the tapenade, mint, lemon zest and juice and pepper. If, after combining the ingredients, the tapenade seems too dry, add up to 2 tablespoons oil until it reaches your desired consistency. Set aside until serving.

2 Prepare the grill for grilling/direct cooking over high heat (230–290°C/450–550°F).

3 Combine the rub ingredients. Lightly brush the tuna steaks on both sides with oil and season evenly with the rub. Grill the steaks over *grilling/direct high heat* for 2–3 minutes, with the lid open, until cooked to rare doneness, turning once. Remove from the grill and serve right away with the tapenade spooned on top.

For medium-rare doneness, grill the tuna for 3–4 minutes, turning once.

For medium doneness, grill the tuna for about 5 minutes, turning once.

SEARED SPICY TUNA AND AVOCADO ROLLS

SERVES: 4 | PREP TIME: 45 minutes | GRILLING TIME: 1½–2 minutes | SPECIAL EQUIPMENT: bamboo sushi mat

400 g/13 oz raw sushi rice
4 tablespoons seasoned rice vinegar
4 teaspoons honey
¾ teaspoon sea salt
125 ml/4 fl oz mayonnaise
2 tablespoons toasted sesame oil
4 teaspoons wasabi paste
1 tuna steak, about 500 g/1 lb and 2.5 cm/1 inch thick
8 sheets nori, each about 19 by 20 cm/7½ by 8 inches
1 avocado, halved and cut crossways into 24 slices
4 teaspoons sesame seeds, toasted
125 ml/4 fl oz soy sauce
1 tablespoon hot chilli-garlic sauce
Pickled ginger (optional)

1 Cook the rice according to package instructions. Cool thoroughly. Combine the vinegar, honey and salt and whisk until the salt is dissolved. Pour the mixture over the cooled rice and mix gently but thoroughly.

2 Prepare the grill for grilling/direct cooking over high heat (230–290°C/450–550°F).

3 Combine the mayonnaise, half the oil, and the wasabi paste. Reserve 4 tablespoons for serving.

4 Coat the tuna steak on both sides with the remaining 1 tablespoon oil. Grill over *grilling/direct high heat* for 1½–2 minutes, with the lid open, until the tuna is browned on the outside and just barely warm but still red in the centre, turning once. Remove from the grill and cool completely. Cut the steak lengthways into eight 1-cm/½-inch slices.

5 Arrange the sushi mat with the slats running horizontally. Place one sheet of nori, shiny side down, on the mat, lining up a long edge with the edge of the mat nearest you. With wet hands, spread an eighth of the rice on to the nori in a thin, even layer, leaving a 1-cm/½-inch border on the long end opposite you. Spread 2 teaspoons of the mayonnaise mixture in a horizontal stripe about 1.5 cm/¾ inch wide across the rice, 5 cm/2 inches from the side nearest you. Put one slice of the tuna on top of the mayonnaise and then three slices of avocado over the tuna. Top with ½ teaspoon sesame seeds.

6 Beginning with the edge nearest you, lift up the nori and fold the bottom up and over the filling, tightly rolling the sushi into a thick cylinder, using the mat to assist in rolling. Once rolled, wrap the sushi in the mat and gently squeeze to shape and seal. If the 1-cm/½-inch border of nori doesn't stick, moisten lightly with water and press to seal securely. Repeat with the remaining nori and filling.

7 Combine the soy sauce and the hot chilli-garlic sauce. Transfer the rolls, seam side down, to a chopping board. Dip a sharp, thin knife into water and shake off any excess. Using a sawing motion, cut the rolls crossways into 6–8 equal pieces. Serve with the soy sauce mixture, the reserved mayonnaise and the pickled ginger, if using.

> TIP To make spreading the mayonnaise over the rice easier, put the mixture in a resealable plastic bag, cut off a corner and squeeze the mixture out of the bag.

1 Buy sushi-grade tuna and sear it quickly over high heat, leaving the centre raw.

2 Arrange the tuna in a line on the mayonnaise, followed by the avocado and the sesame seeds.

3 Lift up the nori and fold the bottom up and over the filling, rolling the sushi into a tight cylinder.

4 Roll the mat outside the cylinder to help create a nice round, compact shape.

OPEN-FACED SALMON BURGERS
WITH WASABI MAYO

SERVES: 4 | PREP TIME: 35 minutes | CHILLING TIME: 1–2 hours | GRILLING TIME: 6–7 minutes

BURGERS

1 skinless salmon fillet, about 750 g/1½ lb, pin
    bones removed, cut into 2.5 cm/1-inch chunks
6 tablespoons panko breadcrumbs
2 tablespoons cottage cheese
1 large egg, lightly beaten
3 spring onions, finely chopped (white and light
    green parts only)
1 tablespoon peeled, grated fresh ginger
Finely grated zest of 1 large lime
½ teaspoon sea salt
¼ teaspoon freshly ground black pepper

6 tablespoons mayonnaise
1 teaspoon prepared wasabi paste
Olive oil cooking spray
2 muffins, split
1 avocado, cut lengthways into thin slices
8 slices tomato

1 In a food processor combine the burger ingredients.
Pulse until the salmon chunks are evenly chopped,
4–6 pulses, being careful not to purée the mixture.

2 With wet hands and handling the mixture as little as
possible, gently form four burgers of equal size, each

about 1.5 cm/¾ inch thick. Place the burgers on a large
plate, cover loosely with clingfilm, and refrigerate for at
least 1 hour or up to 2 hours.

3 Prepare the grill for grilling/direct cooking over high
heat (230–290°C/450–550°F).

4 Whisk the mayonnaise and the wasabi together. Cover
and refrigerate until ready to serve.

5 Lightly coat the salmon burgers with olive oil spray on
both sides. Grill the burgers over *grilling/direct high
heat* for about 4 minutes, with the lid closed (do not move
the burgers during this time or they may fall apart). Using a
metal spatula, carefully turn the burgers over and continue
cooking for 2–3 minutes more, until they are firm and
cooked through. During the last minute of grilling time,
lightly toast the muffins, cut side down, over *grilling/direct
heat*. Remove the burgers and the muffins from the grill.

6 Place the muffins, cut side up, on a serving plate. Fan a
quarter of the avocado slices on top of each muffin half,
and place a salmon burger on the avocado. Top each burger
with two slices of tomato and a dollop of wasabi mayo.
Serve immediately.

CEDAR-PLANKED SALMON FILLETS
WITH TENDERSTEM BROCCOLI

SERVES: 4 | PREP TIME: 20 minutes | GRILLING TIME: 12–15 minutes
SPECIAL EQUIPMENT: 1 untreated cedar plank, 30–37 cm/12–15 inches long and about 18 cm/7 inches wide

1 salmon fillet (with skin), about 1 kg/2 lb and
    2.5–3.5 cm/1–1½ inches thick, pin bones removed
2 tablespoons Dijon mustard
2 tablespoons light brown sugar
500 g/1 lb tenderstem broccoli, stem ends trimmed and
    split lengthways 1 cm/½ inch below the florets
2½ tablespoons extra-virgin olive oil
1½ teaspoons finely grated orange zest
Sea salt
Freshly ground black pepper

1 Soak the cedar plank in water for at least 1 hour.

2 Prepare the grill for grilling/direct cooking over medium heat (180–230°C/350–450°F).

3 Carefully cut the salmon fillet crossways into four equal pieces and generously season with salt and pepper. Stir the mustard and the brown sugar into a paste. Spread the paste all over the salmon. Toss the broccoli with the oil, ¾ teaspoon salt and ½ teaspoon pepper.

4 Place the soaked cedar plank over *grilling/direct medium heat* and close the lid. After 5–10 minutes, when the plank begins to smoke and char, turn the plank over. Place the fillets, skin side down, in a single layer on the plank, leaving a little room between the fillets, and place the broccoli at right angles to the bars on the cooking grates. Grill the fillets and the broccoli over *grilling/direct medium heat* for 12–15 minutes, with the lid closed, until the salmon is cooked to your desired doneness and the broccoli is crisp-tender, turning the vegetables and checking the salmon for doneness every 5 minutes. The broccoli will char a little on the floret ends. Remove the fillets from the plank and transfer the broccoli to a large bowl. Add the orange zest to the broccoli and toss to combine. Serve immediately.

TIP Splitting the broccoli stems in half means they will cook faster. Char the cedar plank on one side before adding the salmon.

SALMON AND VEGETABLE KEBABS
WITH LEMON-HERB VINAIGRETTE

SERVES: 4 | PREP TIME: 30 minutes | GRILLING TIME: 8–10 minutes | SPECIAL EQUIPMENT: 8 metal or bamboo skewers

VINAIGRETTE
4 tablespoons fresh lemon juice
3 tablespoons finely chopped fresh coriander
3 tablespoons finely chopped fresh flat-leaf parsley
4 garlic cloves, finely chopped or crushed
1½ teaspoons paprika
¾ teaspoon ground cumin
¼ teaspoon ground cayenne pepper

Extra-virgin olive oil
750 g/1½ lb skinless centre-cut salmon fillet, cut into
    3-cm/1¼-inch cubes, pin bones removed
2 courgettes, cut into 2.5-cm/1-inch-thick half-moons
2 yellow courgettes, cut into 2.5-cm/1-inch-thick
    half-moons
½ large red onion, cut lengthways into quarters, each
    quarter cut crossways into 2 pieces
Sea salt
Freshly ground black pepper
1 lemon, quartered

1 If using bamboo skewers, soak in water for at least 30 minutes.

2 Prepare the grill for grilling/direct cooking over medium-high heat (200–260°C/400–500°F).

3 Combine the vinaigrette ingredients, including 1 teaspoon salt. Gradually add 125 ml/4 fl oz oil, whisking constantly until emulsified. Set aside until ready to serve.

4 Thread the salmon cubes on to four skewers. Thread the green and yellow courgettes and onion alternately on to four more skewers. Generously brush the salmon and the vegetables all over with oil and season evenly with salt and pepper.

5 Grill the kebabs over *grilling/direct medium-high heat* for 8–10 minutes, with the lid closed, until the vegetables are crisp-tender and the salmon is crusty and golden outside and beginning to turn opaque in the centre but still moist, turning four times. Remove the kebabs from the grill and serve immediately with the vinaigrette and the lemon quarters.

MARINATED SALMON
WITH RED CURRY AND ROASTED PEPPER SAUCE

SERVES: 4 | PREP TIME: 25 minutes | MARINATING TIME: 30 minutes | GRILLING TIME: 18–24 minutes

MARINADE
450-ml/15-fl oz can unsweetened coconut milk
2 tablespoons fresh lime juice
1 tablespoon rapeseed oil
1½ teaspoons Thai red curry paste

4 salmon fillets (with skin), each 175–250 g/6–8 oz and
    about 2.5 cm/1 inch thick, pin bones removed
1 large red pepper
1 garlic clove, finely chopped or crushed
1 tablespoon peeled, grated fresh ginger
1 teaspoon sea salt
4 tablespoons finely chopped fresh coriander
250 g/8 oz cooked rice
Baby spinach, to serve (optional)

1 Combine the marinade ingredients. Place the salmon fillets in a large, resealable plastic bag and pour in the marinade. Press the air out of the bag and seal tightly. Turn the bag to distribute the marinade, place on a plate and marinate at room temperature for 30 minutes, turning occasionally.

2 Prepare the grill for grilling/direct cooking over high heat (230–290°C/450–550°F).

3 Grill the red pepper over *grilling/direct high heat* for 10–12 minutes, with the lid closed, until blackened and blistered all over, turning occasionally. Put the pepper in a bowl and cover with clingfilm to trap the steam. Let stand for about 10 minutes. Peel away and discard the charred skin. Cut off and discard the stem and seeds, then roughly chop the pepper. Transfer the pepper to a food processor.

4 Remove the fish from the bag and pour the marinade into the food processor with the pepper. Add the garlic, ginger and salt and process until smooth. Transfer to a saucepan and bring to the boil over a medium-high heat. Reduce the heat to a simmer and cook for 2–3 minutes. Keep warm.

5 Grill the fish fillets, flesh side down first, over *grilling/direct high heat* for 6–8 minutes, with the lid closed, until you can lift the fillets off the cooking grates without sticking. Turn the fillets over and continue to cook to your desired doneness, 2–4 minutes more for medium rare. Slip a spatula between the skin and the flesh and transfer the fillets to serving plates. Serve the salmon warm with the sauce, and garnish with the coriander. Serve with the rice and baby spinach, if desired.

SALMON CHAR
WITH SPICY TOMATO AND OLIVE RELISH

SERVES: 4 | PREP TIME: 30 minutes | GRILLING TIME: 6–7 minutes

RELISH

3 large plum tomatoes, deseeded and finely diced
75 g/3 oz black olives, such as kalamata, each cut in half
75 g/3 oz green olives, such as Cerignola, each cut
   in half (or quartered if large)
3 tablespoons extra-virgin olive oil
2 tablespoons capers, rinsed and drained
1 tablespoon white balsamic vinegar
2 anchovy fillets packed in olive oil, drained and
   finely chopped
2 garlic cloves, finely chopped or crushed
½ teaspoon crushed red pepper flakes
¼ teaspoon freshly ground black pepper

4 Arctic salmon fillets, each 175–250 g/6–8 oz and
   about 1 cm/½ inch thick
1 tablespoon extra-virgin olive oil
¾ teaspoon sea salt
½ teaspoon freshly ground black pepper
15 g/½ oz fresh basil, chopped

1 Combine the relish ingredients. Set aside at room temperature until ready to serve.

2 Prepare the grill for grilling/direct cooking over high heat (230–290°C/450–550°F).

3 Brush the fish fillets on both sides with the oil and season evenly with the salt and pepper. Grill the fillets over *grilling/direct high heat* for about 4 minutes, with the lid closed, until you can lift them off the cooking grate without sticking. Turn the fish over and continue cooking to your desired doneness, 2–3 minutes more for medium rare. Remove from the grill.

4 Stir the basil into the relish. Generously spoon the relish over the fish and serve immediately.

TIP Instead of salmon you could substitute halibut or swordfish. The relish is also great served over chicken.

BASIL- AND CITRUS-STUFFED WHOLE SEA BASS
WITH PESTO

SERVES: 4 | PREP TIME: **20 minutes** | GRILLING TIME: **30–40 minutes** | SPECIAL EQUIPMENT: **kitchen string**

2 tablespoons extra-virgin olive oil
2 whole sea bass, each 750 g–1 kg/1½–2 lb, gutted, scaled
   and fins removed
¾ teaspoon sea salt
½ teaspoon freshly ground black pepper
3 large lemons
2 oranges
5 tablespoons shop-bought pesto
30 fresh basil leaves

1 Prepare the grill for roasting/indirect cooking over medium heat (180–230°C/350–450°F).

2 Rub the oil evenly on the inside and outside of each fish, and season evenly inside and outside with the salt and pepper. Set aside.

3 Grate the zest of one of the lemons and one of the oranges into the pesto. Add the juice from one lemon half into the pesto and stir to combine. Cut the remaining 2½ lemons and both oranges into slices 5 mm/¼ inch thick, discarding the ends. Cut four of the lemon slices in half and two of the orange slices into quarters. Fill each fish cavity with four of the halved lemon slices, four of the quartered orange slices and 15 basil leaves.

4 Cut four 45-cm/18-inch lengths of kitchen string. Place two pieces of string parallel and about 3.5 cm/1½ inches apart from each other. Put one orange and one lemon slice in the centre of each piece of string. Place one fish on top of the fruit slices, then put another orange and lemon slice side by side on top of the fish. Wrap each piece of string around the fish and tie, securing the fruit to the fish. Repeat with the other fish.

5 Grill the fish over *roasting/indirect medium heat* for 30–40 minutes, with the lid closed, until the flesh is opaque near the bone but still juicy, turning once. Remove from the grill and let rest for about 2 minutes.

6 Arrange the remaining lemon and orange slices on a small serving plate. Remove the string from each fish, discard the grilled fruit slices, then cut off the head and tail. Cut along the backbone and open the fish like a book. Remove the basil, the lemon and orange slices and the bones. Lift the flesh off the skin. Place the filleted fish on the prepared serving plate and drizzle with 2 tablespoons of the pesto. Serve the fish warm with the remaining pesto.

SWORDFISH
WITH ROASTED TOMATOES AND OLIVES

SERVES: 4 | PREP TIME: 20 minutes | GRILLING TIME: 14–18 minutes

1 kg/2 lb plum tomatoes
Extra-virgin olive oil
1 large garlic clove, finely chopped or crushed
¼ teaspoon crushed red chilli flakes, or to taste
75 g/3 oz kalamata olives, cut in half lengthways
2 teaspoons fresh thyme *or* 1 teaspoon dried thyme
4 swordfish steaks, each about 250 g/8 oz and
    2.5 cm/1 inch thick
Sea salt
Freshly ground black pepper

1 Prepare the grill for grilling/direct cooking over medium heat (180–230°C/350–450°F).

2 Core the tomatoes and cut them in half lengthways. Scoop out the seeds and discard. Toss the tomatoes with 2 tablespoons oil and lightly season with salt. Grill the tomatoes, cut side down first, over *grilling/direct medium heat* for 6–8 minutes, with the lid closed, until blackened and blistered in spots, turning once or twice. Transfer the tomatoes to a bowl. When the tomatoes are cool enough to handle, remove and discard the skin. Coarsely chop the tomato flesh and return to the bowl.

3 Warm 1 tablespoon oil in a large saucepan over a medium heat. Add the garlic and chilli flakes and sauté for about 1 minute until fragrant without letting the garlic brown. Add the tomatoes along with any oil left in the bowl and then add the olives and thyme. Simmer for about 20 minutes until thickened, stirring occasionally.

4 Lightly brush the swordfish steaks on both sides with 1 tablespoon oil and season evenly with salt and pepper. Grill the steaks over *grilling/direct medium heat* for 8–10 minutes, with the lid closed, until they are just opaque in the centre but still juicy, turning once. Serve warm with the sauce spooned over the top.

PACIFIC RIM SWORDFISH
WITH CUCUMBER SALAD

SERVES: 4 | PREP TIME: 20 minutes | GRILLING TIME: 4–5 minutes

DRESSING
5 spring onions, thinly sliced (white and light green
    parts only)
1½ tablespoons seasoned rice vinegar
1½ tablespoons mirin (sweet rice wine)
1½ tablespoons fish sauce
1 tablespoon soy sauce
2 teaspoons fresh lemon juice
1 teaspoon toasted sesame oil
¼ teaspoon crushed red chilli flakes

1 cucumber, deseeded and cut into large matchsticks
Rapeseed oil
1 tablespoon finely chopped fresh coriander
4 centre-cut swordfish steaks, each about 175 g/6 oz
    and 1.5 cm/¾ inch thick
½ teaspoon sea salt
¼ teaspoon freshly ground black pepper

1 Whisk the dressing ingredients together in a small bowl. Transfer half the dressing (about 4 tablespoons) to another bowl. If time allows, refrigerate the bowl, covered, for up to 1 hour (if the dressing is chilled, the cucumber salad will be crisper). Set aside the remaining dressing in the small bowl for the swordfish.

2 Prepare the grill for grilling/direct cooking over high heat (230–290°C/450–550°F).

3 Add the cucumber, 1 tablespoon rapeseed oil and the coriander to the chilled dressing. Toss to coat thoroughly with the dressing.

4 Lightly brush the swordfish steaks on both sides with rapeseed oil and season evenly with the salt and pepper. Grill the steaks over *grilling/direct high heat*, with the lid closed, for 2 minutes without moving them, then turn the steaks and continue cooking for 2–3 minutes more, until the flesh is just opaque in the centre but still juicy. Swordfish dries out quickly, so be careful not to overcook it. Remove the fish from the grill and let rest for about 2 minutes. Transfer the fish to serving plates and mound some of the cucumber salad on the side. Spoon a little of the reserved dressing over the top of each steak and serve immediately.

DIJON AND GARLIC SWORDFISH KEBABS
WITH LEMON VINAIGRETTE

SERVES: 4 | PREP TIME: 20 minutes | MARINATING TIME: 30 minutes | GRILLING TIME: 6–8 minutes
SPECIAL EQUIPMENT: 8 metal or bamboo skewers

MARINADE

3 tablespoons Dijon mustard
Grated zest of 1 lemon
2 teaspoons chopped fresh rosemary
2 garlic cloves, finely chopped or crushed
¾ teaspoon sea salt
¼ teaspoon freshly ground black pepper

Extra-virgin olive oil
4 swordfish steaks, each about 250 g/8 oz and
   2.5 cm/1 inch thick, cut into 2.5-cm/1-inch pieces
2 peppers, each about 250 g/8 oz, preferably
   1 red and 1 green, cut into 2.5-cm/1-inch squares

VINAIGRETTE

2 tablespoons fresh lemon juice
1 teaspoon Dijon mustard
½ teaspoon sea salt
¼ teaspoon freshly ground black pepper

250 g/8 oz cooked rice

1 If using bamboo skewers, soak them in water for at least 30 minutes.

2 Prepare the grill for grilling/direct cooking over medium heat (180–230°C/350–450°F).

3 In a bowl whisk the marinade ingredients together, including 4 tablespoons oil. Place the swordfish pieces in the bowl, turn to coat, cover and marinate at room temperature for 30 minutes. In another bowl toss the pepper squares with 2 teaspoons oil.

4 Whisk the vinaigrette ingredients together, including 4 tablespoons oil.

5 Thread the swordfish and the peppers alternately on to the skewers. Discard any remaining marinade. Grill the kebabs over *grilling/direct medium heat* for 6–8 minutes, with the lid closed, until the swordfish is just opaque in the centre but still juicy, turning several times. Remove from the grill. Divide the rice among four plates and place two kebabs on each serving of rice. Drizzle the swordfish and the rice with the vinaigrette and serve immediately.

TIP Mild and versatile, swordfish has a firm, meaty flesh that absorbs marinades nicely. The texture also holds up well on kebabs, but be careful about adding a lot of other ingredients to the skewers. Cubes of swordfish and squares of pepper are perfectly grilled in the same amount of time, but if you try adding a lot of other seafood or vegetables you are bound to get some pieces that are either undercooked or overcooked. When in doubt, separate the ingredients so that each skewer has only one ingredient that you have cut into even pieces. That way, every ingredient can get just the right time and temperature it needs.

FISH TACOS
WITH PINEAPPLE AND RADISH SALSA

SERVES: 4 | PREP TIME: 30 minutes | GRILLING TIME: 7–9 minutes

SALSA
300 g/10 oz fresh pineapple, diced
8 radishes, grated on the large holes of a box grater
4 tablespoons fresh lime juice
1 serrano chilli, deseeded and finely chopped, or to taste
2 tablespoons finely chopped fresh chives
½ teaspoon ground cumin
½ teaspoon sea salt

PASTE
2 tablespoons extra-virgin olive oil
2 tablespoons prepared chilli seasoning
2 teaspoons ground cumin

4 skinless cod fillets, each about 175 g/6 oz and
    1 cm/½ inch thick
8 corn tortillas (15 cm/6 inches)

1 Prepare the grill for grilling/direct cooking over high heat (230–290°C/350–450°F).

2 Combine the salsa ingredients.

3 Whisk the paste ingredients together. Spread the paste evenly on both sides of the cod fillets.

4 Wrap four tortillas in each of two foil packets.

5 Grill the fish over *grilling/direct high heat* for 4 minutes, with the lid closed. Using a metal spatula, turn the fillets over and continue cooking for 2–4 minutes more, until the flesh barely begins to flake when poked with the tip of a knife. Remove from the grill. Break the fish into large chunks.

6 Warm the tortillas over *grilling/direct high heat* for about 1 minute, turning once. Remove from the grill and divide the tortillas among four serving plates. Fill the tortillas with cod and salsa and serve immediately.

GRIDDLED COD
WITH SWEET PICKLE TARTARE SAUCE

SERVES: 4 | PREP TIME: 10 minutes | GRILLING TIME: about 6 minutes | SPECIAL EQUIPMENT: grill-proof griddle or cast-iron frying pan

SAUCE
150 ml/¼ pint mayonnaise
3 tablespoons sweet pickle (cucumber) relish
2 tablespoons finely chopped shallots
1 tablespoon capers, rinsed, drained and chopped
2 teaspoons fresh lemon juice
¼ teaspoon dried tarragon

4 skinless cod fillets, each 175–200 g/6–7 oz and
    1.5 cm/¾ inch thick
Extra-virgin olive oil
½ teaspoon sea salt
¼ teaspoon freshly ground black pepper

1 Prepare the grill for grilling/direct cooking over high heat (230–290°C/350–450°F) and preheat a grill-proof griddle for about 10 minutes.

2 Whisk the sauce ingredients together. Cover and refrigerate until ready to use.

3 Lightly brush both sides of the fish with oil and season evenly with the salt and pepper. Place the fillets on the griddle and cook over *grilling/direct high heat* for about 6 minutes, with the lid closed, until the fish just begins to flake when poked with the tip of a knife, carefully turning with a spatula after 4 minutes. Remove the fillets from the griddle and serve warm with the tartare sauce.

> **TIP** Using a grill-proof griddle on your grill is a great way to get a nice crust on fish fillets. One of the keys to success when making this dish is allowing the griddle plenty of time to preheat. Once it is thoroughly heated, cook the fish a little longer on the first side than on the second side.

CRISPY TROUT
WITH HERB SALAD AND SHALLOT-LEMON VINAIGRETTE

SERVES: 4 | PREP TIME: **30 minutes** | GRILLING TIME: **about 10 minutes**

VINAIGRETTE
50 g/2 oz shallots, finely chopped
2½ tablespoons white balsamic vinegar
2 teaspoons finely grated lemon zest
2 tablespoons fresh lemon juice
125 ml/4 fl oz extra-virgin olive oil
1 teaspoon sea salt
¾ teaspoon freshly ground black pepper
¾ teaspoon granulated sugar

75 g/3 oz fresh basil
50 g/2 oz fresh flat-leaf parsley
75 g/3 oz fresh mint
4 tablespoons small fresh dill sprigs
50 g/2 oz panko breadcrumbs
1 tablespoon finely grated lemon zest
4 large trout fillets (with skin), each 175–250 g/6–8 oz
2 teaspoons ground fennel
1 teaspoon sea salt
1 teaspoon freshly ground black pepper

1 Whisk the shallots, vinegar, lemon zest and lemon juice. Add the oil in a steady stream, whisking constantly to emulsify. Whisk in the salt, pepper and sugar.

2 Combine the basil, parsley, mint and dill. Cover and refrigerate while preparing the trout.

3 Prepare the grill for roasting/indirect cooking over high heat (230–290°C/350–450°F).

4 Combine the breadcrumbs and the lemon zest. Coat the flesh side of each trout fillet with 1 tablespoon of the vinaigrette and season evenly with the fennel, salt and pepper. Press the breadcrumb mixture evenly on to the flesh side of each fillet.

5 Grill the fillets, skin side down, over *roasting/indirect high heat* for about 10 minutes, with the lid closed, until the flesh is opaque in the centre, the skin is lightly charred and the breadcrumbs are crisp and golden brown (do not turn). Transfer the fish to serving plates.

6 Toss the herb salad with enough of the vinaigrette to coat lightly. Divide the herb salad among the serving plates, spoon any remaining vinaigrette over the fish and serve immediately.

TROUT FILLETS
WITH WATERMELON SALSA

SERVES: 6 | PREP TIME: 30 minutes | GRILLING TIME: about 10 minutes

125 g/4 oz fresh basil leaves
250 g/8 fl oz extra-virgin olive oil

SALSA
500 g/1 lb seedless watermelon, finely diced
2 tablespoons finely chopped shallots
2 tablespoons finely chopped fresh mint
1 tablespoon balsamic vinegar
¼ teaspoon sea salt
½ teaspoon coarsely ground black pepper

6 large trout fillets (with skin), each 175–250 g/6–8 oz

1 Prepare a bowl of iced water and spread kitchen paper on a work surface. Bring a large saucepan of water to the boil over a high heat. Add the basil leaves to the saucepan and blanch for 10 seconds. Using a slotted spoon, transfer the leaves to the iced water to stop them from cooking. Using your hands, gently squeeze the basil to remove any excess water, place them on the kitchen paper and blot dry.

2 In a food processor or blender combine the basil leaves and the oil and purée until smooth. Transfer to a small covered container. (The basil oil can be kept for up to 2 weeks, covered, in the refrigerator. Bring to room temperature before using.)

3 Prepare the grill for roasting/indirect cooking over high heat (230–290°C/350–450°F).

4 Gently combine the salsa ingredients.

5 Brush 1 tablespoon of the basil oil on the flesh side of each trout fillet. Grill the fillets, skin side down, over *roasting/indirect high heat* for about 10 minutes, with the lid closed, until the flesh is opaque in the centre and the skin is lightly charred (do not turn). Transfer the fish to serving plates. Serve warm with the salsa and a drizzle of the basil oil over each fillet.

VEGETABLES & SIDES

GRILLING VEGETABLES

TYPE	THICKNESS / SIZE	APPROXIMATE GRILLING TIME
Artichoke hearts	whole	**14–18 minutes:** boil 10–12 minutes; cut in half and grill 4–6 minutes grilling/direct medium heat
Asparagus	1-cm/½-inch diameter	**6–8 minutes** grilling/direct medium heat
Beetroot (175 g/6 oz)	whole	**1–1½ hours** roasting/indirect medium heat
Pepper	whole	**10–12 minutes** grilling/direct medium heat
Carrot	2.5-cm/1-inch diameter	**7–11 minutes:** boil 4–6 minutes, grill 3–5 minutes grilling/direct high heat
Corn, leaves removed		**10–15 minutes** grilling/direct medium heat
Corn, leaves intact		**20–30 minutes** grilling/direct medium heat
Aubergine	1-cm/½-inch slices	**8–10 minutes** grilling/direct medium heat
Garlic	whole	**45 minutes–1 hour** roasting/indirect medium heat
Mushroom, button or shiitake		**8–10 minutes** grilling/direct medium heat
Mushroom, portobello		**8–12 minutes** grilling/direct medium heat
Onion	halved	**35–40 minutes** roasting/indirect medium heat
	1-cm/½-inch slices	**8–12 minutes** grilling/direct medium heat
Potato, new	halved	**15–20 minutes** grilling/direct medium heat
Potato, baking	whole	**45 minutes–1 hour** roasting/indirect medium heat
	1-cm/½-inch slices	**9–11 minutes** grilling/direct medium heat
Potato, sweet	whole	**45 minutes–1 hour** roasting/indirect high heat
	1-cm/½-inch slices	**12–15 minutes** grilling/direct medium heat
Spring onion	whole	**3–4 minutes** grilling/direct medium heat
Squash (750 g/1½ lbs)	halved	**40 minutes–1 hour** roasting/indirect medium heat
Tomato, garden or plum	whole	**8–10 minutes** grilling/direct medium heat
	halved	**6–8 minutes** grilling/direct medium heat
Courgette	1-cm/½-inch slices	**4–6 minutes** grilling/direct medium heat

Just about everything from artichoke hearts to courgettes tend to cook best over grilling/direct medium heat. The temperature on the grill's thermometer should be somewhere between 180 and 230°C/350° and 450°F.

MEXICAN-STYLE CORN ON THE COB

SERVES: 4 | PREP TIME: 10 minutes | GRILLING TIME: 10–15 minutes

SPREAD
3 tablespoons mayonnaise
1–2 tablespoons soured cream
1 tablespoon fresh lime juice

TOPPING
3 tablespoons grated Cotija or Parmesan cheese
¾ teaspoon prepared chilli seasoning
¼ teaspoon chipotle chilli powder

4 fresh corn cobs, outer leaves and silk removed

1 Prepare the grill for grilling/direct cooking over medium heat (180–230°C/350–450°F).

2 In a small bowl combine the spread ingredients. In another bowl combine the topping ingredients.

3 Grill the corn over *grilling/direct medium heat* for 10–15 minutes, with the lid closed, until the kernels are browned in spots and tender, turning occasionally.

4 Remove from the grill, brush the corn all over with the spread and then season evenly with the topping. Serve right away.

Try the recipe with butter and lime juice instead of the spread. Here's how:

In a small bowl combine 65 g/2½ oz melted unsalted butter with 1 tablespoon fresh lime juice. Lightly brush the corn all over with about half the butter mixture. Grill the corn as directed in step 3, above. Remove from the grill and brush the corn all over with the remaining butter mixture. Sprinkle the corn evenly with the topping.

CORN ON THE COB

It's summer's sweetest gift – a crunchy, juicy, silk-wrapped side dish often more celebrated than the main course. And just when you think it can't get any better, you introduce it to the grill.

This grain-in-vegetable's-clothing is naturally sweet, thanks to its abundance of the plant-based sugar dextrose. The starchy compound gives corn its sublime flavour, but also its potential to burn. Luckily, fresh corn needs only a few minutes over a fire to achieve perfection.

There are several great methods for grilling corn. The first two call for pulling the leaves back but not off, stripping off the silk, replacing the leaves, and then securing them shut with either a piece of kitchen string or a sliver of leaf. Soak the cobs in their leaves in cold water (optional), and then do one of two things: place them over grilling/direct medium heat for 20–30 minutes with the lid closed, or nestle them in the hot embers of a charcoal fire for about 10 minutes. The latter method requires frequent turning and undivided attention, but the kernels caramelize rather than steam, producing that coveted sweet-savoury flavour.

The third method happens to be our favourite (and the easiest). Remove the silk and leaves, lightly oil the cobs and place over a direct fire for 10–15 minutes with the lid closed. A tasty, caramelized char dapples the kernels, thanks to direct exposure to the heat. Beyond tasting fantastic, it looks impressive, and your guests aren't having to remove the leaves from a piping hot corn over their dinner.

A little butter and salt is plenty of adornment, but we love the style of street vendors in Mexico: with a squeeze of lime and a sprinkle of chilli powder.

ROASTED CORN AND RED PEPPER SALAD

SERVES: 4–6 | PREP TIME: 20 minutes | GRILLING TIME: 14–17 minutes

40 g/1½ oz unsalted butter, melted
1 tablespoon finely chopped fresh basil
⅛ teaspoon hot pepper sauce or ground cayenne pepper
2 fresh corn cobs, outer leaves and silk removed
2 large red peppers
3 tablespoons extra-virgin olive oil
4 teaspoons fresh lime juice
1 tablespoon mayonnaise
1½ teaspoons spicy brown mustard
125 g/4 oz green cabbage, roughly chopped
50 g/2 oz baby rocket
40 g/1½ oz fresh basil
4 spring onions, finely chopped (white and light green parts only)
Sea salt
Freshly ground black pepper

1 Prepare the grill for grilling/direct cooking over high heat (230–290°C/450–550°F).

2 Whisk the butter, chopped basil, hot pepper sauce, ¼ teaspoon salt and ⅛ teaspoon pepper. Place both corn cobs on one sheet of aluminium foil, about 37 cm/ 15 inches long, and brush the corn all over generously with the butter mixture. Wrap up the corn, crimping the edges of the foil tightly to trap the steam and prevent the parcel from leaking.

3 Grill the corn parcel and the peppers over *grilling/direct high heat* for 10–12 minutes, with the lid closed, until the peppers are blackened and blistered all over, turning occasionally. Remove the corn parcel from the grill after 10 minutes. Put the peppers in a bowl and cover with clingfilm to trap the steam. Let stand for about 10 minutes. Meanwhile, carefully unwrap the corn and return to the grill over *grilling/direct high heat* for 4–5 minutes until browned in spots and tender. Remove from the grill.

4 When the peppers are cool enough to handle, peel away and discard the charred skin. Cut off and discard the stalks and seeds, then cut the peppers into 5-mm/¼-inch dice. Cut the kernels off the cobs into a large bowl.

5 To the bowl with the corn, add the oil, lime juice, mayonnaise, mustard, ¼ teaspoon salt and ¼ teaspoon pepper. Toss to combine evenly. Fold in the red peppers, cabbage, rocket, basil and spring onions. Serve warm or at room temperature.

SUMMER CORN, TOMATO AND AVOCADO SALAD

SERVES: 4 | PREP TIME: 15 minutes | GRILLING TIME: 10–15 minutes

2 fresh corn cobs, outer leaves and silk removed
Extra-virgin olive oil
2 tablespoons fresh lime juice
½ teaspoon ground cumin
1 large avocado, cut into 1-cm/½-inch dice
375 g/12 oz cherry tomatoes, halved
1 red onion, finely chopped
4 tablespoons chopped fresh flat-leaf parsley
Sea salt
Freshly ground black pepper

1 Prepare the grill for grilling/direct cooking over medium heat (180–230°C/350–450°F).

2 Brush the corn all over with oil and lightly season with salt. Grill over *grilling/direct medium heat* for 10–15 minutes, with the lid closed, until browned in spots and tender, turning occasionally. Remove from the grill. When the corn is cool enough to handle, cut the kernels from the cobs into a large bowl.

3 Whisk 3 tablespoons oil, the lime juice, cumin, ½ teaspoon salt and ¼ teaspoon pepper. Set the dressing aside.

4 To the bowl with the corn, add the avocado, tomatoes, onion and parsley. Pour the dressing on top. Toss gently to combine and season with more salt and pepper, if desired. Serve immediately.

TIP This versatile salad can be varied in many ways. Try replacing the parsley with coriander and serving it as a salsa alongside chicken or fish. For a more substantial salad, spoon the vegetables over a bed of mixed salad leaves. Select a firm but ripe avocado for this recipe, so that the pieces will maintain their shape when tossed with the other ingredients.

CHARRED CARROT SALAD
WITH SPINACH AND PARMESAN

SERVES: 6 | PREP TIME: 15 minutes | MARINATING TIME: 30 minutes–2 hours | GRILLING TIME: 8–10 minutes
SPECIAL EQUIPMENT: perforated grill pan

750 g/1½ lb carrots, peeled and cut diagonally
   into slices about 5 cm/2 inches long and
   1 cm/½ inch thick
3 tablespoons extra-virgin olive oil
1 teaspoon Dijon mustard
3 tablespoons red wine vinegar
175 g/6 oz fresh baby spinach leaves
2 tablespoons chopped fresh chives
50 g/2 oz Parmesan cheese, shaved into strips with a
   vegetable peeler
Sea salt
Freshly ground black pepper

1 Toss the carrots with 1 tablespoon of the oil. Lightly season with salt and pepper and set aside at room temperature for at least 30 minutes or up to 2 hours.

2 Prepare the grill for grilling/direct cooking over medium heat (180–230°C/350–450°F) and preheat a perforated grill pan.

3 Remove the carrots from the bowl and let the excess oil drip back into the bowl. Spread the carrots in a single layer on the grill pan and grill over *grilling/direct medium heat* for 8–10 minutes, with the lid closed, until crisp-tender and lightly charred, turning once or twice. Remove from the grill.

4 In a small bowl whisk the mustard and the vinegar. Add the remaining 2 tablespoons oil in a steady stream, whisking constantly to emulsify. Season with salt and pepper.

5 Put the spinach, chives and carrots in a bowl and toss with the vinaigrette. Top the salad with the cheese and serve immediately.

TIP To make the salad a little more complex, toss in a handful of pine nuts or toasted walnuts.

ROASTED BEETROOT
WITH ROCKET, GOATS' CHEESE AND PISTACHIOS

SERVES: 6 | PREP TIME: 20 minutes | GRILLING TIME: 45 minutes–1 hour

6 golden or red beetroots, 750 g–1 kg/1½–2 lb total,
    leafy tops and root ends removed
Extra-virgin olive oil

DRESSING
2 tablespoons fresh lemon juice
1 tablespoon red wine vinegar
1 teaspoon honey
½ teaspoon sea salt
½ teaspoon freshly ground black pepper

150 g/5 oz baby rocket
125 g/2 oz goats' cheese, crumbled
3 tablespoons roughly chopped fresh tarragon leaves
50 g/2 oz shelled and roasted salted pistachios

We love homemade salad dressing, but preparing it does pose a too-many-tasks-not-enough-hands problem. By wrapping a tea towel around the base of the bowl, it stays put while you whisk with one hand and pour the oil with the other. Problem solved.

1 Prepare the grill for roasting/indirect cooking over medium heat (180–230°C/350–450°F).

2 Scrub the beetroots under cold water, and then lightly brush them all over with oil. Grill them over *roasting/indirect medium heat* for 45 minutes–1 hour, with the lid closed, until they are tender but not too soft when pierced with the tip of a knife, turning once or twice. Remove from the grill and put them in a bowl. Cover with clingfilm and let stand at room temperature until cool enough to handle.

3 Whisk the dressing ingredients together. Add 4 tablespoons oil in a steady stream, whisking constantly to emulsify. Set aside.

4 Remove the beetroots from the bowl and, using a sharp paring knife, cut off the stalk ends and remove the peel. Cut each beetroot in half horizontally, and then cut each half into quarters or eighths. Put the beetroots in a bowl, drizzle with 4 tablespoons of the dressing and gently toss to coat. Put the rocket in another bowl, drizzle with enough of the remaining dressing to coat the leaves very lightly and toss. Arrange the rocket on a serving plate or on individual plates. Spoon the beetroots over the rocket. Top with the goats' cheese, tarragon and pistachios. Serve immediately.

GRILLED VEGETABLE GRATIN
WITH RICOTTA AND BASIL

SERVES: 4–6 | PREP TIME: 45 minutes | GRILLING TIME: 43–52 minutes
SPECIAL EQUIPMENT: 18-by-25-cm/7-by-10-inch or 20-cm/8-inch-square grill-proof baking dish or 23-cm/9-inch cast-iron frying pan

2 large red peppers
2 small aubergines, about 500 g/1 lb total, ends trimmed,
    cut crossways into 5-mm/¼-inch slices
Extra-virgin olive oil
3 green courgettes, about 500 g/1 lb total, cut crossways into
    5-mm/¼-inch slices
3 yellow courgettes, about 500 g/1 lb total, cut crossways
    into 5-mm/¼-inch slices
1 large egg
375 g/12 oz full-fat ricotta cheese
6 tablespoons chopped fresh basil
1 garlic clove, finely chopped or crushed
50 g/2 oz Parmesan cheese, finely grated
Sea salt
Freshly ground black pepper

1 Prepare the grill for grilling/direct and roasting/indirect cooking over medium heat (180–230°C/350–450°F).

2 Grill the peppers over *grilling/direct medium heat* for 10–12 minutes, with the lid closed, until blackened and blistered all over, turning occasionally. Put the peppers in a bowl and cover with clingfilm to trap the steam. Let stand for about 10 minutes. Remove the peppers from the bowl and peel away and discard the charred skin. Cut off and discard the stalks and seeds, and cut each pepper into four pieces.

3 Generously brush the aubergines on both sides with oil. Lightly brush the courgettes on both sides with oil. Season the vegetables evenly with ½ teaspoon salt and ¼ teaspoon pepper. Grill the vegetables over *grilling/ direct medium heat* for 8–10 minutes, with the lid closed, until nicely marked and tender but not too soft, for the aubergines, and 4–6 minutes for the courgettes, turning once or twice.

4 Lightly oil an 18-by-25-cm/7-by-10-inch grill-proof baking dish or frying pan. In a bowl whisk the egg, ricotta, 4 tablespoons of the basil, the garlic, ½ teaspoon salt and ½ teaspoon pepper. Using half the vegetables, arrange a layer of aubergines, then courgettes, then peppers, overlapping the slices slightly. Spread half the ricotta mixture over the vegetables in an even layer and top with half the cheese. Repeat with the remaining vegetables, ricotta mixture and cheese. Cook over *roasting/indirect medium heat* for 25–30 minutes, with the lid closed, until the cheese is melted and bubbly, rotating the dish occasionally. Remove from the grill and let cool slightly. Serve warm or at room temperature, garnished with the remaining basil.

> **TIP** Grilled summer vegetables are the stars of this cheesy gratin that's redolent of fresh basil. Choose courgettes and aubergines with similar diameters for the prettiest dish. If the aubergines are wider, cut each slice in half or in quarters after grilling.

GLOBE AUBERGINE
WITH SUN-DRIED TOMATO VINAIGRETTE

SERVES: 4 | PREP TIME: 15 minutes | GRILLING TIME: 8–10 minutes

VINAIGRETTE
4 sun-dried tomato halves packed in oil,
   drained and finely chopped
2 tablespoons balsamic vinegar
1 tablespoon finely chopped shallots
1 teaspoon dried oregano
1 teaspoon honey

Extra-virgin olive oil
2 large rounded aubergines, each about 500 g/1 lb,
   ends trimmed
Sea salt
Freshly ground black pepper

1 Prepare the grill for grilling/direct cooking over medium heat (180–230°C/350–450°F).

2 Whisk the vinaigrette ingredients, including ¼ teaspoon salt and ⅛ teaspoon pepper. Add 5 tablespoons oil in a steady stream, whisking constantly to emulsify. Set aside.

3 Cut the aubergines crossways into 1-cm/½-inch slices. Brush both sides of each slice with oil and season evenly with ¼ teaspoon salt and ¼ teaspoon pepper. Grill over *grilling/direct medium heat* for 8–10 minutes, with the lid closed, until well marked and tender, turning once or twice. Place the slices on a serving plate. Immediately spoon the vinaigrette over the top. Serve warm or at room temperature.

STUFFED PEPPERS
WITH BEEF, RICE AND FETA

SERVES: 4; 8 as a side dish | PREP TIME: 40 minutes | GRILLING TIME: 20–30 minutes

Extra-virgin olive oil
500 g/1 lb minced beef (80% lean)
2 onions, finely chopped
3 large garlic cloves, finely chopped or crushed
2 plum tomatoes, deseeded and finely diced
1 jalapeño chilli, deseeded and finely chopped
4 tablespoons tomato purée
1 teaspoon sea salt
1 teaspoon paprika
1 teaspoon ground cumin
½ teaspoon freshly ground black pepper
½ teaspoon ground coriander
275 g/9 oz steamed long- or medium-grain white rice
175 g/6 oz feta cheese, crumbled
6 tablespoons finely chopped fresh flat-leaf parsley
4 tablespoons finely chopped fresh mint
4 large red peppers, each cut in half lengthways, seeds and ribs removed, stalks left on

1 Warm 1 tablespoon oil in a large frying pan over a medium heat. Crumble the mince into the frying pan and cook for 6–8 minutes until browned, stirring to break up any clumps. Using a slotted spoon, transfer to a bowl. Pour off the fat from the pan and wipe clean. Add 1 tablespoon oil and the onions to the pan and sauté over a medium heat for 5–7 minutes until softened. Add the garlic, tomatoes and chilli and cook for 1 minute, stirring frequently. Return the meat to the frying pan. Add the tomato purée, salt, paprika, cumin, pepper and coriander. Cook for about 1 minute, until the flavours are blended, stirring often. Remove from the heat. Gently stir in the rice, 125 g/4 oz of the feta, 4 tablespoons of the parsley and the mint.

2 Prepare the grill for roasting/indirect cooking over medium heat (180–230°C/350–450°F).

3 Firmly pack the filling into the pepper halves, mounding it about 1 cm/½ inch above the rim. Top evenly with the remaining 50 g/2 oz feta. Grill the stuffed peppers over *roasting/indirect medium heat* for 20–30 minutes, with the lid closed, until the peppers are tender and the filling is hot. Transfer to a serving plate. Drizzle the peppers with a little oil and garnish with the remaining parsley. Serve warm.

CHARRED ASPARAGUS
WITH BASIL-LIME DIPPING SAUCE

SERVES: 4–6 | PREP TIME: 15 minutes | GRILLING TIME: 6–8 minutes

SAUCE
250 ml/8 fl oz mayonnaise
2 tablespoons finely chopped fresh basil
Finely grated zest of 1 lime
2 teaspoons fresh lime juice
1 garlic clove, finely chopped or crushed
⅛ teaspoon ground cayenne pepper

1 kg/2 lb asparagus
2 tablespoons extra-virgin olive oil
½ teaspoon sea salt
½ teaspoon freshly ground black pepper

1 Whisk the sauce ingredients together. Transfer to a small serving bowl and refrigerate, covered, until ready to serve.

2 Prepare the grill for grilling/direct cooking over medium heat (180–230°C/350–450°F).

3 Remove and discard the tough bottom of each asparagus spear by grasping each end and bending it gently until it snaps at its natural point of tenderness, usually about two-thirds of the way down the spear. Brush the asparagus with the oil and season evenly with the salt and pepper.

4 Grill the asparagus over *grilling/direct medium heat* for 6–8 minutes, with the lid closed, until nicely marked and crisp-tender, rolling occasionally. Remove from the grill and serve warm with the sauce.

GRILLED POTATO PLANKS
WITH LEMON AIOLI

SERVES: 6–8 | PREP TIME: 15 minutes | GRILLING TIME: 9–11 minutes

AIOLI
250 ml/8 fl oz mayonnaise
2 tablespoons fresh lemon juice
1 tablespoon finely chopped garlic

6 tablespoons extra-virgin olive oil
1 teaspoon finely chopped garlic
6 baking potatoes, each about 175 g/6 oz, unpeeled,
    scrubbed and cut lengthways into 1-cm/½-inch planks
1 tablespoon finely chopped fresh flat-leaf parsley
Sea salt
Freshly ground black pepper

1 Prepare the grill for grilling/direct cooking over medium heat (180–230°C/350–450°F).

2 Combine the aioli ingredients, including ⅛ teaspoon pepper. Set aside at room temperature for about 15 minutes to allow the flavours to blend. Taste and add salt, if liked.

3 Stir together the oil and the garlic. Brush the potato planks on both sides with the garlic oil, making sure to distribute the garlic bits evenly, and season with ½ teaspoon salt and ½ teaspoon pepper.

4 Grill the potato planks over *grilling/direct medium heat* for 9–11 minutes, with the lid closed, until they are tender when pierced with a fork, turning once after 5–6 minutes. If some of the potatoes start to become too dark before they are done, move them to a cooler part of the grill. Remove from the grill, top with the parsley and serve warm with the lemon aioli.

ROASTED POTATOES
STUFFED WITH MUSHROOMS AND CHEDDAR CHEESE

SERVES: 4; 8 as a side dish | PREP TIME: 20 minutes | GRILLING TIME: 40–45 minutes

4 large baking potatoes, each about 250 g/8 oz, unpeeled, scrubbed, halved horizontally and pierced with a fork
250 g/8 oz large button mushrooms, stalks removed
1 tablespoon extra-virgin olive oil
2 spring onions, ends trimmed, finely chopped (dark green tops reserved)
125 ml/4 fl oz soured cream
125 g/4 oz mature Cheddar cheese, grated
Sea salt
Freshly ground black pepper

1 Prepare the grill for roasting/indirect cooking over medium heat (180–230°C/350–450°F).

2 Brush the potato halves and the mushrooms all over with the oil. Grill the potato halves over *roasting/indirect medium heat* for 25–30 minutes, with the lid closed, until they are just tender when pierced with a fork, turning occasionally. At the same time, grill the mushrooms over *roasting/indirect medium heat* for about 15 minutes until tender, turning once. Remove from the grill as they are done.

3 When cool enough to handle, scoop out the interior of each potato half, leaving a shell about 1 cm/½ inch thick. Place the potato flesh in a medium bowl and coarsely mash with a fork. Add the white and light green parts of the spring onions, the soured cream and the cheese. Roughly chop the mushrooms, add to the potato mixture, and stir to combine. Season with salt and pepper. Stuff each of the potato skins with an equal amount of the potato mixture. (At this point the potatoes can be covered loosely with clingfilm and kept at room temperature for up to 2 hours.)

4 Grill the stuffed potatoes over *roasting/indirect medium heat* for about 15 minutes, with the lid closed, until the cheese is melted and the potatoes are heated through. Garnish with the reserved dark green spring onion tops and serve right away.

SPANISH FRITTATA
WITH BABY POTATOES AND PEPPERS

SERVES: 4; 8 as a side dish | PREP TIME: 30 minutes | GRILLING TIME: 25–31 minutes
SPECIAL EQUIPMENT: 23-cm/9-inch cast-iron frying pan

8 large eggs
2 tablespoons extra-virgin olive oil
250 g/8 oz baby new potatoes, unpeeled, scrubbed and
    thinly sliced
½ large red onion, thinly sliced
1 red pepper, cut into thin strips
2 teaspoons smoked paprika
150 g/6 oz frozen petits pois peas, thawed
2 garlic cloves, finely chopped or crushed
65 g/2½ oz soft garlic-and-herb cheese, broken into
    small pieces
2 tablespoons finely chopped fresh flat-leaf parsley
2 tablespoons capers, rinsed and drained
Sea salt
Freshly ground black pepper

1 Prepare the grill for grilling/direct cooking over medium heat (180–230°C/350–450°F) and preheat a 23-cm/9-inch cast-iron frying pan.

2 Whisk the eggs with ½ teaspoon salt and ¼ teaspoon black pepper.

3 Add the oil to the frying pan and then add the potatoes, onion and pepper. Cook over *grilling/direct medium heat* for 1 minute, with the lid closed, stirring occasionally. Season evenly with 1 teaspoon salt, ½ teaspoon pepper and 1½ teaspoons of the paprika and stir to combine. Continue cooking for 13–15 minutes, with the lid closed, until the potatoes are tender when pierced with a fork and the vegetables are lightly browned, stirring frequently so that the vegetables cook evenly and don't stick to the pan. Add the peas and the garlic and cook for 1–2 minutes more.

4 Spread the vegetables evenly in the pan. Pour the eggs on top of the vegetables and then add the cheese. Cook over *grilling/direct medium heat* for 10–13 minutes, with the lid closed, until the eggs are puffed and just firm in the centre, lowering the heat if needed to prevent the frittata from getting too brown on the bottom. Wearing insulated barbecue mitts or oven gloves, remove the frying pan from the grill. Top evenly with the parsley, the remaining ½ teaspoon paprika and the capers. Serve the frittata from the pan, either warm or at room temperature.

TIP The Italian version of an omelette, a frittata, is usually made in a frying pan on top of the stove and then finished in the oven to lightly brown the eggs on the top. This version, which is cooked in a frying pan on the grill from beginning to end, gets its Spanish flavour from the combination of potatoes, peppers, smoked paprika and capers. It is substantial enough to serve four as a simple supper, with two generous wedges per person. A green salad tossed with a sherry vinaigrette and some grilled Continental bread would be fitting side dishes.

SPICED SWEET POTATO FRIES
WITH CHILLI SOURED CREAM

SERVES: 4 | PREP TIME: **15** minutes | GRILLING TIME: **12–15** minutes | SPECIAL EQUIPMENT: perforated grill pan

CHILLI SOURED CREAM

250 ml/8 fl oz soured cream
2 tablespoons finely chopped fresh coriander
1 tablespoon fresh lime juice
1 teaspoon hot chilli-garlic sauce
1 large garlic clove, finely chopped
1 teaspoon sea salt

SEASONING

2 teaspoons paprika
2 teaspoons sea salt
1 teaspoon freshly ground black pepper
1 teaspoon ground cumin
½ teaspoon ground coriander
½ teaspoon ground cayenne pepper, or to taste

2 sweet potatoes, each about 500 g/1 lb, peeled
2 tablespoons extra-virgin olive oil

1 Prepare the grill for grilling/direct cooking over medium heat (180–230°C/350–450°F) and preheat a perforated grill pan.

2 Whisk the chilli soured cream ingredients together.

3 Combine the seasoning ingredients. Scrub the sweet potatoes under cold water and then dry them with kitchen paper. Cut the potatoes into 10-by-1-by-1-cm/ 4-by-½-by-½-inch sticks. Toss the potatoes thoroughly with the oil and the seasoning.

4 Spread the potatoes in a single layer on the grill pan and grill over *grilling/direct medium heat* for 12–15 minutes, with the lid closed, until they are tender when pierced with a knife, turning occasionally to brown all sides. Remove from the grill and serve warm with the chilli soured cream.

SWEET POTATOES
WITH HONEY-CASHEW BUTTER

SERVES: 4–6 | PREP TIME: 10 minutes | GRILLING TIME: 45 minutes–1 hour

4 sweet potatoes, each about 250 g/8 oz
40 g/1½ oz unsalted butter, softened
1 tablespoon honey
40 g/1½ oz unsalted cashews, toasted and roughly chopped
½ teaspoon sea salt
¼ teaspoon chipotle chilli powder

1 Prepare the grill for roasting/indirect cooking over high heat (230–290°C/450–550°F).

2 Scrub the sweet potatoes under cold water, and then dry them with kitchen paper. Wrap the potatoes individually in sheets of aluminium foil. Grill over *roasting/indirect high heat* for 45 minutes–1 hour, with the lid closed, until they are soft when squeezed with a pair of tongs. Remove from the grill and let cool for about 5 minutes.

3 While the potatoes are grilling, make the honey-cashew butter. Using a rubber spatula, mash the butter and the honey together. Stir in the cashews, salt and chilli powder. Set aside.

4 Remove the potatoes from the foil, and then slip off and discard the skins. Cut the potatoes into 1-cm/½-inch slices, put in a serving bowl, and dollop the honey-cashew butter all over. Serve warm.

TIP Choose cylindrical potatoes of a similar size and thickness so they cook evenly.

SOUTHWEST GRILLED RED POTATO SALAD
WITH CHORIZO

SERVES: 4–6 | PREP TIME: 15 minutes | GRILLING TIME: 27–35 minutes | SPECIAL EQUIPMENT: perforated grill pan

1 large red onion, cut crossways into 1-cm/½-inch slices
1 large green pepper
Extra-virgin olive oil
2 fresh chorizo sausages or 3 hot Italian sausages, about 250 g/8 oz total
1 kg/2 lb red potatoes, 3–3.5 cm/1½–2 inches in diameter, unpeeled, scrubbed, each cut into quarters
Sea salt

DRESSING
4 tablespoons mayonnaise
2 tablespoons chopped fresh coriander
1 tablespoon fresh lime juice
¼ teaspoon prepared chilli seasoning
¼ teaspoon ground cumin
⅛ teaspoon chipotle chilli powder

1 Prepare the grill for grilling/direct cooking over medium heat (180–230°C/350–450°F).

2 Lightly brush the onion and the pepper all over with oil. Grill the onion, pepper and sausages over *grilling/ direct medium heat* for 12–15 minutes, with the lid closed, until the onions are tender, the pepper is blackened and blistered all over, and the sausages are fully cooked, turning occasionally. Remove the vegetables and the sausages from the grill. Place the pepper in a bowl and cover with clingfilm to trap the steam. Let stand for about 10 minutes. Preheat a perforated grill pan over grilling/direct medium heat for about 10 minutes.

3 Remove the pepper from the bowl and peel away and discard the charred skin, cut off the stalk and remove the seeds. Cut the pepper, onion and sausages into small pieces. Toss the potatoes with 2 tablespoons oil and ½ teaspoon salt.

4 Spread the potatoes in a single layer on the grill pan and grill over *grilling/direct medium heat* for 15–20 minutes, with the lid closed, until they are tender inside and crispy outside, turning occasionally. Meanwhile, combine the dressing ingredients.

5 Remove the potatoes from the grill. To the bowl with the dressing, add the potatoes, onion, pepper and sausages; toss to coat. Season with salt. Serve at room temperature.

BLACK BEAN BURGERS
WITH CHIPOTLE CREAM AND AVOCADO

SERVES: 4 | PREP TIME: 20 minutes | CHILLING TIME: 2–24 hours | GRILLING TIME: 8–10 minutes

BURGERS
Extra-virgin olive oil
1 large red onion, finely chopped
2 small red peppers, finely chopped
2 garlic cloves, finely chopped or crushed
2 cans (each 475 g/15 oz) black beans, rinsed, drained
    and patted dry
75 g/3 oz salted tortilla chips, crushed
1 large egg
1 canned chipotle chilli pepper in adobo sauce, finely
    chopped with 1 teaspoon of the adobo sauce
3 tablespoons chopped fresh coriander
1 tablespoon tomato purée
1 teaspoon ground cumin
½ teaspoon sea salt

CHIPOTLE CREAM
125 ml/4 fl oz soured cream
2 teaspoons adobo sauce from the canned chipotle chilli
Finely grated zest of ½ lime
1 teaspoon fresh lime juice

4 hamburger buns, split
1 large avocado, mashed
4 lettuce leaves
8 slices tomato

1 Warm 1 tablespoon oil in a nonstick frying pan over a
medium heat. Add the onion, peppers and garlic and
cook for 3–5 minutes until tender, stirring occasionally.
Add the black beans and cook for about 2 minutes just
until any excess moisture from the beans is evaporated,
stirring occasionally. Remove from the heat and let cool for
10 minutes. Transfer the bean mixture to a food processor.
Add the remaining ingredients and pulse 10–12 times until
the beans are coarsely puréed. Let stand for 5 minutes.
With wet hands, gently form four burgers, each about
10 cm/4 inchesin diameter and 1.5 cm/¾ inch thick. Place
on a greaseproof paper-lined roasting tray and cover with
clingfilm. Refrigerate for at least 2 hours or up to 24 hours
(If not, they will be too soft to turn on the grill.)

2 Mix the chipotle cream ingredients. Cover and refrigerate.

3 Prepare the grill for grilling/direct cooking over medium
heat (180–230°C/350–450°F). Brush the burgers on both
sides with oil. Grill over *grilling/direct medium heat* for
8–10 minutes, with the lid closed, until heated through,
turning once. During the last minute of grilling, toast the
buns, cut side down, over *grilling/direct heat*. Spread the top
bun halves with avocado. Top the bottom bun halves with
lettuce, tomato, a burger and chipotle cream. Serve warm.

SMOKY VEGETARIAN CHILLI
WITH PINTO BEANS

SERVES: 6 | PREP TIME: 30 minutes | GRILLING TIME: about 50 minutes
SPECIAL EQUIPMENT: 1 large handful mesquite wood chips, cast-iron casserole

3 courgettes, trimmed and cut in half lengthways
2 large Portobello mushrooms, stems and gills removed
Extra-virgin olive oil
3 fresh corn cobs, outer leaves and silk removed
3 large red peppers
3 white onions, finely chopped
2 garlic cloves, finely chopped or crushed
1 jalapeño chilli, deseeded and finely chopped
2 tablespoons smoked paprika
1½ teaspoons ground cumin
½ teaspoon chipotle chilli powder
875 g/1¾ lb canned Italian plum tomatoes in juice,
    roughly chopped, juice reserved
250 ml/8 fl oz tomato-vegetable juice
475 g/15-oz can pinto beans, rinsed and drained
Grated Cheddar cheese
Sea salt
Freshly ground black pepper

1 Soak the wood chips in water for at least 30 minutes. Prepare the grill for grilling/direct cooking over medium heat (180–230°C/350–450°F).

2 Brush the courgettes and the mushrooms on both sides with oil. Grill the courgettes, mushrooms, corn cobs and peppers over *grilling/direct medium heat*, with the lid closed, turning as needed. The courgettes will take 4–6 minutes, the mushrooms 6–8 minutes, the corn about 8 minutes and the peppers 10–12 minutes. Remove from the grill as they are done. Put the peppers in a bowl and cover with clingfilm to trap the steam. Let stand for about 10 minutes. Peel away and discard the charred skin from the peppers. Cut off and discard the stems and seeds. Cut the peppers, courgettes and mushrooms into 1-cm/½-inch dice. Cut the corn kernels off the cobs.

3 Warm 2 tablespoons oil in a large cast-iron casserole over *grilling/direct medium heat*. Add the onion, garlic and jalapeño and cook for about 3 minutes, with the lid closed, until the onion is softened. Stir in the paprika, cumin and chilli powder. Add the canned tomatoes and juice, the tomato-vegetable juice, courgettes, mushrooms, corn and peppers. Drain and add the wood chips to the charcoal or to the smoker box of a gas grill, following manufacturer's instructions. Simmer the chilli for about 30 minutes, uncovered, with the lid closed, until the juices are thickened, stirring occasionally. If it is cooking too quickly, move over roasting/indirect heat. During the last 5 minutes, stir in the beans and season. Serve warm, topped with cheese.

SPINACH AND RICOTTA CALZONES

SERVES: 4–6 | PREP TIME: 25 minutes | RISING TIME: 1½–1¾ hours | GRILLING TIME: 16–20 minutes
SPECIAL EQUIPMENT: pizza stone

DOUGH
375 g/12 oz plain flour, plus more as needed
Extra-virgin olive oil
1¾ teaspoons sea salt
1½ teaspoons fast-action dried yeast
250 ml/8 fl oz very warm water (46–49°C/115–120°F)

FILLING
1 courgette, ends trimmed, cut lengthways into 1-cm/
   ½-inch slices
175 g/6 oz fresh spinach, coarsely chopped
½ teaspoon garlic granules
150 g/6 oz ricotta cheese
50 g/2 oz Parmesan cheese, freshly grated
50 g/2 oz provolone cheese, grated
1 plum tomato, 125–150 g/4–5 oz, cored, seeded and chopped
4 tablespoons chopped fresh basil
½ teaspoon dried oregano
¼ teaspoon sea salt
¼ teaspoon freshly ground black pepper

Yellow cornmeal
Tomato sauce (optional)

1 In a food processor combine the flour, 1 tablespoon oil, the salt and the yeast. With the motor running, add the warm water through the feed tube to make a ball of dough that is soft but not sticky and rides on top of the blade (there will be some crumbles of dough, too). If the dough is too moist, dust with 1 tablespoon of flour. If it is too dry, sprinkle with 1 teaspoon water. Process briefly, check the dough again, and repeat until the dough is the correct texture.

2 Coat a bowl with oil. Shape the dough into a ball, put it in the bowl and turn to coat with the oil. Cover the bowl with clingfilm and let stand in a warm, draught-free place until the dough is doubled in volume, 1¼–1½ hours.

3 Prepare the grill for grilling/direct cooking over medium heat (180–230°C/350–450°F).

4 Brush the courgettes on both sides with 1 teaspoon oil and grill over *grilling/direct medium heat* for 4–6 minutes, with the lid closed, until grill marks appear and the courgettes are crisp-tender, turning once. Coarsely chop and put the pieces in a medium bowl. In a large sauté pan over a medium-high heat, warm 2 teaspoons of oil. Add the spinach and garlic granules and cook for 2–3 minutes until the spinach is wilted, stirring occasionally. Add the spinach and the remaining filling ingredients to the bowl with the courgettes, and stir to combine.

5 Turn the dough out on to a lightly floured work surface and divide it into four equal pieces. Shape each into a ball. Working with one ball of dough at a time, press it into a 10-cm/4-inch disc, then use a rolling pin to roll it into an 20-cm/8-inch round, dusting the work surface lightly with flour and turning the dough as needed. Repeat with the remaining dough balls. Loosely cover the rounds with clingfilm and allow them to stand for 10 minutes. During this resting time the gluten in the dough will relax, making the dough easier to work with. The dough rounds may also shrink slightly.

6 Preheat a pizza stone following the manufacturer's instructions for at least 15 minutes. Some stones need to be placed on a cold grill before they are heated. If this is the case, place the pizza stone on the grill when preheating it to cook the courgettes.

7 Sprinkle a large baking sheet with a light coating of cornmeal. Reroll one piece of dough, if necessary, so that it forms a 20-cm/8-inch round again. Place a quarter of the filling on half of the round, spreading it out but leaving a 1–1.5-cm/½–¾-inch border uncovered. Moisten the border with water and fold the unfilled half of the dough over the filling to make a half-moon shape. Lightly press on the top of the calzone to remove any air, then firmly twist and crimp the edges with your fingers to seal. Place the calzone on the baking sheet and repeat with the remaining dough and the remaining filling. Cover the calzones with clingfilm and let stand for 15–20 minutes until very slightly puffy.

8 Brush the tops and the crimped edges of the calzones with oil. Carefully place them on the pizza stone at least 2.5 cm/1 inch apart. Grill over *grilling/direct medium heat* for 12–14 minutes, with the lid closed, until the dough is lightly browned and crisp. Remove from the grill and immediately brush the calzones with more oil. Let stand for 3 minutes. Serve with tomato sauce, if using.

TIP The dough for this recipe, which is made using fast-action yeast and a food processor, couldn't be simpler, but 750 g/1½ lbs of prepared pizza dough could be substituted. If you like, have your favourite homemade or shop-bought tomato sauce warmed and ready for dipping.

BUTTERMILK-CHEDDAR CORN BREAD

SERVES: 8 | PREP TIME: 15 minutes | GRILLING TIME: 30–35 minutes | SPECIAL EQUIPMENT: 25-cm/10-inch cast-iron frying pan

1 tablespoon vegetable oil
250 g/8 oz plain flour
150 g/5 oz yellow cornmeal
125 g/4 oz granulated sugar
2 teaspoons baking powder
1 teaspoon bicarbonate of soda
1 teaspoon sea salt
350 ml/12 fl oz buttermilk
2 large eggs
150 g/5 oz unsalted butter, melted and cooled
225 g/7½ oz Cheddar cheese, grated
30 g/1¼ oz chives, finely chopped

1 Prepare the grill for roasting/indirect cooking over medium-high heat (about 220°C/425°F).

2 Add the oil to a 25-cm/10-inch cast-iron frying pan, and place the frying pan over *roasting/indirect medium-high heat* for 5 minutes while the grill preheats. Wearing insulated barbecue mitts or oven gloves, swirl the frying pan so that the oil coats the bottom and sides.

3 In a large bowl whisk the flour, cornmeal, sugar, baking powder, bicarbonate of soda and salt.

4 In another bowl whisk the buttermilk, eggs and 125 ml/4 fl oz of the melted butter until smooth. Stir in the cheese and the chives. Pour the wet ingredients over the dry ingredients all at once, and stir gently with a rubber spatula just until blended. Pour the batter into the hot frying pan and gently smooth the top.

5 Grill over *roasting/indirect medium-high heat* for 25–30 minutes, with the lid closed, until the top is golden brown on the edges and a skewer or a cocktail stick inserted into the centre comes out moist but not wet. Wearing insulated barbecue mitts, remove the pan from the grill, run a knife around the edges to loosen the corn bread, and carefully invert on to a cutting board. Flip the corn bread over and brush the top with the remaining melted butter. Serve warm or at room temperature.

CHEESY GARLIC BREAD
WITH SUN-DRIED TOMATOES

SERVES: 8–10 | PREP TIME: 10 minutes | GRILLING TIME: 9–14 minutes

25 g/1 oz sun-dried tomatoes packed in oil
8 garlic cloves, finely chopped or crushed
1 teaspoon dried oregano
¼ teaspoon crushed red chilli flakes
25 g/1 oz unsalted butter, softened
1 loaf French or flat bread, about 500 g/1 lb, cut crossways in
    half, each half cut lengthways to make 4 pieces
175 g/6 oz grated mozzarella and Cheddar cheese,
    blended together

1 Prepare the grill for grilling/direct and roasting/indirect cooking over medium heat (180–230°C/350–450°F).

2 Drain the tomatoes, reserve 3 tablespoons of the oil and chop the tomatoes. In a small frying pan over a medium heat, warm the reserved oil. Add the garlic, oregano and chilli flakes, and cook for 2½–3 minutes until the garlic just barely starts to brown, stirring occasionally. Remove from the heat and transfer to a bowl. Add the butter and stir until the butter is melted and the mixture is well combined.

3 Tear off two long sheets of aluminium foil and place two bread pieces, cut side up, on each piece. Brush with an equal amount of the butter mixture, and then close the bread like a sandwich, with the cut sides facing each other. Wrap the bread in the foil.

4 Grill the bread over *grilling/direct medium heat* for 5–8 minutes, with the lid closed, until heated through, turning every 2 minutes. Remove from the grill, open the foil and set the bread halves, cut side up, next to each other on the foil. Top with the cheese and the sun-dried tomatoes. Return the bread to the grill, leaving the halves on top of the foil and unwrapped. Grill over *roasting/indirect medium heat* for 4–6 minutes, with the lid closed, until the cheese melts. Remove from the grill and cut into 5-cm/2-inch pieces. Serve warm or at room temperature.

BEER AND CHEDDAR BREAD

SERVES: 8 | PREP TIME: 20 minutes | RISING TIME: about 2¼ hours | GRILLING TIME: 1¼–1½ hours
SPECIAL EQUIPMENT: electric mixer (optional), pizza peel (optional), pizza stone, spray bottle

1 bottle (350 ml/12 fl oz) beer, at room temperature
2 tablespoons granulated sugar
25 g/1 oz unsalted butter, softened, plus more for the bowl
1 sachet (5 g/¼ oz) fast-action dried yeast
1½ teaspoons table salt
1½ teaspoons dried thyme
½ teaspoon garlic granules
½ teaspoon onion flakes
¼ teaspoon crushed red chilli flakes
550 g/1 lb 2 oz unbleached, plain flour, plus more as needed
125 g/4 oz mature Cheddar cheese, diced
Extra-virgin olive oil

1 MIXER METHOD: In the bowl of a electric mixer, mix the beer, sugar, butter, yeast, salt, thyme, garlic granules, onion flakes and chilli flakes. Attach the bowl to the mixer and affix the paddle beater. With the mixer on low speed, gradually add enough of the flour to make a soft dough that does not stick to the bowl. Turn off the mixer, cover the bowl with a towel and let stand for 10 minutes. Switch from the paddle to the dough hook. With the mixer on medium-low speed, knead the dough for about 8 minutes, adding more flour as needed to keep it from sticking, until the dough is smooth and elastic.

HAND METHOD: To make the dough by hand, in a large bowl using a wooden spoon, mix the beer, sugar, butter, yeast, salt, thyme, garlic granules, onion flakes and chilli flakes. Gradually stir in enough of the flour as necessary to make a stiff dough that cannot be stirred any more. Turn out on to a well-floured work surface. Knead by hand for about 10 minutes, adding more flour as needed, until the dough is smooth and elastic and does not stick to the work surface.

2 Grease a large bowl with butter. Shape the dough into a ball. Put the dough in the bowl, smooth side down, and then turn smooth side up, coating the dough with butter. Cover with clingfilm and let stand in a warm, draught-free place for about 1½ hours until the dough is doubled in volume.

3 Place a 30-cm/12-inch square of baking paper on a pizza peel (or a rimless baking sheet). Set aside.

4 On a lightly floured surface, gently roll the dough into a 33-by-23-inch/13-by-9-inch rectangle. Scatter the cheese over the dough. Starting at a short end, roll the dough to enclose the cheese. Tuck the ends of the dough underneath and shape the dough into a ball. Place the dough, smooth side up, on the lined pizza peel. Coat a large piece of clingfilm with oil. Cover the dough loosely with the clingfilm, oiled side down, and let stand in a warm, draught-free place for about 45 minutes until the loaf looks inflated, but not doubled. Remove the clingfilm.

5 Prepare the grill for roasting/indirect cooking over medium heat (about 190°C/375°F) and preheat a pizza stone for about 15 minutes, following the manufacturer's instructions.

6 Fill a spray bottle with water. Slide the loaf with the baking paper on to the pizza stone. Quickly spray the surface of the loaf with water. Grill over *roasting/indirect medium heat* for 1¼–1½ hours, with the lid closed, until the bread is golden brown and sounds hollow when tapped on the bottom. (Some cheese may ooze on to the stone.) Remove the loaf from the stone, transfer to a wire cooling rack and let cool for at least 30 minutes before cutting into slices.

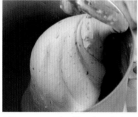

1 You can make the dough in an electric mixer fitted with a paddle beater first and then a dough hook for the final mixing. When you pull it out of the bowl, it should be smooth and elastic.

2 You can also make the dough entirely by hand, mixing it first in a bowl and then kneading it on a floured work surface. It is ready when the surface is completely smooth.

3 The little pieces of cheese that you scatter over the dough and roll inside it will melt slowly and will ooze into the bread pockets.

4 As you slide your dough on to the pizza stone, spray the top with water, which will keep the surface moist and soft enough for the dough to rise fully.

PORTOBELLO MUSHROOM AND CHEESE PANINI

SERVES: 4 | PREP TIME: 20 minutes | MARINATING TIME: 30 minutes–1 hour | GRILLING TIME: 10–16 minutes
SPECIAL EQUIPMENT: cast-iron grill press (optional)

MARINADE
250 ml/8 fl oz extra-virgin olive oil
5 tablespoons balsamic vinegar
2 tablespoons finely chopped garlic
2 teaspoons dried oregano
½ teaspoon crushed red chilli flakes
1 teaspoon sea salt
½ teaspoon freshly ground black pepper

8 Portobello mushrooms, each about 10 cm/4 inches in
   diameter, stalks trimmed evenly with the bottoms
4 round crusty rolls, split
200 g/7 oz fontina or mozzarella cheese, grated
50 g/2 oz baby rocket

1 Whisk the marinade ingredients together. Spread the
mushrooms in a single layer on a rimmed baking sheet
and spoon the marinade over them. Turn to coat both sides
generously. Let stand at room temperature for 30 minutes–
1 hour.

2 Prepare the grill for grilling/direct cooking over medium
heat (180–230°C/350–450°F).

3 Grill the mushrooms over *grilling/direct medium heat*
for 8–12 minutes, smooth side facing up first, with the
lid closed, until juicy and tender, turning once or twice
and brushing with the marinade left on the baking sheet.
Remove from the grill.

4 Reduce the temperature of the grill to low heat
(130–180°C/250–350°F).

5 Sprinkle the bottom half of each roll with 4 tablespoons
of the cheese. Stack two mushrooms on each roll, then top
the mushrooms with another 4 tablespoons of the cheese, a
quarter of the rocket and the top half of the roll. Press the
top of the roll firmly to compress. Place the sandwiches
over *grilling/direct low heat* and press them down, one at
a time, with a grill press or a wide, sturdy spatula. Grill for
2–4 minutes until the bread is toasted and the cheese is
melted, turning once and pressing them flat after turning.
Remove from the grill, cut in half and serve immediately.

TIP Be sure to use sturdy rolls. The mushrooms give off
deliciously dark juices, and a thin roll will get soggy.

BAGUETTE SANDWICHES
OF GRILLED COURGETTES AND PESTO CREAM CHEESE

SERVES: 4 | PREP TIME: 15 minutes | GRILLING TIME: 3–5 minutes

3 tablespoons extra-virgin olive oil
½ teaspoon dried oregano
½ teaspoon sea salt
¼ teaspoon freshly ground black pepper
750 g/1½ lb green and/or yellow courgettes, ends trimmed, cut lengthways into 5-mm/¼-inch slices
125 g/4 oz whipped cream cheese, softened
5 tablespoons shop-bought basil pesto
Finely grated zest of 1 lemon
5 fresh basil leaves, finely chopped (optional)
1 French baguette, about 250 g/8 oz, cut crossways into 4 pieces, each halved horizontally
250 g/8 oz roasted red peppers (in a jar), drained and cut into flat strips
125 g/4 oz smoked Gouda, provolone or mozzarella cheese, cut into thin slices

1 In a baking dish whisk the oil, oregano, salt and pepper. Add the courgettes and turn to coat evenly. Set aside at room temperature.

2 Combine the cream cheese, pesto, lemon zest and basil (if using).

3 Prepare the grill for grilling/direct cooking over medium heat (180–230°C/350–450°F).

4 Grill the courgettes over *grilling/direct medium heat* for 3–5 minutes, with the lid closed, until tender and nicely marked, turning once or twice. During the last minute of grilling time, toast the baguette pieces, cut side down, over grilling/direct medium heat. Remove the courgettes and the baguette pieces from the grill.

5 Spread a thin layer of the cream cheese mixture over the cut side of each baguette piece. Build the sandwiches with equal amounts of the courgettes, peppers and cheese. Serve warm.

DESSERTS

GRILLING FRUIT

TYPE	THICKNESS / SIZE	APPROXIMATE GRILLING TIME
Apple	whole	**35–40 minutes** roasting/indirect medium heat
	1-cm/¹⁄₂-inch slices	**4–6 minutes** grilling/direct medium heat
Apricot	halved lengthways	**4–6 minutes** grilling/direct medium heat
Banana	halved lengthways	**3–5 minutes** grilling/direct medium heat
Nectarine	halved lengthways	**6–8 minutes** grilling/direct medium heat
Peach	halved lengthways	**6–8 minutes** grilling/direct medium heat
Pear	halved lengthways	**6–8 minutes** grilling/direct medium heat
Pineapple	1-cm/¹⁄₂-inch slices or 2.5-cm/1-inch wedges	**5–10 minutes** grilling/direct medium heat
Plum	halved lengthways	**6–8 minutes** grilling/direct medium heat
Strawberry	whole	**4–5 minutes** grilling/direct medium heat

Just about everything from apples to strawberries tends to cook best over grilling/direct medium heat. The temperature on the grill's thermometer should be somewhere between 180° and 230°C/350° and 450°F.

PEAR UPSIDE-DOWN CAKE

SERVES: 8–10 | PREP TIME: 30 minutes | GRILLING TIME: 47 minutes–1 hour | SPECIAL EQUIPMENT: 30-cm/12-inch cast-iron frying pan

75 g/3 oz unsalted butter
7 firm but ripe pears, about 1.5 kg/3 lb total, peeled, halved and cored
125 g/4 oz light brown sugar
½ teaspoon sea salt
¼ teaspoon ground cinnamon
¼ teaspoon ground ginger

SPONGE
50 g/5 oz plain flour
1 teaspoon baking powder
¼ teaspoon bicarbonate of soda
¼ teaspoon ground cinnamon
¼ teaspoon ground ginger
¼ teaspoon sea salt
125 ml/4 fl oz full-fat milk
125 ml/4 fl oz soured cream
2 large eggs
2 teaspoons pure vanilla extract
125 g/4 oz unsalted butter, softened
75 ml/3 fl oz granulated sugar

Lightly sweetened whipped cream

1 Prepare the grill for grilling/direct and roasting/indirect cooking over medium heat (180–230°C/350–450°F).

2 Melt 25 g/1 oz of the butter. Brush the butter on both sides of the pear halves. Grill the pears over *grilling/direct medium heat* for 10–12 minutes, with the lid closed, until nicely marked, turning once. Remove from the grill and let cool.

3 In a 30-cm/12-inch cast-iron frying pan combine the remaining butter, the brown sugar, salt, cinnamon and ground ginger. Close the lid and cook over *grilling/direct medium heat* for 2–3 minutes until the sugar is melted and the liquid starts to bubble slightly around the edges. Wearing insulated barbecue mitts or oven gloves, remove the frying pan from the grill and place on a roasting tray. Arrange the pear halves in the pan, flat side down and overlapping if necessary, starting at the edge of the pan and working in towards the centre. Set aside.

4 In a bowl combine the cake flour, baking powder, bicarbonate of soda, cinnamon, ginger and salt. In a small bowl whisk the milk, soured cream, eggs and vanilla extract. In a large bowl using an electric mixer on medium-high speed, cream the butter and sugar for 2–3 minutes until light and fluffy. With the mixer on low, add the milk mixture and then the flour mixture. Blend until smooth, scraping down the sides of the bowl as necessary. Pour the mixture evenly over the pears in the pan, smoothing it with a rubber spatula, if necessary.

5 Bake the cake over *roasting/indirect medium heat* for 35–45 minutes, with the lid closed, keeping the temperature as close to 180°C/350°F as possible, until the top is golden brown and a skewer or a cocktail stick inserted into the centre comes out clean. Wearing insulated barbecue mitts or oven gloves, remove the pan from the grill and let cool for 10 minutes. (If the cake stays in the pan longer than 10 minutes, the topping will begin to harden and it will be difficult for the cake to release.)

6 Remove the cake from the pan by running a paring knife around the edge to loosen it. Place a serving plate large enough to hold the cake over the top of the pan. Carefully invert the pan and plate at the same time, and then slowly remove the pan. If any pears have stuck to the bottom of the pan, use a spatula to remove them and replace them on top of the cake. Let the cake cool slightly before cutting it into wedges. Serve warm or at room temperature topped with whipped cream.

CARAMELIZED PEARS
WITH TOASTED ALMONDS AND LEMON CREAM

SERVES: 6 | PREP TIME: **10 minutes** | GRILLING TIME: **6–8 minutes**

25 g/1 oz flaked unblanched almonds
175 ml/6 fl oz soured cream
Finely grated zest of 1 large lemon
1 tablespoon honey, or to taste
3 large, firm but ripe pears, halved and cored
1½ tablespoons balsamic vinegar
2 teaspoons light brown sugar

1 Prepare the grill for grilling/direct cooking over medium heat (180–230°C/350–450°F).

2 In a small, dry frying pan over medium heat, toast the almonds for 2–3 minutes until golden brown, stirring frequently and watching closely to avoid burning. Transfer to a chopping board and roughly chop.

3 Whisk the soured cream, lemon zest and honey together.

4 Grill the pear halves, cut side down, over *grilling/direct medium heat* for 4–5 minutes, with the lid closed, until lightly charred. Turn the pears cut side up, then brush generously with the vinegar, and grill for 2–3 minutes more, until warmed through and beginning to soften. Remove from the grill. Mound about 2 tablespoons of lemon cream into the centre of each pear half, top evenly with the brown sugar and almonds and serve immediately.

PINEAPPLE WEDGES
WITH RUM BUTTER AND TOASTED COCONUT

SERVES: 4 | PREP TIME: **10 minutes** | MARINATING TIME: **about 1 hour** | GRILLING TIME: **8–10 minutes**

75 g/3 oz unsalted butter, softened
2 tablespoons dark or spiced rum
2 tablespoons dark brown sugar
3 tablespoons dessicated coconut
1 pineapple, peeled, cut lengthways into 8 spears,
    core removed
⅛ teaspoon sea salt
⅛ teaspoon freshly ground black pepper

1 Combine the butter, rum and 1 tablespoon of the brown sugar. Beat with a wooden spoon or mix with an electric hand whisk on medium speed until smooth and fluffy and the rum is completely incorporated.

2 In a frying pan over low heat, toast the coconut, about 3 minutes. Watch it closely, as it can burn quickly. Pour the coconut into a small bowl and set aside.

3 Put the pineapple spears in a non-reactive baking dish just large enough to hold them. Combine the remaining brown sugar, the salt and the pepper and season the pineapple evenly with the sugar and spices. Allow the pineapple to stand at room temperature for 1 hour, brushing the liquid released from the pineapple over the spears once or twice.

4 Prepare the grill for grilling/direct cooking over medium heat (180–230°C/350–450°F).

5 Grill the spears over *grilling/direct medium heat* for 8–10 minutes, with the lid closed, until nicely marked, turning once or twice. Remove from the grill and immediately spoon the rum butter over the spears to melt. Top with the coconut and serve immediately.

TIP To choose a ripe pineapple, first press the base and lower sides of the pineapple. It should give slightly under pressure. Next, sniff the bottom of the fruit. If it is ripe, it will have a distinct pineapple smell. If either one of these signs is missing, keep looking.

PINEAPPLE, MANGO AND STONE FRUIT SALAD

SERVES: 6–8 | PREP TIME: 20 minutes | GRILLING TIME: 8–10 minutes

1 pineapple, peeled, cut crossways into 1-cm/½-inch slices, core removed
2 large, ripe but slightly firm mangoes, peeled and cut into 8 slices
3 firm but ripe peaches, each cut in half
3 firm but ripe nectarines, each cut in half
3 firm but ripe plums, each cut in half
Vegetable oil

DRESSING
2 tablespoons chopped fresh mint
2 teaspoons finely grated lime zest
2 tablespoons fresh lime juice
2 tablespoons honey

1 Prepare the grill for grilling/direct cooking over medium heat (180–230°C/350–450°F).

2 Lightly brush the fruit all over with oil. Grill the fruit, placing the peaches, nectarines and plums cut side down first, over *grilling/direct medium heat*, with the lid closed, until lightly charred and beginning to soften, 8–10 minutes for the pineapple; 6–8 minutes for the peaches, nectarines and plums; and 4–6 minutes for the mangoes, turning once. Remove from the grill as they are done and let cool for 10 minutes. Cut the pineapple and mangoes into 2.5-cm/1-inch pieces. Cut each peach, nectarine and plum half into four wedges.

3 In a large bowl combine the dressing ingredients. Add the grilled fruit and toss gently to combine. Serve immediately or refrigerate for up to 4 hours before serving.

WHAT THE GRILL DOES FOR FRUIT

Think for a second about the difference between a marshmallow right out of the bag and one that you have just toasted over a campfire so that it is richly golden and lightly charred on the surface. It's as if the fire and smoke have wrapped the marshmallow in a warm, fragile crust that oozes with sweetness.

The difference between raw fruit and grilled fruit is like that, only better, because you start with something much more flavourful than a marshmallow. You start with a ripe piece of glistening fruit whose natural flavours have matured and deepened slowly on the tree or vine. When you grill that fruit, the juices sizzle and change almost immediately. They turn deliciously caramelized and intensely concentrated while the interior of the fruit warms and softens to the point that it nearly melts on your tongue. Now that's a difference worth grilling for.

MAPLE GRILLED PEACHES
WITH VANILLA ICE CREAM AND TOASTED PECANS

SERVES: 6 | PREP TIME: 10 minutes | GRILLING TIME: about 8 minutes

SAUCE
5 tablespoons maple syrup
25 g/1 oz unsalted butter
¼ teaspoon ground cinnamon
¼ teaspoon sea salt

6 firm but ripe peaches, each cut in half
1½ tablespoons vegetable oil
1 litre/1¾ pints vanilla ice cream
40 g/1½ oz toasted pecans, chopped

1 Prepare the grill for grilling/direct cooking over medium-low heat (about 180°C/350°F).

2 In a saucepan combine the sauce ingredients. Cook over medium heat for 2–3 minutes until the butter melts, stirring constantly. Remove from the heat and set aside.

3 Brush the peach halves with the oil. Grill the peaches, cut side down, over *grilling/direct medium-low heat* for about 4 minutes, with the lid closed, until they are lightly charred and starting to soften. Turn the peaches over and brush with a little of the sauce. Continue to grill for about 4 minutes more, until the peaches are tender. Transfer the peaches to a chopping board and let rest for 5 minutes. Cut the peaches into wedges.

4 To serve, scoop ice cream into six serving bowls. Divide the peaches evenly among the bowls and drizzle with the remaining sauce. Top with the toasted pecans.

FRENCH TOAST
WITH GRILLED PEACHES AND BLUEBERRY SYRUP

SERVES: 4 | PREP TIME: 25 minutes | GRILLING TIME: 20–26 minutes | SPECIAL EQUIPMENT: grill-proof griddle or cast-iron frying pan

175 g/6 oz fresh blueberries
175 ml/6 fl oz maple syrup
Finely grated zest of 1 lemon
25 g/1 oz unsalted butter, melted
2 tablespoons granulated sugar
4 firm but ripe peaches, each cut in half
4 large eggs
150 ml/¼ pint single cream
1 teaspoon pure vanilla extract
½ teaspoon ground cinnamon
¼ teaspoon sea salt
8 slices day-old brioche bread, each about 1.5 cm/
   ¾ inch thick
Unsalted butter

1 Prepare the grill for grilling/direct cooking over medium heat (180–230°C/350–450°F).

2 In a saucepan over a medium-high heat, combine the blueberries, syrup and lemon zest and bring to the boil. Reduce the heat to low and simmer for 3 minutes. Remove from the heat. Keep warm, if liked.

3 Combine the melted butter and 1 tablespoon of the sugar and stir until the sugar is dissolved. Brush the peach halves all over with the butter mixture. Grill over *grilling/direct medium heat* for 8–10 minutes, with the lid closed, until they are browned in spots and warm throughout, turning every 3 minutes or so. Transfer to a chopping board. When cool enough to handle, cut into wedges.

4 Preheat a grill-proof griddle over *grilling/direct medium heat* for about 10 minutes. In a baking dish whisk the eggs, single cream, the remaining sugar, the vanilla extract, cinnamon and salt until thoroughly combined. Working in batches, place the brioche in the egg mixture, soak for 2 minutes, and turn once. Butter the griddle. Using tongs, remove the brioche from the egg mixture, allowing any excess to drip back into the dish. Place the brioche on the griddle and cook for 6–8 minutes with the lid closed, until golden brown on both sides, turning once. Remove from the griddle and keep warm. Repeat with the remaining brioche. Serve the French toast topped with the grilled peaches and the blueberry syrup.

APRICOT SUNDAES
WITH GELATO AND AMARETTI

SERVES: 4 | PREP TIME: 15 minutes | GRILLING TIME: 4–6 minutes

SAUCE
125 g/4 oz granulated sugar
2 tablespoons water
125 ml/4 fl oz whipping cream
50 g/2 oz unsalted butter, softened
2 teaspoons fresh lemon juice

6 firm but ripe apricots, each cut lengthways in half
1 tablespoon vegetable oil
1 tablespoon granulated sugar
475 ml/16 fl oz vanilla ice cream
40 g/1½ oz amaretti biscuits, coarsely crushed

1 In a small, heavy saucepan combine the sugar with the water. Without touching the sugar, allow it to melt and turn golden brown (but not burnt) over a medium heat, 9–11 minutes, occasionally swirling the saucepan by the handle to be sure all the sugar caramelizes evenly. Meanwhile, in another pan, bring the cream and the butter to a simmer over a medium heat, and then remove it from the heat. When the sugar mixture is golden brown throughout, remove it from the heat. Add the cream mixture to the sugar mixture very slowly (it will bubble up). Then add the lemon juice and whisk the sauce until smooth. Let cool until just slightly warm. If necessary, warm the sauce again over a very low heat.

2 Prepare the grill for grilling/direct cooking over medium heat (180–230°C/350–450°F).

3 Brush the apricots with the oil. Sprinkle with the sugar. Grill the apricots, cut side down, over *grilling/direct medium heat* for 4–6 minutes, with the lid closed, until heated through, turning once. (Cooking times will vary depending on the ripeness of the apricots.) Remove from the grill.

4 To serve, stack one apricot half, one scoop of ice cream, some crushed biscuits and a spoonful of caramel sauce in each dessert dish. Repeat, and finish with an apricot half, a drizzle of sauce and more crushed biscuits. Serve the sundaes immediately.

GRILLED ORANGES
WITH CHOCOLATE SAUCE AND WHIPPED CREAM

SERVES: 4 | PREP TIME: 15 minutes | GRILLING TIME: about 2 minutes

250 ml/8 fl oz whipping cream
2 teaspoons icing sugar
½ teaspoon vanilla extract
4 large oranges
Vegetable oil
Shop-bought chocolate sauce

1 Prepare the grill for grilling/direct cooking over medium heat (180–230°C/350–450°F).

2 In a bowl, using an electric hand whisk on medium speed, beat the cream for about 3 minutes until the trail from the beaters is just visible. Add the icing sugar and vanilla extract and continue to beat until soft peaks form. Cover and refrigerate until ready to use.

3 Cut away the skin and pith of the oranges, and then cut the oranges crossways into 5-mm/¼-inch slices. Lightly brush both sides of the orange slices with oil.

4 Grill the orange slices over *grilling/direct medium heat* for about 2 minutes, with the lid closed, until nicely marked on both sides, turning once.

5 Warm the chocolate sauce. Divide the orange slices among four serving bowls, overlapping the slices slightly. Top with a generous dollop of the whipped cream and drizzle with chocolate sauce. Serve immediately.

TOASTED SPONGE CAKE
WITH WARM STRAWBERRIES AND ICE CREAM

SERVES: 6 | PREP TIME: 10 minutes | GRILLING TIME: 7–9 minutes | SPECIAL EQUIPMENT: 25-cm/10-inch cast-iron frying pan

1 kg/2 lb fresh strawberries, hulled and each cut
    vertically in half
75 g/3 oz granulated sugar
4 tablespoons dark rum
1 teaspoon vanilla extract
40 g/1½ oz unsalted butter
1 shop-bought sponge cake, 300–375 g/10–12 oz, cut
    into 12 slices
1 litre/1¾ pints strawberry ice cream

1 Combine the strawberries, sugar, rum and vanilla
extract. Set aside at room temperature, and stir the
mixture occasionally.

2 Prepare the grill for grilling/direct cooking over
medium-low heat (about 180°C/350°F) and preheat
a 25-cm/10-inch cast-iron frying pan.

3 Add the butter to the pan and stir with a long-handled
spoon until the butter is melted. Add the strawberry
mixture, close the lid and cook over *grilling/direct
medium-low heat* for 7–9 minutes until the strawberries
start to soften, stirring occasionally. During the last
2 minutes of grilling time, grill the cake slices over
grilling/direct medium-low heat until lightly marked,
turning once. Remove the pan and the cake from the grill.

4 Place two slices of cake on each of six serving plates
and top with an equal amount of the strawberry ice
cream. Spoon the strawberries and any sauce in the pan
over the cake and the ice cream. Serve immediately.

BANANA AND COCONUT SUNDAES
WITH BOURBON-CARAMEL SAUCE

SERVES: 6 | PREP TIME: **15 minutes** | GRILLING TIME: **3–5 minutes**

SAUCE
125 g/4 oz granulated sugar
2 tablespoons water
125 ml/4 fl oz heavy whipping cream
50 g/2 oz unsalted butter, softened
2 tablespoons bourbon
2 teaspoons fresh lemon juice

1 tablespoon granulated sugar
¾ teaspoon ancho chilli powder
3 firm but ripe bananas, each cut lengthways in half
40 g/1½ oz unsalted butter, melted
475 ml/16 fl oz vanilla ice cream
250 ml/8 fl oz coconut sorbet
4 tablespoons dessicated coconut, toasted

Grill banana halves in their skins to hold the fruit together.

1 Prepare the grill for grilling/direct cooking over medium heat (180–230°C/350–450°F).

2 In a small, heavy saucepan combine the sugar with the water. Without touching the sugar, allow it to melt and turn golden brown (but not burnt) over a medium heat, 9–11 minutes, occasionally swirling the saucepan by the handle to be sure all the sugar caramelises evenly. Meanwhile, in another pan, bring the cream, butter and bourbon to a simmer over a medium heat, then remove it from the heat. When the sugar mixture is golden brown throughout, remove it from the heat. Add the cream mixture to the sugar mixture very slowly (it will bubble up). Then add the lemon juice and whisk until smooth. Let cool until slightly warm.

3 Combine the sugar and the chilli powder. Brush the cut side of the bananas with the melted butter and season with the sugar mixture. Grill the bananas, cut side down, over *grilling/direct medium heat* for 3–5 minutes, with the lid closed, until warm and nicely marked (do not turn). Remove from the grill, peel the bananas and cut them into 1.5-cm/¾-inch pieces. If necessary, warm the sauce again over very low heat. Divide the ice cream and the sorbet evenly among six bowls. Top with bananas, sauce and toasted coconut flakes. Serve immediately.

CHOCOLATE CHIP AND PEANUT BUTTER COOKIES

MAKES: 36 cookies | PREP TIME: 20 minutes | GRILLING TIME: about 45 minutes | SPECIAL EQUIPMENT: pizza stone

600 g/1 lb 5 oz plain flour
1 teaspoon bicarbonate of soda
¾ teaspoon table salt
125 g/4 oz unsalted butter, softened
125 g/4 oz peanut butter
175 g/6 oz granulated sugar
175 g/6 oz light brown sugar
2 large eggs, at room temperature
2 teaspoons vanilla extract
375 g/12 oz plain chocolate chips

1 Sift the flour, bicarbonate of soda and salt into a large bowl.

2 In another large bowl combine the butter, peanut butter and both sugars and beat until smooth. One at a time, beat in the eggs, followed by the vanilla extract. Gradually add in the flour mixture. Mix in the chocolate chips. Refrigerate the dough while you preheat the grill.

3 Prepare the grill for roasting/indirect cooking over medium-low heat (180–190°C/350–375°F) and preheat a pizza stone over *roasting/indirect medium-low heat* for at least 15 minutes, following manufacturer's instructions.

4 One heaped tablespoon at a time, scoop the dough into 36 balls. Arrange about 12 balls in even rows at least 5 cm/2 inches apart on the pizza stone. Refrigerate the remaining balls until ready to grill. Bake the cookies over *roasting/indirect medium-low heat for* 12–15 minutes, with the lid closed, until lightly browned around the edges. Transfer the cookies to a wire cooling rack and let cool for 3–5 minutes. Repeat the process with the remaining dough. Serve the cookies warm.

TIP You'll be happy to have a thermometer on your grill's lid for this recipe, as these cookies will be most successful if you keep a steady baking temperature of 180–190°C/350–375°F.

WARM MOLTEN CHOCOLATE CAKES
WITH FRESH BERRIES

SERVES: 4 | PREP TIME: **10 minutes** | GRILLING TIME: **10–14 minutes** | SPECIAL EQUIPMENT: **12-hole muffin tin**

60 g/2½ oz unsalted butter
125 g/4 oz top-quality plain chocolate
2 large eggs
50 g/2 oz granulated sugar
1 tablespoon plain flour
125 ml/4 fl oz cold whipped cream
250 g/8 oz fresh raspberries

1 Using 5 g/¼ oz of the butter, grease the four holes down the centre of a 12-hole muffin tin.

2 In a bowl set over a pan of barely simmering water, melt the chocolate and the remaining 75 g/3 oz butter, stirring occasionally until smooth. In another bowl whisk the eggs and the sugar for about 20 seconds, until light and fluffy. Add the warm chocolate mixture to the egg mixture and mix until smooth. Then add the flour and mix until you no longer see specks of flour.

3 Fill the four greased holes with the batter (almost to the top rim, but not all the way). If not ready to cook, refrigerate for as long as 3 hours.

4 Prepare the grill for roasting/indirect cooking over medium heat (ideally 200°C/400°F).

5 Place the muffin tin over *roasting/indirect medium heat* and bake for about 10 minutes (or as long as 14 minutes if the batter has been refrigerated) with the lid closed, until the cake tops no longer jiggle when you shake the pan. Remove from the grill and let rest for 5–10 minutes.

6 Run a knife around the outer rim of each cake to make sure it is not stuck to the tin. On top of the muffin tin place a chopping board or a plate that is slightly larger than the tin. Holding the tin and chopping board together, invert them so that the cakes fall out of the tin. Serve immediately with whipped cream and raspberries.

TIP Each hole in the muffin tin should measure 6.5 cm/2¾ inches in diameter by 3 cm/1¼ inches high, and each should hold 125 ml/4 fl oz by volume.

RUBS, BRINES, MARINADES & SAUCES

RUBS

MAKING RUBS

A rub is a mixture of spices, herbs and other seasonings (often including sugar) that can quickly give a boost of flavours to foods before grilling. This page provides some mighty good examples, but dare to be different. One of the steps towards developing your own style at the grill is to concoct a signature rub recipe or two. Only you will know exactly what ingredients are blended in your special jar of 'magic dust'.

A word about freshness: ground spices lose their aromas in a matter of months (8–10 months maximum). If you have been holding on to a little jar of coriander for years, waiting to blend the world's finest version of curry powder, forget about it. Dump the old, tired coriander and buy some freshly ground. Better yet, buy whole coriander seeds and grind them yourself. Whatever you do, store your spices and spice rubs in airtight containers away from light and heat, to best preserve their flavours and fragrances.

BEEF RUB

Makes: 2 tablespoons

2 teaspoons sea salt
1 teaspoon garlic granules
1 teaspoon freshly ground black pepper
1 teaspoon smoked paprika
½ teaspoon ground coriander
½ teaspoon ground cumin

LAMB RUB

Makes: 2 tablespoons

2 teaspoons sea salt
1 teaspoon paprika
1 teaspoon curry powder
1 teaspoon freshly ground black pepper
½ teaspoon onion flakes
½ teaspoon aniseed

PORK RUB

Makes: about 1½ tablespoons

2 teaspoons sea salt
1 teaspoon ground cumin
½ teaspoon freshly ground black pepper
½ teaspoon dried oregano
½ teaspoon light brown sugar
¼ teaspoon chipotle chilli powder

HOW LONG?

If you leave a rub on for a long time, the seasonings intermix with the juices in the meat and produce more pronounced flavours as well as a crust. This is good to a point, but a rub with a lot of salt or sugar will draw moisture out of the meat over time, making the meat tastier, yes, but also drier. So how long should you use a rub? Here are some guidelines.

TIME	TYPES OF FOOD
Up to 15 minutes	Small foods, such as shellfish, cubed meat for kebabs and vegetables
15–30 minutes	Thin cuts of boneless meat, such as chicken breasts, fish fillets, pork fillets, chops and steaks
30 minutes–1½ hours	Thicker cuts of boneless or bone-in meat, such as leg of lamb, whole chickens and beef joints
½–8 hours	Big or tough cuts of meat, such as racks of ribs, whole hams, pork shoulders and turkeys

POULTRY RUB

Makes: about 3 tablespoons

2 teaspoons sea salt
2 teaspoons dried thyme
1 teaspoon dried oregano
1 teaspoon onion flakes
1 teaspoon ground coriander
1 teaspoon freshly ground black pepper
½ teaspoon chilli powder

SEAFOOD RUB

Makes: about 2 tablespoons

2 teaspoons sea salt
1 teaspoon chilli powder
1 teaspoon garlic granules
½ teaspoon ground coriander
½ teaspoon celery seeds
½ teaspoon freshly ground black pepper

VEGETABLE RUB

Makes: 2 tablespoons

1 teaspoon mustard powder
1 teaspoon onion flakes
1 teaspoon paprika
1 teaspoon sea salt
½ teaspoon garlic granules
½ teaspoon ground coriander
½ teaspoon ground cumin
½ teaspoon freshly ground black pepper

MARINADES

MAKING MARINADES

It's what's inside that counts – and that's flavour, where marinades are concerned. Letting food sit in a mixture of acidic liquid, oil, herbs and seasonings does wonders to kick-start items that might need a little boost, like leaner cuts of meat and even vegetables, in addition to keeping them moist on the grill. Bold ingredients work best – think garlic, rosemary, or soy sauce – to maximize the marinade's effect, and the right combinations can give your meal a regional or ethnic flair.

FIESTA MARINADE

While this festive marinade is reminiscent of a margarita, be sure to save your best tequila for cocktails, and choose a lower-shelf option for the marinade.

Good with: beef, chicken, fish, prawns
Makes: about 300 ml/½ pint

125 ml/4 fl oz fresh orange juice
4 tablespoons fresh lime juice
4 tablespoons gold tequila
1 large jalapeño chilli, including seeds, finely chopped
3 tablespoons agave nectar
2 tablespoons soy sauce
2 teaspoons ground cumin
4 garlic cloves, finely chopped or crushed

1 Whisk all of the ingredients in a bowl.

INDIAN MARINADE

Good with: chicken, fish, vegetables
Makes: about 250 ml/8 fl oz

125 ml/4 fl oz full-fat yogurt
4 tablespoons extra-virgin olive oil
2 tablespoons fresh lemon juice
1 tablespoon peeled, finely grated fresh ginger
2 teaspoons ground cardamom
3 large garlic cloves, finely chopped
1 teaspoon ground coriander
1 teaspoon sea salt
1 teaspoon freshly ground black pepper

1 Whisk all of the ingredients in a bowl.

MOROCCAN MARINADE

This potent marinade is commonly used with fish, but equally delicious with lamb, beef, chicken, prawns and hearty vegetables, such as aubergine and cauliflower. It will keep for up to 2 days refrigerated, but its flavour is freshest when used within 1 day. If refrigerating, pour a thin layer of olive oil over the top before covering to prevent discoloration.

Good with: beef, lamb, chicken, fish, prawns, vegetables
Makes: about 250 ml/8 fl oz

75 ml/3 fl oz extra-virgin olive oil
2 teaspoons finely grated lemon zest
4 tablespoons fresh lemon juice
4 tablespoons roughly chopped fresh coriander
4 tablespoons roughly chopped fresh flat-leaf parsley
3 garlic cloves, finely chopped or crushed
2 teaspoons smoked paprika
1 teaspoon ground cumin
1 teaspoon ground coriander
1 teaspoon sea salt

1 Whisk all of the ingredients in a bowl.

SMOKY MARINADE

Chipotle chillies add smoke and heat to this feisty marinade, which is smoothed and sweetened with ketchup and brown sugar. This is a great marinade for flavouring and tenderizing tough cuts of meat, such as skirt steak and top rump.

Good with: beef, pork, chicken, prawns
Makes: about 250 ml/8 fl oz

4 canned chipotle chillies in adobo sauce, finely chopped
4 tablespoons fresh lime juice
3 tablespoons tomato ketchup
2 tablespoons extra-virgin olive oil
1 tablespoon dark brown sugar
4 garlic cloves, finely chopped or crushed
2 teaspoons sea salt
1 teaspoon ground cumin
1 teaspoon chilli powder

1 Whisk all of the ingredients in a bowl.

HOW LONG?	TIME	TYPES OF FOOD
The right length of time varies, depending on the strength of the marinade and the food you are marinating. If your marinade includes intense ingredients like soy sauce, hard liquor, or hot chillies and strong spices, don't overdo it. A fish fillet should still taste like fish, not like a burning-hot, salt-soaked piece of protein. Also, if an acidic marinade is left on meat or fish too long, it can turn the surface dry or mushy. Here are some guidelines to get you going.	15–30 minutes	Small foods, such as shellfish, fish fillets, cubed meat for kebabs, and tender vegetables
	1–3 hours	Thin cuts of boneless meat, such as chicken breasts, pork tenderloins, chops, steaks and sturdy vegetables
	2–6 hours	Thicker cuts of boneless or bone-in meat, such as leg of lamb, whole chickens and beef roasts
	6–12 hours	Big or tough cuts of meat, such as racks of ribs, whole hams, pork shoulders and turkeys

GO-TO FAVOURITE MARINADE

A generous amount of grated onion with its juice adds the necessary sweetness to round out this simple marinade.

Good with: chicken, fish, prawns, scallops, vegetables
Makes: about 300 ml/½ pint

1 small onion, grated, with juice
4 tablespoons fresh lemon juice
3 tablespoons extra-virgin olive oil
3 tablespoons soy sauce
2 tablespoons Dijon mustard
1 teaspoon freshly ground black pepper

1 Whisk all of the ingredients in a bowl.

SWEET AND SIMPLE MARINADE

Classic barbecue sauce ingredients come together in this sweet and sharp marinade.

Good with: beef, pork, chicken
Makes: about 250 ml/8 fl oz

125 ml/4 fl oz soy sauce
4 tablespoons bourbon or whisky
4 tablespoons honey
2 tablespoons tomato ketchup
2 tablespoons Dijon mustard
1 tablespoon cider vinegar
1 tablespoon extra-virgin olive oil
4 garlic cloves, finely chopped or crushed

1 Whisk all of the ingredients in a bowl.

CORIANDER: LOVE IT OR HATE IT

Coriander has a secure home among the likes of black liquorice, mayonnaise and musical theatre – in the 'you either love it or you hate it' ranks.

'Corianderphiles' cite the herb's fresh, vibrant flavour and unparalleled ability to tame the heat of spicy foods (hence its popularity in Asia and Latin America), while 'corianderphobes' think that any food it has touched tastes drenched in washing-up liquid or, even worse, insects.

Oddly enough, there are scientific theories for this culinary schism. Some studies have shown that there is an anti-coriander gene, and others found that the aroma of coriander has smelly cousins that are by-products of soaps and lotions and yes, even some insects. Since taste and smell are strong triggers of memories, experiences with cleaning agents or with an infestation are probably not what you want to recall when diving into corn chips and guacamole.

For the lucky ones that don't have that strong reaction, a sprinkling of chopped coriander leaves can lighten rich or heavy flavours and deliciously balance acidic ones. Try coriander pesto as a fantastic alternative to the traditional basil variety. But if you're among the 'forget it' crowd and are looking to substitute coriander in a recipe, some bright, lemony parsley can do the trick. Or just omit the herb part altogether.

If you are a lover of coriander and want to cook with it for a crowd, wonderful. But don't say we didn't warn you.

SAUCES

MAKING SAUCES

No matter what you grill or what sorts of regional styles you prefer, chances are very good that you will brush, ladle or drizzle some sort of sauce on your food. Without it, your meal could be missing an essential range of flavour, an important degree of texture or a beautiful boost of colour – or all three. Grilling sauces are usually pretty easy to make. Sometimes the prep is as simple as whisking a handful of ingredients, most of which are probably in your store cupboard or refrigerator already. Whichever type of sauce you choose, keep in mind the all-important principle of balance. Whether you are making a fresh salsa, a lively vinaigrette or a sweet and smoky barbecue sauce, you should first understand some fundamentals about taste.

TASTE 101

SWEETNESS

As humans we are wired to like sweetness, even in savoury sauces. It is a nice counterpoint to acidity or spiciness, as it rounds out the sharp edges. The right level of sweetness varies according to the particular sauce. For example, in barbecue sauces the sweetness is usually much higher than the acidity, but in a herb sauce like pesto there is only a trace of sweetness. Sweet condiments include white and brown sugar, black treacle, honey, maple syrup, ketchup, apple juice and hoisin sauce. You can also add sweetness with fruits, peppers and sweetcorn.

SOURNESS

Sourness is the acidity that keeps sweetness in check and is also crucial for bringing some zip and tang to rich sauces that would otherwise taste flat. Imagine how boring and one-dimensional a vinaigrette would be if it had no acidity. Sour ingredients include vinegars (cider, wine, rice, balsamic), some citrus juices, mustards, yogurt and sharp and tangy vegetables, such as tomatillos.

SALTINESS

Saltiness is absolutely critical. Salt itself is the single best ingredient for exciting our taste buds and amplifying other flavours. Even sweet sauces like caramel benefit from salt. But, of course, too much saltiness will disrupt the other features of any good sauce, so start with just a little and add more slowly. If a sauce actually tastes salty, you've gone too far. Your choice of ingredients includes, of course, sea salt, but also soy sauce, Worcestershire sauce, fish sauce and capers.

BITTERNESS

A lot of us have bad associations with bitterness. It reminds us of extreme examples like burnt Brussels sprouts and liver, but keep in mind that a little bitterness is often an essential component of great wine, beer, coffee and, yes, even some sauces. It balances out sweetness and provides a little edginess. Delicious choices for bitterness (in small amounts) include cranberry juice, olives and horseradish – but not all together.

SPICINESS

Spiciness is not really a taste. It is a combination of both flavour and sensation; that is, you taste it and you feel it. Depending on the type of sauce, your choice of spices can emphasize specific regions and ethnic traditions. Usually the spicier sauces are tempered with sweetness. Some of the most popular spicy ingredients include fresh ginger and garlic, chilli powder, fresh chillies and bottled hot sauces.

UMAMI

This is the taste that is as much fun to say (uuu-mah-mee) as it is to eat. Umami is the deep, rich savouriness that usually comes from concentrated, aged or fermented ingredients like Parmesan cheese, bacon and red wine. When a sauce seems a little thin or bland, try adding some umami. Other potent sources are Worcestershire sauce, beef stock and sun-dried tomatoes.

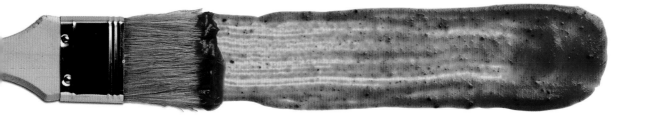

BARBECUE SAUCES

The barbecue sauces hundreds of years ago were basting liquids, or 'mops', made from just butter, vinegar, salt and pepper, to add moisture and an extra touch of good taste to meat as it sizzled over a fire. Time and regional differences introduced additional ingredients, such as tomatoes, sugar, mustard and mayonnaise, leading to a wide variety of traditions and flavour profiles – not to mention evangelising followers. Today you will find a nearly endless assortment of barbecue sauces, yet they all share some elements. Whether it's a vinegar- or mustard-based Carolina sauce, a tomato-enriched Kansas City sauce or a soy-and-ginger Asian-inspired sauce, all good barbecue sauces find a balance of sweetness, sourness, spiciness and saltiness – and the best ones have a good dose of umami from something like Worcestershire sauce.

CLASSIC RED BARBECUE SAUCE

Ketchup provides the base flavour and the smooth, thick body of this sauce. Apple juice bumps up the sweetness quite a bit, while cider vinegar provides the required acidity.

Makes: about 300 ml/½ pint
175 ml/6 fl oz apple juice
125 ml/4 fl oz tomato ketchup
3 tablespoons cider vinegar
2 teaspoons soy sauce
1 teaspoon Worcestershire sauce
½ teaspoon chilli powder
1 garlic clove, finely chopped or crushed
¼ teaspoon freshly ground black pepper

1 In a small saucepan mix the ingredients. Simmer for a few minutes over a medium heat, and then remove the saucepan from the heat.

APPLE CIDER VINEGAR SAUCE

Vinegar sauce is usually thin enough that it can penetrate the meat while basting. Sugar, salt and pepper usually offset its pronounced acidity. This version uses cider for sweetness, hot sauce and mustard for spiciness, and soy and Worcestershire sauces for umami.

Makes: about 400 ml/14 fl oz
250 ml/8 fl oz cider
4 tablespoons cider vinegar
4 tablespoons Dijon mustard
2 tablespoons soy sauce
2 tablespoons Worcestershire sauce
1 teaspoon sea salt
1 teaspoon hot pepper sauce

1 In a saucepan over a high heat, whisk the ingredients and bring to the boil. Remove the pan from the heat.

SAUCES

PASILLA BARBECUE SAUCE

For this chilli-based sauce, the preparation begins by browning onion and garlic to sweeten them a bit, but the more dominant effects come from the spiciness of roasted chillies, the acidity of tomatoes and vinegar, and the slight bitterness of beer. The oregano and the seasoning fill out the flavour profile with more complexity.

Makes: about 500 ml/17 fl oz

2 tablespoons extra-virgin olive oil
6 garlic cloves, peeled
1 small red onion, finely chopped
2 dried pasilla chillies, deseeded and cut into strips
250 ml/8 fl oz canned diced tomatoes in juice
250 ml/8 fl oz amber Mexican beer
1 tablespoon cider vinegar
1 teaspoon sea salt
½ teaspoon dried oregano
¼ teaspoon freshly ground black pepper

1 In a small heavy saucepan over a medium heat, warm the oil and cook the garlic for 4–5 minutes until lightly browned, turning occasionally. Add the onion and the chillies and cook for about 3 minutes, stirring occasionally. Add the remaining ingredients, bring to the boil and simmer for 15 minutes. Remove the saucepan from the heat and let the mixture stand for 15 minutes to soften the chillies and blend the flavours. Purée in a blender.

HERB SAUCES

Herb sauces are bold, coarsely chopped or pulsed condiments made in a variety of styles all over the world. Whether it's Argentinian chimichurri, Italian pesto or Moroccan chermoula, all herb sauces feature soft leafy herbs, good oil, garlic and salt. The flavour balance is not as sweet as it is in most barbecue sauces. Instead, there is an emphasis on sour, acidic ingredients, such as vinegar, citrus or tomatillos, which help to preserve freshness and boost the herbal flavour. Some form of saltiness is universally important, as it supports each sauce's finished flavours. In addition to sea salt, anchovies, fish sauce, capers or olives may be used.

CHERMOULA

Chermoula is a North African sauce typically used to garnish fish, but it's also delicious with meat, chicken and vegetables.

Makes: about 300 ml/½ pint

75 ml/3 fl oz extra-virgin olive oil
4 tablespoons fresh lemon juice
4 tablespoons chopped fresh flat-leaf parsley
4 tablespoons chopped fresh coriander
1 tablespoon finely chopped garlic
1½ teaspoons paprika
1 teaspoon ground cumin
1 teaspoon sea salt
½ teaspoon freshly ground black pepper
¼ teaspoon ground cayenne pepper

1 Combine all of the ingredients in a bowl.

CHIMICHURRI

Chimichurri is an Argentinian condiment served with grilled beef as a garnish or a dipping sauce. Classic chimichurri features parsley; however, oregano, coriander or basil is sometimes added for extra flavour.

Makes: about 375 ml/13 fl oz
2 large garlic cloves
125 g/4 oz fresh flat-leaf parsley leaves and tender stems
2 tablespoons fresh oregano
125 ml/4 fl oz extra-virgin olive oil
2 tablespoons red wine vinegar
1 teaspoon sea salt
½ teaspoon freshly ground black pepper
¼ teaspoon crushed red chilli flakes

1 In a food processor finely chop the garlic. Add the parsley and the oregano. Pulse to finely chop the herbs. Then slowly add the oil in a steady stream. Add the remaining ingredients and mix well.

CORIANDER PESTO

Pesto is a well-known and beloved herb sauce that hails from the Liguria region of northern Italy. It is traditionally prepared with fresh basil; however, it can be made with other leafy herbs, such as fresh coriander or parsley (or even rocket). As with most herb sauces, the leaves are ground with olive oil, garlic and nuts to achieve a coarse consistency. Parmesan or pecorino cheese can be added at the end for saltiness and umami.

Makes: about 250 ml/8 fl oz
2 tablespoons coarsely chopped walnuts
2 garlic cloves
65 g/2½ oz fresh coriander leaves and tender stems
25 g/1 oz fresh flat-leaf parsley leaves and tender stems
½ teaspoon sea salt
¼ teaspoon freshly ground black pepper
4 tablespoons extra-virgin olive oil

1 In a food processor finely chop the walnuts and the garlic. Scrape down the sides of the bowl. Add the coriander, parsley, salt and pepper and process until finely chopped. With the motor running, slowly add the oil to create a smooth purée.

SALSAS

The conquistadores gave salsas their name when they came to the Americas, yet the origins of these sauces extend as far back as the days of the Aztecs. So let's just say salsas have stood the test of time. The best-known version today is a blend of tomatoes, onions and chillies (salsa roja). It is distinguished by a chunky texture that shows off the main components.

When making your own salsa, bear in mind the idea that 'what grows together, goes together'. If you are making a Caribbean-style salsa, use tropical ingredients, such as mango and pineapple for sweetness and citrus juice for sourness. A Mexican-style salsa might include tomatoes and corn for sweetness and pickled jalapeños for sourness, not to mention spiciness. And no matter where you are going with your salsa, don't forget the salt.

SAUCES

BLACK BEAN AND AVOCADO SALSA

Makes: about 1 litre/1¾ pints
475-g/15-oz can black beans, rinsed and drained
1 large avocado, diced
1 red pepper, finely diced
175 g/6 oz fresh corn kernels
1 small red onion, finely diced
25 g/1 oz fresh coriander, coarsely chopped
4 tablespoons fresh lime juice
2 tablespoons extra-virgin olive oil
1 teaspoon ground cumin
1 teaspoon sea salt
½ teaspoon freshly ground black pepper
¼ teaspoon ground cayenne pepper

1 Combine all of the ingredients in a large bowl.

ROASTED TOMATILLO SALSA

Salsa ingredients are not always raw. Grilling coaxes natural plant sugars out of many vegetables and introduces a nice smoky char to the mix.

Makes: about 500 ml/17 fl oz
1 onion, cut crossways into 1-cm/½-inch slices
Extra-virgin olive oil
10 tomatillos, about 250 g/8 oz total, husked and rinsed, or green tomatoes
1 small jalapeño chilli, stem removed
4 tablespoons fresh coriander leaves and tender stems
1 garlic clove
½ teaspoon dark brown sugar
½ teaspoon sea salt

1 Prepare the grill for grilling/direct cooking over high heat (230–290°C/450–550°F).

2 Lightly brush the onion slices on both sides with oil. Grill the onion slices, tomatillos and chilli over *grilling/direct high heat for* 6–8 minutes, with the lid closed, until lightly charred, turning once or twice and swapping their positions as needed for even cooking. Be sure the tomatillos are completely soft as you remove them from the grill. In a food processor combine the onion slices, tomatillos and chilli, along with all the remaining ingredients. Pulse until blended but still chunky.

NECTARINE, RED PEPPER AND ONION SALSA

This sweeter-style salsa goes well with fish or chicken.

Makes: about 600 ml/1 pint
2 firm but ripe nectarines, about 500 g/1 lb total, diced
1 small red pepper, diced
1 red onion, diced
1 jalapeño chilli, deseeded and finely chopped
2 tablespoons finely chopped fresh mint
2 tablespoons finely chopped fresh flat-leaf parsley
1 tablespoon fresh lime juice
1 tablespoon honey
¼ teaspoon crushed red chilli flakes
¼ teaspoon sea salt

1 Combine all of the ingredients in a large bowl.

VINAIGRETTES

If you think a vinaigrette is just for salads, then think again. In the world of grilling, it plays many roles, first as a fully loaded marinade for lean items like chicken breasts, prawns and vegetables. It also works nicely as a basting sauce or a moisturiser for almost anything on the grill, including pork chops and large mushrooms. Finally, you can spoon a vinaigrette over whatever has just come hot off the grill. It's a brilliant way to dress up a simple steak or a platter of grilled vegetables.

A vinaigrette is actually one of the original 'mother sauces' of French cuisine, but that shouldn't intimidate you. Just whisk some vinegar with three or four times as much oil and season to taste. That temporary emulsion can go in any flavour direction you like.

FRENCH VINAIGRETTE

This is the classic version that you might serve with a salad. It shouldn't be too sweet. Cider vinegar and olive oil form its base. To that, shallots and mustard add sharpness, lemon zest adds brightness, and salt and pepper do what they always do well.

Makes: about 175 ml/6 fl oz

3 tablespoons cider vinegar
1 tablespoon finely chopped shallots
2 teaspoons finely grated lemon zest
1 teaspoon Dijon mustard
125 ml/4 fl oz extra-virgin olive oil
½ teaspoon sea salt
¼ teaspoon freshly ground black pepper

1 In a small bowl whisk the vinegar, shallots, lemon zest and mustard. Slowly drizzle and whisk in the oil until it is emulsified. Season with the salt and pepper.

BALSAMIC VINAIGRETTE

Rich and sweet balsamic vinegar stands up well to more pronounced flavours including brown sugar (sweet), mustard (sharp) and garlic (spice).

Makes: about 250 ml/8 fl oz

4 tablespoons balsamic vinegar
2 teaspoons light brown sugar
1 teaspoon mustard powder
1 small clove garlic, finely chopped
½ teaspoon sea salt
½ teaspoon freshly ground black pepper
175 ml/6 fl oz extra-virgin olive oil

1 In a small bowl whisk all of the ingredients except the oil. Then slowly drizzle and whisk in the oil until the vinaigrette is emulsified.

SAUCES

ASIAN VINAIGRETTE

A combination of rice vinegar and lime juice plus olive oil and toasted sesame oil team up to achieve a 3:1 ratio in this Asian-inspired vinaigrette. Honey adds sweetness. Coriander, ginger, garlic and chilli sauce add spice. Soy sauce adds salt.

Makes: about 250 ml/8 fl oz

2 tablespoons rice vinegar
1 tablespoon fresh lime juice
1 tablespoon finely chopped fresh coriander
2 teaspoons honey
2 teaspoons soy sauce
2 teaspoons peeled, finely grated fresh ginger
1 teaspoon hot chilli-garlic sauce
1 small garlic clove, finely chopped
125 ml/4 fl oz extra-virgin olive oil
2 teaspoons toasted sesame oil

1 Whisk all of the ingredients except the oils in a bowl. Then slowly drizzle and whisk in the olive oil and sesame oil until the vinaigrette is emulsified.

WHITE SAUCES

The term 'white sauces' is meant to capture all the creamy emulsions and dairy-based sauces used for dipping and garnishing grilled beef, lamb, pork, poultry, fish, vegetables and bread. Besides a common colour, they also usually share a generous kick of garlic. The base might include mayonnaise, egg and oil, yogurt or soured cream. To increase sweetness, sweet pickles, red peppers or a pinch of sugar may be added. Onions, lemon juice, gherkins, capers, mustard and vinegar provide sharpness and sourness. They get their umami from things like Worcestershire sauce and anchovies.

RÉMOULADE

Mayonnaise-based rémoulade is inherently sweet. To balance that taste, it needs some vinegar, pickles, capers and mustard. Spicy Louisiana-style rémoulade can include Creole seasoning, mustard, paprika, parsley and horseradish. French rémoulade is less sweet and often includes gherkins, capers, chives and tarragon.

Makes: about 175 ml/6 fl oz

125 ml/4 fl oz mayonnaise
1 tablespoon capers, drained and chopped
1 tablespoon sweet pickle relish
1 tablespoon finely chopped fresh tarragon
2 teaspoons finely chopped shallots
1 teaspoon tarragon vinegar or white wine vinegar
½ teaspoon Dijon mustard
1 small garlic clove, finely chopped or crushed
¼ teaspoon paprika
¼ teaspoon sea salt

1 Whisk the ingredients in a bowl. If not using right away, cover and refrigerate for as long as 24 hours.

LEMON-BASIL AIOLI

Aioli is a Provençal-style emulsion of oil, egg and garlic. Purists will make it with raw egg yolks, but a high-quality mayonnaise makes a fine substitute.

Makes: about 125 ml/4 fl oz

4 tablespoons mayonnaise
1 tablespoon finely chopped fresh basil
1½ teaspoons finely grated lemon zest
2 teaspoons fresh lemon juice
1 small garlic clove, finely chopped or crushed
¼ teaspoon sea salt

1 Combine the ingredients in a small bowl and mix together thoroughly.

TZATZIKI

Tzatziki is the cooler, creamier version of white sauces. It's less sweet than mayo-rich rémoulade, and it gets a burst of acidity from yogurt and lemon juice. Chopped or grated cucumber cools the yogurt's tang. Garlic, hot pepper sauce or cayenne pepper is added for punch. Mint, dill or parsley contributes traditional flavour and colour. Variations include adding red peppers for a sweeter North African-style sauce, or blending bread or potatoes into the mix for Greek skordalia.

Makes: about 375 ml/13 fl oz

250 ml/8 fl oz full-fat Greek yogurt
½ cucumber, finely diced
4 tablespoons chopped fresh mint
1 tablespoon fresh lemon juice
2 garlic cloves, finely chopped or crushed
1 teaspoon sea salt
½ teaspoon freshly ground black pepper
¼ teaspoon hot pepper sauce

1 Combine the ingredients in a bowl. Refrigerate until ready to use.

BRINES
MAKING BRINES

Good grillers love to brine, and for good reason. A nice, salty soak in a brine will ensure that meats, especially lean varieties, such as chicken breast and pork loin, stay moist, tender and flavourful against the high heat and/or long cooking times of certain recipes. Brines penetrate meat's cellular structure both to break down the tough stuff and to plump it all up. There's an art — and a science — to brining, starting with the ratios. You'll need ½–1 cup of sea salt for every gallon of water. Meat likes balance, so it will absorb salt until it matches the levels in the brine. See the chart below for some guidelines.

ITALIAN BRINE

Good with: pork, chicken, turkey
Makes: enough brine for 1.5 kg/3 lb of meat
475 ml/16 fl oz water
1 orange, quartered
1 lemon, quartered
1 small yellow onion, quartered
50 g/2 oz granulated sugar
50 g/2 oz sea salt
4 sprigs fresh oregano or thyme
2 teaspoons black peppercorns
4 fresh sage leaves
2 garlic cloves, peeled and smashed
2 bay leaves
475 ml/16 fl oz dry white wine

1 Pour the water into a saucepan, and then add the orange and lemon quarters, squeezing the juice into the water. Add the remaining brine ingredients except the wine. Heat over medium-low heat, stirring to dissolve the sugar and salt. Remove from the heat and add the wine. Cool completely. Before grilling, remove the meat from the brine and discard the brine. Rinse the meat and pat dry with paper towels, inside and outside the cavity, if using a whole bird. Refrigerate for at least 1 hour, uncovered, to dry thoroughly.

BUTTERMILK BRINE

Good with: pork, chicken, turkey, game
Makes: enough brine for 1.5 kg/3 lb of meat
475 ml/16 fl oz buttermilk
150 g/5 oz finely chopped onion
2 tablespoons granulated sugar
2 tablespoons sea salt
3 fresh thyme sprigs
2 garlic cloves, peeled and smashed
2 fresh or dried bay leaves, torn
1 teaspoon black peppercorns

1 Combine the ingredients and whisk until the sugar and salt are dissolved. Remove the meat from the brine and discard the brine. Rinse the meat and pat dry with paper towels, inside and outside the cavity for a whole bird. Refrigerate for 1 hour, uncovered, to dry thoroughly.

NORMANDY BRINE

Good with: pork, chicken, turkey
Makes: enough brine for 1.5 kg/3 lb of meat
475 ml/16 fl oz apple cider
75 g/3 oz packed dark brown sugar
75 g/3 oz sea salt
4 fresh thyme sprigs
6 whole cloves, smashed
1 tablespoon yellow mustard seed
2 teaspoons black peppercorns
2 bay leaves, torn
475 ml/16 fl oz water

1 In a medium saucepan over medium-low heat, combine all of the ingredients, except the water, whisking to dissolve the sugar and salt. Remove from the heat and add the water. Cool completely. Before grilling, remove the meat from the brine and discard the brine. Rinse the meat and pat dry with paper towels, inside and outside the cavity, if using a whole bird. Refrigerate for 1 hour, uncovered, or until dry.

HOW LONG?

TIME	TYPES OF FOOD
Up to 30 minutes	Small foods, such as shellfish, cubed meat for kebabs, and vegetables
30 minutes–1 hour	Thin cuts of boneless meat, such as chicken breasts, fish fillets, pork tenderloins, chops and steaks
2–4 hours	Thicker cuts of boneless or bone-in meat, such as leg of lamb, whole chickens and beef roasts
4–12 hours	Big or tough cuts of meat, such as racks of ribs, whole hams, pork shoulders and turkeys

INDEX

USEFUL EQUIVALENT WEIGHTS & MEASURES

CUP EQUIVALENTS FOR DIFFERENT TYPES OF INGREDIENTS

A standard cup measure of a dry or solid ingredient will vary in weight depending on the type of ingredient. A standard cup of liquid is the same volume for any type of liquid. Use the following chart when converting from grams (weight) or millilitres (volume) to cups.

Standard cup	Fine powder (e.g., flour)	Grain (e.g., rice)	Granular (e.g., sugar)	Liquid solids (e.g., butter)	Liquid (e.g., milk)
1/8	18 g	19 g	24 g	25 g	30 ml
1/4	35 g	38 g	48 g	50 g	60 ml
1/3	47 g	50 g	63 g	67 g	80 ml
1/2	70 g	75 g	95 g	100 g	120 ml
2/3	93 g	100 g	125 g	133 g	160 ml
3/4	105 g	113 g	143 g	150 g	180 ml
1	140 g	150 g	190 g	200 g	240 ml

USEFUL EQUIVALENTS FOR LIQUID INGREDIENTS BY VOLUME

1/4 tsp						=	1 ml
1/2						=	2 ml
1 tsp						=	5 ml
3 tsp	=	1 tbs			=	1/2 fl oz	=	15 ml
		2 tbs	=	1/8 cup	=	1 fl oz	=	25 ml
		4 tbs	=	1/4 cup	=	2 fl oz	=	50 ml
		5 1/3 tbs	=	1/3 cup	=	3 fl oz	=	75 ml
		8 tbs	=	1/2 cup	=	4 fl oz	=	125 ml
		10 2/3 tbs	=	2/3 cup	=	5 fl oz	=	150 ml
		12 tbs	=	3/4 cup	=	6 fl oz	=	175 ml
		16 tbs	=	1 cup	=	8 fl oz	=	250 ml
			=	2 cups	=	16 fl oz	=	500 ml
			=	4 cups	=	32 fl oz	=	1 litre

USEFUL EQUIVALENTS FOR COOKING/OVEN TEMPERATURES

	Celsius	Fahrenheit	Gas Mark
Freezing point	0°C	32°F	
Room temperature	20°C	68°F	
Boiling point	100°C	212°F	
Bake	170°C	325°F	3
	180°C	350°F	4
	190°C	375°F	5
	200°C	400°F	6
	220°C	425°F	7
	230°C	450°F	8

USEFUL EQUIVALENTS FOR DRY INGREDIENTS BY WEIGHT

To convert ounces to grams, multiply the number of ounces by 30.

1 oz	=	$1/16$ lb	=	30 g
4 oz	=	$1/4$ lb	=	120 g
8 oz	=	$1/2$ lb	=	240 g
12 oz	=	$3/4$ lb	=	360 g
16 oz	=	1 lb	=	480 g

USEFUL EQUIVALENTS FOR LENGTH

To convert inches to centimeters, multiply the number of inches by 2.5.

1 in						=	2.5 cm		
6 in	=	$1/2$ ft				=	15 cm		
12 in	=	1 ft				=	30 cm		
36 in	=	3 ft	=	1 yd		=	90 cm		
40 in						=	100 cm	=	1 m

CREDITS

ORIGINAL EDITION (OXMOOR HOUSE, 2013)

AUTHOR
Jamie Purviance

MANAGING EDITOR
Marsha Capen

EDITORIAL, DESIGN AND PRODUCTION
rabble+rouser, inc.:
Christina Schroeder, Chief Creative
Marsha Capen, Editorial Director
Shum Prats, Creative Director
Abby Wilson, Assistant Editor

PHOTOGRAPHY
Tim Turner, Photographer and Photo Art Direction
Christy Clow, Digital Guru
Takamasa Ota, Photo Assistant
Joe Bankmann, Photo Assistant

FOOD STYLING
Lynn Gagné, Food Stylist
Nina Albazi, Assistant Food Stylist

CONTRIBUTORS
Lynda Balslev, Brigit Binns, Lena Birnbaum, David Bonom, Angela Brassinga, Tara Duggan, Sarah Epstein, Mary Goodbody, Gina Hodgson, Michael Kalhorn, Shannon Kinsella, Rick Rodgers, Cheryl Sternman Rule, Mark Scarbrough, Manuela Tar, Jess Thomson, Kerry Trotter, Amy Vogler, Bruce Weinstein, Sharron Wood, Terri Pischoff Wuerthner

WEBER-STEPHEN PRODUCTS LLC
Mike Kempster, Chief Marketing Officer
Brooke Jones, Director of Marketing

PUBLISHING CONSULTANT
Susan Maruyama, Round Mountain Media

OXMOOR HOUSE
Jim Childs, Publisher
Leah McLaughlin, Editorial Director

UK EDITION (OCTOPUS PUBLISHING GROUP, 2014)

WEBER-STEPHEN PRODUCTS (UK) LTD
Helen Raison, Senior Marketing Executive
Laura Ashall, Director of Marketing
Jo McDonald, Director of Sales

OCTOPUS PUBLISHING GROUP
Eleanor Maxfield, Commissioning Editor
Jo Wilson, Editor
Jonathan Christie, Art Director
Allison Gonzalves, Production Controller
Jeremy Tilston design